HEARTS OF FREEDOM

McGill-Queen's Refugee and Forced Migration Studies

Series editors: Megan Bradley and James Milner

Forced migration is a local, national, regional, and global challenge with profound political and social implications. Understanding the causes and consequences of, and possible responses to, forced migration requires careful analysis from a range of disciplinary perspectives, as well as interdisciplinary dialogue.

The purpose of the McGill-Queen's Refugee and Forced Migration Studies series is to advance in-depth examination of diverse forms, dimensions, and experiences of displacement, including in the context of conflict and violence, repression and persecution, and disasters and environmental change. The series will explore responses to refugees, internal displacement, and other forms of forced migration to illuminate the dynamics surrounding forced migration in global, national, and local contexts, including Canada, the perspectives of displaced individuals and communities, and the connections to broader patterns of human mobility. Featuring research from fields including politics, international relations, law, anthropology, sociology, geography, and history, the series highlights new and critical areas of enquiry within the field, especially conversations across disciplines and from the perspective of researchers in the global South, where the majority of forced migration unfolds. The series benefits from an international advisory board made up of leading scholars in refugee and forced migration studies.

11 Kingdom of Barracks
Polish Displaced Persons in Allied-Occupied Germany and Austria
Katarzyna Nowak

12 Urban Refugees and Digital Technology
Reshaping Social, Political, and Economic Networks
Charles Martin-Shields

13 Migration Governance in North America
Policy, Politics, and Community
Edited by Kiran Banerjee and Craig Damian Smith

14 Write to Return
Huguenot Refugees on the Frontiers of the French Enlightenment
Bryan A. Banks

15 The Politics of Refugee Policy in the Global South
Ola G. El-Taliawi

16 Forced Migration in/to Canada
From Colonization to Refugee Resettlement
Edited by Christina R. Clark-Kazak

17 Sanctuary in Pieces
Two Centuries of Flight, Fugitivity, and Resistance in a North American City
Laura Madokoro

18 Knowledge, Power, and Migration
Contesting the North/South Divide
Edited by Yasmeen Abu-Laban, Mireille Paquet, and Ethel Tungohan

19 Unequal Access
Categorising Refugees in European Resettlement and Humanitarian Admission Programmes
Natalie Welfens

20 Hearts of Freedom
Stories of Southeast Asian Refugees
Peter Duschinsky, Colleen Lundy, Michael J. Molloy, Allan Moscovitch, and Stephanie Phetsamay Stobbe

HEARTS OF FREEDOM

Stories of Southeast Asian Refugees

Peter Duschinsky, Colleen Lundy, Michael J. Molloy, Allan Moscovitch, and Stephanie Phetsamay Stobbe

McGill Queen's University Press
Montreal & Kingston • London • Chicago

ISBN 978-0-2280-2552-8 (paper)
ISBN 978-0-2280-2553-5 (ePDF)
ISBN 978-0-2280-2554-2 (ePUB)

Legal deposit third quarter 2025
Bibliothèque et Archives nationales du Québec

Printed in Canada on acid-free paper that is 100% ancient-forest-free, containing 100% sustainable, recycled fibre, and processed chlorine-free.

This book has been published with the help of a grant from the Local Engagement Refugee Research Network.

Funded by the Government of Canada | Financé par le gouvernement du Canada

Canada Council for the Arts | Conseil des arts du Canada

We acknowledge the support of the Canada Council for the Arts.
Nous remercions le Conseil des arts du Canada de son soutien.

McGill-Queen's University Press in Montreal is on land which long served as a site of meeting and exchange amongst Indigenous Peoples, including the Haudenosaunee and Anishinabeg nations. In Kingston it is situated on the territory of the Haudenosaunee and Anishinaabek. We acknowledge and thank the diverse Indigenous Peoples whose footsteps have marked these territories on which peoples of the world now gather.

Library and Archives Canada Cataloguing in Publication

Title: Hearts of freedom : stories of Southeast Asian refugees / Peter Duschinsky, Colleen Lundy, Michael Molloy, Allan Moscovitch, and Stephanie Phetsamay Stobbe.
Names: Duschinsky, Peter, 1943- author | Lundy, Colleen, 1946- author | Molloy, Michael J., author | Moscovitch, Allan, 1946- author | Stobbe, Stephanie Phetsamay, author
Series: McGill-Queen's refugee and forced migration studies ; 20.
Description: Series statement: McGill-Queen's refugee and forced migration studies ; 20 | Includes bibliographical references and index.
Identifiers: Canadiana (print) 20250147610 | Canadiana (ebook) 20250147637 | ISBN 9780228025528 (paper) | ISBN 9780228025535 (PDF) | ISBN 9780228025542 (EPUB)
Subjects: LCSH: Refugees—Canada—Interviews. | LCSH: Refugees—Southeast Asia—Interviews. | LCSH: Oral history—Southeast Asia. | LCSH: Canada—Emigration and immigration.
Classification: LCC JV7282 .D87 2025 | DDC 305.9/06914—dc23

This book was designed and typeset by studio oneonone in Minion 11/14.
Copyediting by Rachel Taylor.

McGill-Queen's University Press
Suite 1720, 1010 Sherbrooke St West, Montreal, QC, H3A 2R7

Authorized safety representative in the EU: Mare Nostrum Group BV, Mauritskade 21D, 1091 GC Amsterdam, the Netherlands, gpsr@mare-nostrum.co.uk

This book is dedicated to those who fled war and oppression in Vietnam, Cambodia, and Laos during the 1970s, 1980s, and 1990s, including those brave souls who perished in the escape attempt and those who survived to rebuild their lives in Canada and who, with their children, are now a valued and admired part of the Canadian community. This book is also dedicated to the Canadians who played an active part in aiding the movement, arrival, and settlement of Southeast Asian refugees by opening their communities and hearts to the newcomers.

We also dedicate this book to the memory of Dr Nick Kiriakides, a physician with the Department of National Health and Welfare. He was responsible for the medical screening of immigrants and refugees and a member of the team that went to Guam immediately after the fall of Saigon to document Vietnamese refugees interested in coming to Canada. While there, Dr Kiriakides contracted dengue fever and subsequently passed away. His colleagues remember him as a kind and generous man.

A Thank You Note from Canada's Southeast Asian Communities

The Vietnamese, Cambodian, and Laotian communities of Canada would like to acknowledge the federal government ministers who worked to make their welcome to Canada possible: the Right Honourable Pierre Elliot Trudeau; the Right Honourable Joe Clark; the Honourable Flora MacDonald; the Honourable Robert Andras; the Honourable Bud Cullen; the Honourable Ron Atkey; and the Honourable Lloyd Axworthy.

CONTENTS

PART FOUR
CAMBODIAN REFUGEES

PART FIVE
LAOTIAN REFUGEES

APPENDICES

FOREWORD

Canadians are properly proud of the extent and generosity of our welcoming response to the many thousands of refugees forced to flee their homes in Vietnam, Cambodia, and Laos in the 1970s, 1980s, and 1990s. Because of that broad and genuine citizen response, the United Nations High Commissioner for Refugees presented the "people of Canada" with the Nansen Refugee Award in 1986.

But our greater reward has been the extraordinary contributions made by over 200,000 men, women, and children who arrived here as refugees. They have become some of our most constructive citizens forming a bold and inspiring chapter in Canada's continuing story as a diverse country of immigrants and Indigenous communities. Their stories also remind us of the threats, fear, courage, and determination which marked their flight to freedom.

It is estimated that about 3 million people fled their homes, jobs, and families in Southeast Asia, forced to sea in makeshift and dangerous vessels, or to cross rivers and jungles over land. They were often denied the right to dock at safe ports or turned back to extreme danger at land borders. They spent months, sometimes years, in primitive, crowded refugee camps. Too many died, denied their future. But with the help of Canada and other countries, many endured and now enrich their new communities.

The broad strokes of their stories are known: often told by people who experienced or observed those hardships or those triumphs, sometimes conveyed in extraordinary works of art, literature, and reflection. Through in-depth interviews across Canada, the Hearts of Freedom project has recorded a cross-section of the experiences and memories of these refugees, as well as the sponsors, government staff, and others who aided them in their journeys to new lives. This volume tells of lives and hopes brutally interrupted and then – through the commitment of Canadians – renewed.

I was privileged to lead Canada's national government in the period when our country's engagement with these refugees stepped up dramatically. In an important sense, that acceleration was citizen-led. Across Canada, individuals, communities, and nongovernmental organizations became actors as well as advocates, not least in applying the principle of "private sponsorship" which an earlier Parliament had endorsed in 1976. With that citizen support, our government became an active international leader. The party in office had the cooperation of other parliamentarians and, emphatically, the Canadian public service, in Ottawa and the provinces.

Two of my ministers, Flora MacDonald at External Affairs and Ron Atkey at Immigration, were the Cabinet's driving force and public face on the issue. Their determination was matched by the skill and audacity of the professional public servants who had to turn this lofty initiative into action and concrete results. One classic example of that leadership was Jack Manion, then deputy minister of immigration, who deliberately drew his minister's attention to the refusal by Canadian officials in World War II to welcome Jews fleeing Nazi persecution. The deputy asked the minister: What side of history do you want to be on?

Canada's response to the Vietnamese, Cambodian, and Laotian refugees combines two essential strands of our nature as a national community. One element is reflected in our constitution: we are a genuine federation and can't function effectively without truly respecting the federal idea. The second element is our shared tradition of community: different people and regions able to respect the cultures we come from without being antagonistic to people whose roots are different.

It's worth remembering that Canada was formed in a spirit distinct from the other new nation established in North America centuries ago. The proud and ambitious Americans set out to change the world, to be a guide to how other nations should behave. They stepped deliberately away from the traditions of Europe.

Canada's distinctive idea was to transplant the best of those traditions in new and more positive terrain, where differences were accepted and opportunities were open. That instinct is one reason the Southeast Asian refugees were welcomed to Canada with respect as well as refuge, and they have responded with contributions which are as remarkable now as their courage was when they came.

The Right Honourable Joe Clark, PC, CC

PREFACE AND METHODOLOGY

This book is a major deliverable for Hearts of Freedom (HOF), the Canadian Southeast Asian Refugee Historical Research Project at Carleton University. It is based on the review and analysis of 173 video-recorded oral interviews that were conducted by interview teams that travelled to eight locations across Canada to meet with former refugees. The objective was to capture and preserve, in their own words, a sample of the experiences of the over 200,000 refugees who escaped from Vietnam, Cambodia, and Laos and resettled in Canada during the 1970s and 1980s, and to inform future resettlement and integration practices in Canada. The book focuses on the knowledge shared in the interviews and synthesizes the essence of over two hundred hours of video-recorded material.

Oral history video interviews serve as the primary source for the descriptions of the escapes, the refugee camps, the migration, and the settlement experiences in Canada that are the essence of the book. In order to place the interviews within the context of the geopolitical history of Southeast Asia, part I offers an overview of the relevant factors of the historical background and the refugee movement that shaped the global framework at that time.

There is a voluminous body of literature on Southeast Asian history during the Second Indochina War and following the communist conquests in 1975 of Vietnam, Cambodia, and Laos; it contains many different academic views. Except for part 1, which is based on secondary sources, the book refers to relatively few secondary sources. The authors' intention is to present information as narrated in the oral history interviews, free of academic debate. At its core, the book relies on the stories of the interviewees' day-to-day lives. It concentrates on why they decided to undertake dangerous, potentially lethal journeys to escape Southeast Asia, how they initially adapted to Canada, and to what extent they regard themselves as members of Canadian society. The authors do, however, refer to a limited number of published and internet sources throughout the book in order to place the interviews within their historical, political, and social contexts.

The authors are indebted to the Vietnamese Canadian, Cambodian Canadian, and Laotian Canadian communities which, through their participation on the HOF project's Management Committee, supported and publicized the project from coast to coast. The committee identified highly motivated community coordinators who helped recruit the interviewing teams and identified potential interviewees.

The interviews cover several decades in the lives of new Canadians who arrived in Canada as Vietnamese, Cambodian, and Laotian refugees. The interviewees – women and men, on occasion accompanied by other members of the same family – tell gripping stories in English, French, or their mother tongues. Through emotional personal memories, they present accounts of their lives in Southeast Asia, of escapes as refugees, of life in refugee camps in countries of asylum, as well as of their journeys to Canada, their initial adaptation in Canada, and their lives as new Canadians. These primary source oral history interviews are referenced throughout the book by their interview numbers, directing the reader to the video interviews that are available at https://heartsoffreedom.org.

To date, the only major book based on interviews with Southeast Asian refugees who resettled in Canada is Morton Beiser's *Strangers at the Gate*, a study published in 1999 recounting how these refugees resettled in British Columbia following their arrival in Canada (Beiser 1999). However, the Beiser book is limited to the initial ten-year integration period of the refugees' lives in a single Canadian province. The present book is the first effort to present an account based on interviews covering the life stories of Southeast Asian refugees both before and after their arrivals across Canada.

Methodology

The authors collaborated closely throughout the writing process, using the interviewees' deeply personal and often painful experiences as the foundation of the book. All interviewees who consented to share their stories with the public are acknowledged in the text. The book carefully selects elements from the oral histories and shapes them into focused written narratives, ensuring that the voices of the interviewees are preserved by quoting them in their own words whenever possible.

To ensure that the project team was well prepared to conduct oral histories, the authors, interviewers, and camera crews received training inspired by Steven High's methodologies at Concordia University's Centre for Oral History and Digital Storytelling, specifically from the Montreal Life Stories Project (High 2008). Additionally, the team was guided by an Interview and Digital Recording Guide created specifically for the HOF project by former CBC film director Sheila Petzold and videographer Karl Roeder.

The interviewees were from three distinct Southeast Asian countries – Vietnam, Cambodia, and Laos – each with unique national identities, languages, histories, and pre-escape circumstances. They encountered different challenges during their escape, in the refugee camps, and after arriving in Canada. As a result, they established separate ethnic communities and institutions. Recognizing these distinctions, the interviewees were grouped by their communities and interviewed by teams from their own backgrounds. The authors discuss the interviews in dedicated sections of the book: Vietnamese war refugees in part 2, Vietnamese boat people in part 3, Cambodian refugees in part 4, and Laotian refugees in part 5.

The book is structured to address two distinct phases of each national group's story: their lives in Southeast Asia before escaping and their subsequent adaptation to life in Canada. These two stages are explored in separate chapters to provide a clear distinction between their experiences before and after resettlement. Twenty interviewees were chosen for an in-depth examination of both their escape journeys and their adjustment to Canadian society, giving readers a comprehensive understanding of how individual refugees remember their past in their homelands and their lives in Canada.

The use of personal names differs between the three cultures. Consequently, the interviewees' original names in each part of the book are in accordance with the different naming conventions. With some exceptions, the Vietnamese are generally referred to by their family names while the Laotians and Cambodians are referred to by their first names. The videos of oral histories, organized by nationality, are posted under "Interviews" at heartsoffreedom.org.

The book *Running on Empty: Canada and the Indochinese Refugees, 1975–1980*, published in 2017, already provides a detailed account of Canadian policy and its implementation regarding this refugee crisis (Molloy et al. 2017). While the HOF interviews with Canadian officials involved in the Southeast Asian refugee movement are valuable historical resources, they fall outside the scope of this book. However, they are briefly referenced in appendix 3, and their full video-recorded interviews can be accessed under "Canadian Facilitators" at heartsoffreedom.org.

From the late 1970s onward, the media and official sources referred to Vietnamese refugees who escaped by boat across the South China Sea as the "boat people." The late Tove Bording, a Canadian visa officer stationed in Singapore, was responsible for locating refugees with Canadian connections in Malaysia and Thailand between 1975 and 1977. Bording told author Michael Molloy that she had coined the term "boat people" to distinguish them from the overland "truck people" who fled Vietnam in trucks, crossing Laos and seeking asylum in Thailand (Molloy 2014).

During the writing process, the question was raised as to whether Vietnamese Canadians accept being referred to as the boat people or whether they regarded it as a pejorative or racist term. The authors contacted several prominent members of the Vietnamese Canadian community and posed that question. Without exception, the community leaders stated that not only did they accept being called the boat people, but they were proud of this name, as it reminded them of their heroic odyssey to Canada. To demonstrate this pride, two of the authors visited the beautiful Vietnamese Boat People Monument in Mississauga, Ontario, that was funded by the Vietnamese Canadian community. Three of the authors, Mike, Peter, and Stephanie, subsequently visited Journey to Freedom Park and the Vietnamese Boat People Monument in Calgary, Alberta, that was established in 2022 by the Boat People Monument Committee of the Calgary Vietnamese Canadian Association. On the other hand, it is worth noting that members of the Vietnamese, Cambodian, and Laotian communities reject the use of the French colonial term "Indochinese," preferring "Southeast Asian" instead.

Appendices 1 and 2 provide a statistical overview of the Southeast Asian refugee movement to Canada and the demographic profile of the HOF interviewees. Appendix 3 offers a focused summary of twenty-eight oral histories that are outside the scope of this book. Appendix 4 lists the individuals and organizations that funded, supported, or participated in the HOF project.

ACKNOWLEDGMENTS

The Hearts of Freedom (HOF) project was made possible by the generous support of Canadian Heritage's Canada History Fund; the DeFehr Foundation; and Immigration, Refugees, and Citizenship Canada. We are also grateful for the generous community donations to the Canadian Mennonite University and SSHRC to support the HOF travelling exhibition, and to Carleton University who matched donor contributions to support HOF project activities through its Future Funder program. We wish to acknowledge as well the generous support of the Marshall Family Foundation on behalf of Elizabeth Marshall.

The refugee stories are at the heart of this book. We are extremely grateful to the interviewees for allowing us to preserve, in their own words, their memories of escapes from conflict and oppression, and of coming to Canada. We also thank the sponsors, government officials, and community/faith organizations who shared their memories of Canada's response to this refugee movement.

The HOF Management Committee acknowledges the contribution of Minh Nguyen, who was the architect of the new vision and mission of the Vietnamese Canadian Federation's museum project, a vision that paved the way for the creation of the HOF project.

Our heartfelt thanks to the community/city coordinators and interview teams for their compassion and personal connection in capturing the depth of these stories: Mai Nguyen, Uyen Vu, Hanh Hua, Rivaux Lay, Ran Dawn Long, Richard Dang, Som Phouangpraseuth, Jean Legault, Meaghan Brackenbury, Jen Tran, Stella (Nhung) Davis, Pam Sharp, Ari Phanlouvong, and Phuong Nguyen.

We thank Mondy Lim for overseeing the quality control and the transcription of the video-recorded interviews, for setting up the database of facts and statistics to support the authors, and for designing and maintaining the project website where readers can access and view the video interviews that are cited in the book.

We thank Ginette Thomas for lending her research and academic skills and her knowledge of the overall HOF project to the tasks of editing, fact-checking, and proofreading the many drafts and versions of the manuscript for this book.

We are grateful for the photos included in the book provided by HOF interviewees. We thank the United Nations High Commissioner for Refugees for allowing us to use photo images by Kaspar Gaugler, as well as Murray Mosher, Henry Neufeld/the Molloy Collection, and Le Phan and Phan Dam for access to their photo collections.

We are grateful to Sarah Simpkin, librarian at Carleton University, who created the graphic maps for this book. We were fortunate to have the services of our brilliant copyeditor, Rachel Taylor, and our skilled indexer, Alexandra Peace.

Our heartfelt thanks to the volunteers who assisted in the transcribing and translating of the video recordings: Anne Arnott, Diane Burrows, Aliyah Campbell, Gail Devlin, Sylvie Doucet, Megan Evans, Meaghan Fallak, Raphael Girard, Simran Joura, Alexandra Koslock, Amy Ma, Pat Marshall, Phi-Vân Nguyen, Uyiosa Osunde, Ari Phanlouvong, Malinda Pich, and Korri Schneider.

We benefited from the cooperation of the many community organizations and government departments that supported us as we conducted the 173 oral interviews. In Halifax, interview space was graciously provided in Nova Scotia Health's Bethune Building at the Queen Elizabeth II Health Sciences Centre. In Montreal, the Communauté Catholique Vietnamienne de Montréal provided interview space, and Bunkorn Yun, president of Key Development, provided active support for the project. In Ottawa, Carleton University donated interview and office space. In Toronto/Newmarket, Immigration, Refugees and Citizenship Canada generously lent offices, and the Vietnamese Association of Toronto provided community assistance. In Kitchener, the head office of the Mennonite Central Committee provided community assistance. In Winnipeg,

Menno Simons College of the Canadian Mennonite University provided interview and office space. In Edmonton, the Vietnamese Association provided valuable support and assistance for conducting the interviews. In Calgary, the Calgary Vietnamese Canadian Association and the Calgary Vietnamese Canadian Senior Citizens Association supported the interview teams. Finally, in Surrey, British Columbia, St Matthew's Roman Catholic Parish and the Main Branch of the Surrey Public Library provided the team with interview space.

We are deeply grateful to McGill-Queen's University Press for publishing our work, as they previously did with *Running on Empty*. We were especially fortunate to collaborate with senior editor Emily Andrew, whose guidance throughout the rigorous peer review process was invaluable. We also extend our thanks to Kathleen Fraser, the managing editor, for her meticulous editorial direction and support in reviewing the many drafts. We are also thankful to Filomena Falocco and Anna Del Col of the MQUP marketing department for their advice, and to Joanne Pisano, editorial assistant, for her meticulous management of our contract and her careful preparation of the manuscript for the next stage of production.

We extend our sincere gratitude to James Milner and Megan Bradley, coeditors of MQUP's Refugee and Forced Migration Studies series, for their remarkable support of our project. It is a true honour to have our book included in such a respected collection. Finally, thanks to the Canadian Immigration Historical Society for its support and encouragement.

We were privileged to benefit from the insights of three diligent peer reviewers – one anonymous and two prominent migration experts, professor emeritus Dr Marlene Epp and Dr Vic Satzewich. Their thoughtful critiques, observations, and suggestions significantly enhanced the quality of this book.

For a detailed list of the people and organizations involved in the HOF project, please refer to appendix 4.

THE HEARTS OF FREEDOM PROJECT

The project on which this book is based began at the community level. Members of the Vietnamese Canadian community felt that the stories of the Vietnamese boat people's escape from Southeast Asia and resettlement in Canada should be preserved for future generations. In 2015, Dau-Thi Huynh, treasurer of the Vietnamese Canadian Federation, and Minh Nguyen, an artist and volunteer in the Vietnamese community, met with professor emeritus Colleen Lundy of Carleton University's Department of Social Work in Ottawa. Early discussions led to a decision to start Hearts of Freedom (HOF), an oral history project. At a very early stage, HOF was expanded to include the Cambodian and Laotian communities in Canada.

In spring 2018, the initial funding for the project was approved by Canadian Heritage's Canada History Fund. Later, we received supplemental funding from Canadian Heritage, the Winnipeg-based DeFehr Foundation, and Immigration, Refugees and Citizenship Canada that allowed HOF to expand the project to reach more former refugees by conducting interviews in additional locations in Canada. As well, funds were provided by Carleton University's crowdfunding site Future Funder, through which funds donated by private supporters were matched by Carleton University.

The Role of Oral History

Oral history is a "method of gathering, preserving and interpreting the voices and memories of people, communities, and participants in past events" (Stursberg 2006). It allows interviewees to tell their stories in their own words.

HOF's in-person, video-recorded oral interviews were managed by interviewer and camera operator teams who were members of the same ethnic community as the interviewees, who knew their cultures, and could speak their native languages. Participants could bring their spouse or adult children to the interviews for support. Debriefing was with researchers or community elders, and counselling services were offered as needed.

HOF conducted a total of 173 video interviews, which included an additional 24 spouses and adult children who accompanied some of the interviewees and participated in these interviews, assisting with translation and adding their own memories. In the case of 145 of these interviews, the book captures and preserves the experiences and memories of former Vietnamese, Cambodian, and Laotian refugees who resettled in Canada. In the case of the 28 remaining interviews, the book provides a short synopsis of Canadian participation in the resettlement and sponsoring of these refugees in Canada. Some interviewees requested that their names and videos not be made public. As a result, 161 videos are available on the HOF website, heartsoffreedom.org. The interviews expose life before the communist victory and the political, social, and economic conditions in their homelands that prompted their escape journeys, their lives in refugee camps, and the challenges of their resettlement in Canada.

These oral history interviews offered former refugees a unique opportunity to tell their own stories. Ideally, the best way to absorb the information contained in the interviews, with their goldmine of deeply touching recollections, is by listening to all of them. In conducting their analysis, the authors experienced this mammoth undertaking, requiring months of concentrated effort to carefully study the contents of such a large number of interviews. This book organizes and highlights the most important elements of the interviews, while also presenting an in-depth review of a few selected interviews.

Ethics

As with all research with human subjects, attending to ethical guidelines was paramount. A list of available resources was also made available for interviewees, should recalling traumatic events result in undue stress. The project received clearance from the Carleton University Ethics Board on 14 December 2018. The approved consent forms, interview guides, and recruitment materials were translated into French and used by the community interview teams.

Research and Management Committees

A five-member Research Committee was formed and the methodology of oral histories was agreed on early in the life of the project. The committee oversaw project implementation and provided direction on activities of the project staff. The committee included: Colleen Lundy and Allan Moscovitch, two professors emeriti from Carleton University's School of Social Work; Michael Molloy, a former director of refugee policy and senior coordinator of the Indochinese Task Force from 1979 to 1980; Peter Duschinsky, former director, international liaison, for the Department of Citizenship and Immigration; and Stephanie Phetsamay Stobbe, an associate professor of conflict resolution studies at Menno Simons College, a college of Canadian Mennonite University affiliated with the University of Winnipeg. Professors Moscovitch and Lundy served as the project's principal investigators.

An eighteen-member Management Committee provided community input and oversaw HOF's strategic direction. The committee included the Research Committee; former senior Canadian immigration officials; representatives from Canadian Cambodian, Laotian, and Vietnamese associations; representatives from the Canadian Museum of Immigration at Pier 21, the Canadian Museum of History, and the Canadian Immigration Historical Society; and the head of archives and collections at Carleton University. The Management Committee met regularly during the life of the project. Members of the Management Committee are listed in appendix 4.

An important task of the Research and Management Committees was to prepare an interview guide to direct the interview process.

Preparing for the Interviews

Once Canadian Heritage, our principal funder, and Carleton University signed an agreement, the recruitment of staff started with a bilingual project coordinator and a trilingual media coordinator/web designer to support the HOF activities throughout the duration of the project.

Three teams (Cambodian, Laotian, and Vietnamese) conducted the field interviews as required during the project. Each team was comprised of one community coordinator who recruited interviewees, and an interview team consisting of a community interviewer and a camera operator. One of the interviewers assumed the role of coordinator to recruit, liaise with, and interview Canadian private sponsors, government officials, and representatives from nongovernmental organizations.

Of the eleven staff, nine were themselves members of one of the three Southeast Asian communities. In the project's second year, city coordinators from the three Southeast Asian communities were hired to oversee additional interviews in Winnipeg, Edmonton, Calgary, Halifax, and Vancouver. The shared cultural background and language capability proved to be invaluable in contributing to the success of the interviews, as it was possible to conduct interviews in five languages: Khmer, Vietnamese, Lao, French, and English.

The project was launched with a two-day training and team-building session at Carleton University in October 2018 that provided an overview of the project's objectives and the interview guide. Several guest speakers offered contextual background information. Professor Stephane Martelly from Concordia University's Centre for Oral History and Digital Storytelling delivered a lecture on oral history, interviewing techniques, and effective storytelling in an interview setting. Brian Buckley spoke on his experiences researching for his book *Gift of Freedom: How Ottawa Welcomed the Vietnamese, Cambodian, and Laotian Refugees* (Buckley 2008). And Mike Molloy and Peter Duschinsky, members of the Research Committee and coauthors of *Running on Empty: Canada and the Indochinese Refugees, 1975–1980*, provided a comprehensive outline of the history of Canada's involvement in what was then referred to as the Indochinese refugee crisis (Molloy et al. 2017).

In addition, documentary filmmaker Sheila Petzold and videographer Karl Roeder hosted a separate training workshop for the interview teams on quality control, how to properly operate the camera and lighting/sound equipment when recording individuals, and the efficient use of interviewing space through the use of lighting screens and lights.

Recruiting Interview Subjects

Members of the Management Committee referred individuals who have connections with community organizations to work as community and city coordinators. These coordinators reached out and shared information about the project with the community, obtaining the names of former refugees who were interested in sharing their stories on camera. Lists of potential interviewees were provided to the Research Committee for review and for consideration of representation across all groups, gender balance, and language distribution before proceeding.

Creation and Management of a Website

The bilingual HOF website was created to share information about the project. This includes background information about the project, documents related to the project, updates on resources relevant to the refugee crisis in Southeast Asia, commissioned research papers, and most importantly the interview videos that are central to this project. Interview data supported the analysis phase of the research.

The website is the key vehicle for public access to the video interviews which are the primary sources for this book. This is a critical role in HOF project's mandate to preserve the personal histories of refugees from

Southeast Asia and of Canadians who assisted in their resettlement. The Canadian Mennonite University in Winnipeg has offered to serve as the permanent host for the project website.

Interview Administration: Overcoming Challenges

The HOF project followed a flexible trajectory in response to shifts in funding and to public health restrictions during the pandemic.

The first phase of the community/field interviews began in February 2019. The original contribution agreement with Canadian Heritage identified a plan to conduct 110 interviews. The first 40 interviews were conducted at Carleton University for participants from the Ottawa/Gatineau area. Starting in May 2019, the interview teams undertook 32 interviews in Montreal, followed by 40 interviews in the Toronto area. Overall, with the initial available funding, the project completed 112 interviews in these central Canada locations.

In October 2019, the DeFehr Foundation in Winnipeg provided funding to conduct 15 additional interviews in Winnipeg. The project was fortunate to have the opportunity to include an interview with the former minister of employment and immigration who played an active role in the resettlement of these former refugees, the Honourable Lloyd Axworthy. This additional funding allowed the project to grow the total of completed interviews to 127.

In January 2020, the project received additional funding from Canadian Heritage to reach other communities across Canada where former refugees live in large numbers. The project completed fifteen interviews in Edmonton, thirteen interviews in Calgary, and fourteen interviews in Vancouver before the team had to catch flights back home when COVID travel restrictions were imposed in March 2020. This brought the total to 169 completed interviews.

Unfortunately, the ten interviews scheduled for late March 2020 in Halifax had to be postponed, and COVID restrictions over the following months prevented plans to send the interview teams to Halifax. Until the Halifax cancellation, field interviews were conducted in person, focusing on a personal connection with interviewees. Mondy Lim, HOF's media coordinator/web designer developed a hybrid model to facilitate the recording of interviews that would allow the HOF interviewer to still connect with the interviewees. The Halifax city coordinator reached out once more to community organizations and recruited three individuals who, assured that health protocols were in place, agreed to be interviewed remotely. This brought the total to 172 completed interviews.

The final interview was conducted in June 2021 in person in Ottawa with the Right Honourable Joe Clark, former prime minister of Canada. This brought the final total to 173 completed interviews.

The information collected in these interviews forms the basis of the present book.

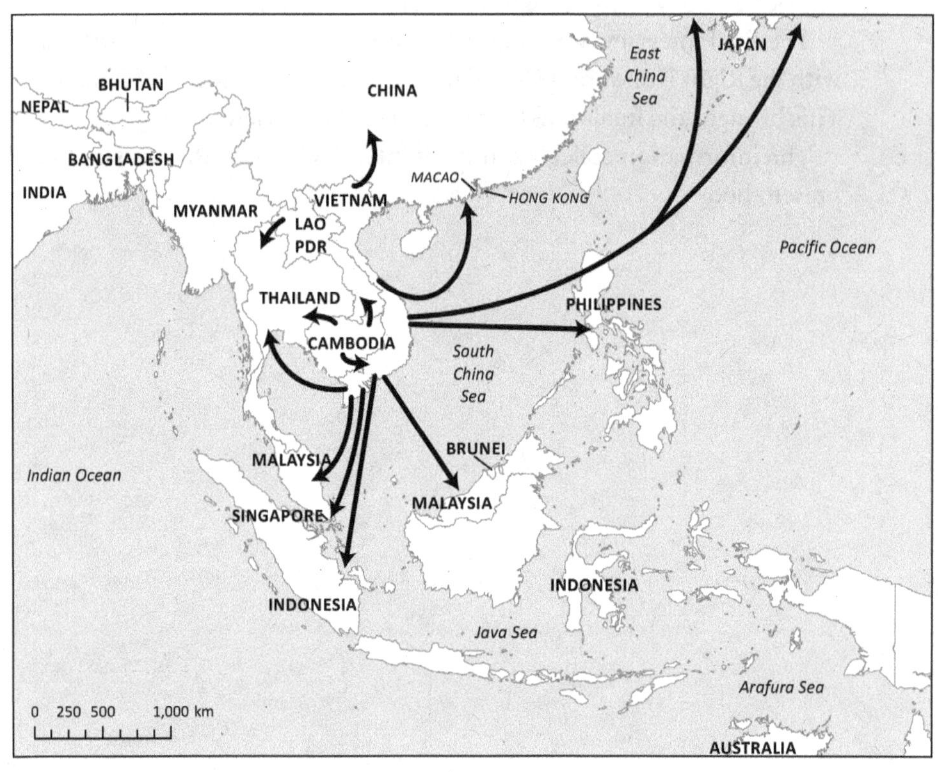

Refugee escape routes from Vietnam, Cambodia, and Lao People's Democratic Republic (PDR).
Commissioned by Hearts of Freedom.

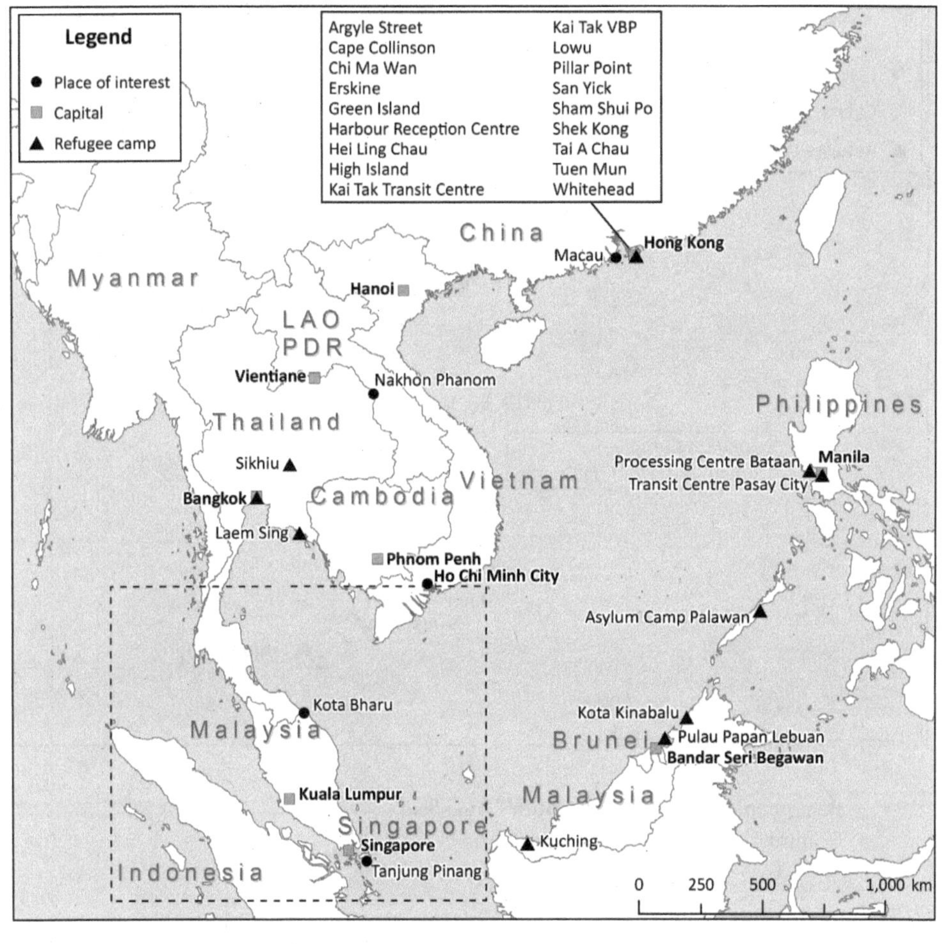

Vietnamese boat people refugee camps, larger Southeast Asia region. For refugee camps inside the dotted line, see the following page. Commissioned by Hearts of Freedom.

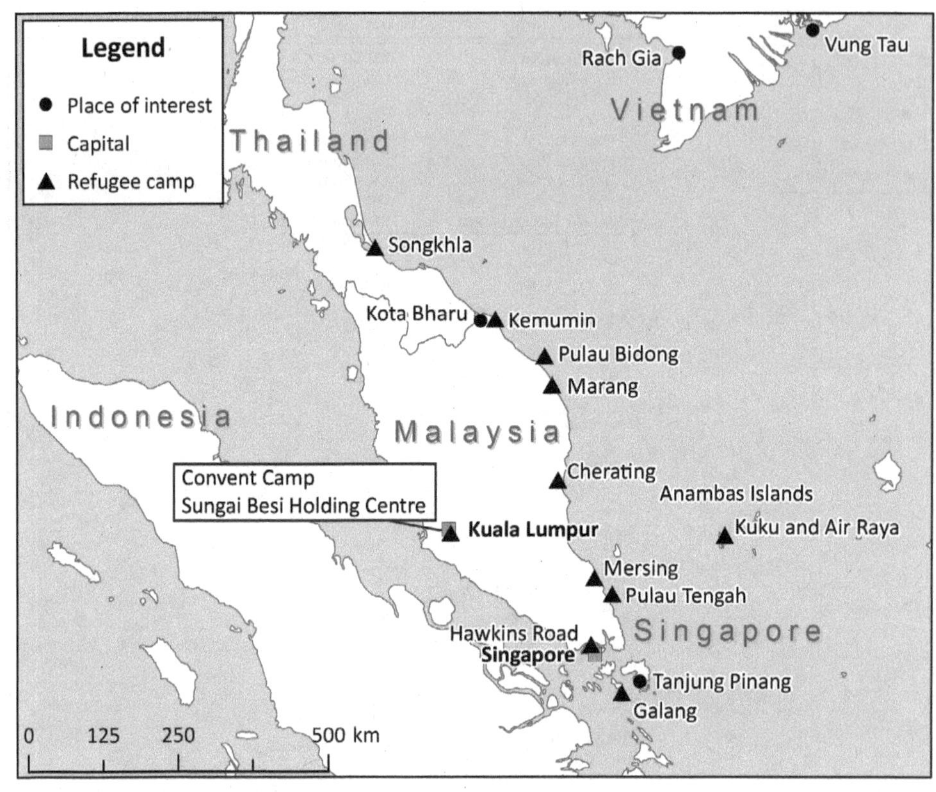

Boat people refugee camps, South China Sea.
Commissioned by Hearts of Freedom.

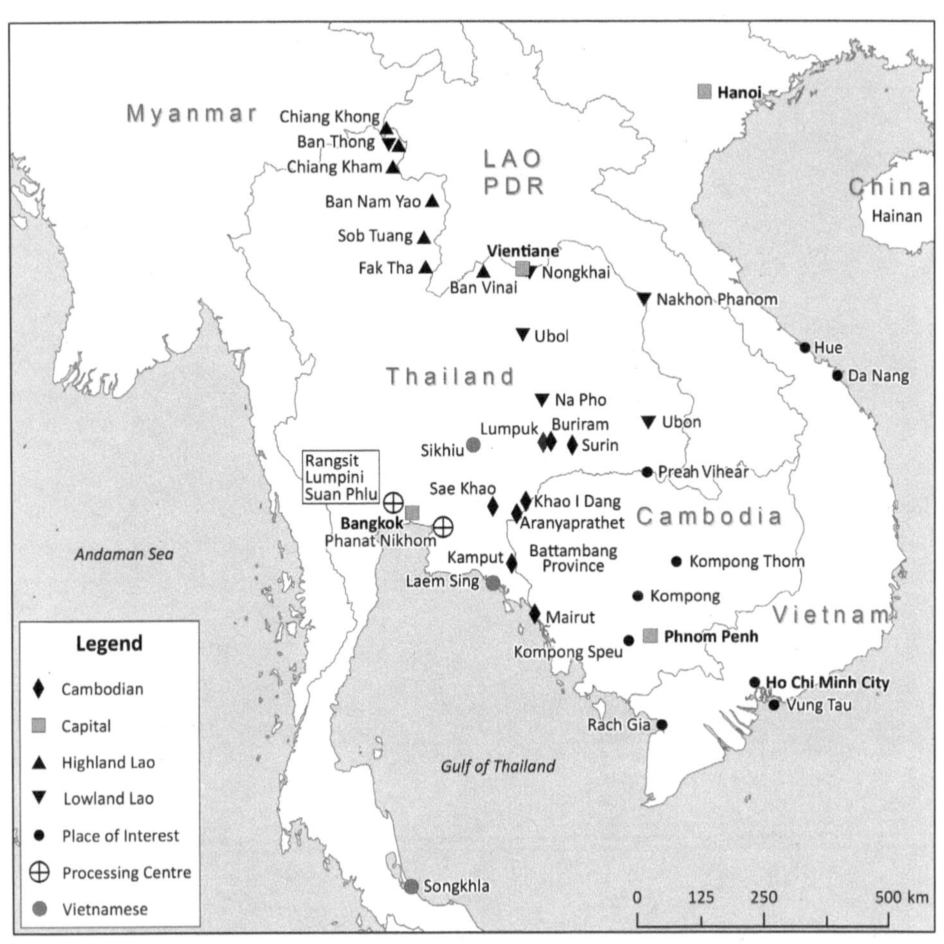

Cambodian, Lao, and Vietnamese refugee camps in Thailand, Lao PDR, and Cambodia.
Commissioned by Hearts of Freedom.

HEARTS OF FREEDOM

INTRODUCTION

According to the Canadian censuses of 2016 and 2021, over 330,000 people of full or part Vietnamese, Cambodian, and Laotian (including Hmong) ethnic background reside in Canada (Statistics Canada 2017, 2023).

As well, there are tens of thousands of Canadians of Chinese ethnicity who originate from the Chinese minority population in Vietnam, Cambodia, and Laos. Most of these people, or their parents, arrived in Canada from Southeast Asia between 1975 and 1997 as refugees, or through family reunification with former refugees who were already Canadian residents.

Hearts of Freedom: Stories of Southeast Asian Refugees is based on oral interviews conducted under Carleton University's Canadian Southeast Asian Historical Research Project: Hearts of Freedom (HOF). It analyzes and narrates the life experiences of refugees as recounted in their own words. It aims to complete the task started by *Running on Empty: Canada and the Indochinese Refugees, 1975–80* which described Canada's programs to resettle these refugees in Canada from the perspective of Canadian immigration officials. This book contains the refugees' own accounts of escaping from Southeast Asia, making their way to Canada, and becoming Canadians (Molloy et al. 2017).

The Evolution of Canada's Approach to Refugee Resettlement

During the decade prior to the Southeast Asian refugee movement's beginnings in 1975, Canada had initiated special programs for refugees from Czechoslovakia, Tibet, Hong Kong, Uganda, Chile, and Argentina and had experimented with varied approaches to refugee resettlement. In

1967, Canada replaced its Eurocentric race-based immigration system with a new universal point system that instead focused on educational and occupational qualifications and connections in Canada. In 1969, Canada became a signatory to the United Nations (UN) Convention Relating to the Status of Refugees, also known as the 1951 Refugee Convention and its 1967 Protocol, opening the possibility of resettlement in Canada for refugees from outside of Europe.

The 1976 Immigration Act provided the legal foundation for the new immigration and refugee system. The new Act's regulatory framework now included provisions for private refugee sponsorship and flexible designated classes for people whose admission to Canada was in line with its traditional concern for the displaced and persecuted. Following Canada's signing of the UN Refugee Convention, the passing of the 1976 Immigration Act embedded Canada's obligation to protect refugees in law and provided a law-based framework for the resettlement of refugees and others in need of resettlement from abroad.

To meet Canada's obligations to asylum seekers who have left their countries and seek protection in Canada while waiting to be recognized legally as refugees, the Act created a tribunal and procedures to examine claims to refugee status from asylum seekers in Canada. To meet Canada's commitments to refugee resettlement, it created a class for refugees who were seeking resettlement in Canada from abroad and authorized the designation of additional humanitarian classes for displaced and persecuted people in need of resettlement (hereafter referred to as designated classes). Finally, the 1976 Act created a legal foundation for the private sponsorship of refugees by civil society institutions and individuals.

Minister of manpower and immigration Robert Andras was responsible for the development of the 1976 Act and its passage in Parliament. When Saigon fell to the North Vietnamese military in April 1975, Andras committed Canada to accept all refugees with relatives in Canada, plus 3,000 additional Convention refugees. He also dispatched teams to Guam, Wake Island, and reception camps in the United States (US) to identify and document those wishing to resettle in Canada.

The changes in the 1976 Immigration Act were so extensive that it took until 1978 to implement them. Andras's successor, Jack (Bud) Cullen, oversaw the implementation of the Private Sponsorship of Refugees

(PSR) program and a new system of selecting refugees and designated classes. Cullen ordered the rescue of 600 refugees from the *Hai Hong*, an overcrowded ship off the shores of Malaysia, in November 1978, and the following month persuaded Cabinet to authorize the resettlement of 5,000 Indochinese, the first tranche of a commitment that would grow into 60,000 (Molloy et al. 2017).

The PSR program gave Canadian citizens and residents a mechanism to become involved in resettling refugees. On 5 March 1979, the Mennonite Central Committee Canada, in the first master agreement signed with the federal government, committed to accepting full liability for one year for refugees sponsored by Mennonite and other congregations. Other churches and dioceses and groups of citizens across Canada soon signed similar agreements, and private sponsorship accounted for 34,000 of the 60,000 Southeast Asian refugees resettled in Canada between 1979 and 1980 (Molloy et al. 2017).

When Joe Clark's Progressive Conservatives formed the government in June 1979, they inherited a new refugee resettlement framework. Seeing the desperate situation in Southeast Asia, two new ministers, Ron Atkey (minister of employment and immigration) and Flora MacDonald (secretary of state for external affairs), determined Canada needed to do more. Atkey immediately increased the resettlement of Southeast Asian refugees from 5,000 to 8,000; this combined with 4,000 through the new private sponsorship program resulted in a total of 12,000 (Molloy et al. 2017).

On 22 July 1979, at a UN conference on the Indochinese refugee crisis in Geneva, Minister MacDonald surprised the international community by announcing that Canada would resettle 50,000 refugees before the end of 1980. This was increased to 60,000 by the addition of 10,000 government-assisted refugees by employment and immigration minister Lloyd Axworthy in March 1980 (Molloy et al. 2017).

The contributions of Prime Minister Joe Clark, Prime Minister Pierre Trudeau, and Ministers Robert Andras, Bud Cullen, Flora MacDonald, Ron Atkey, and Lloyd Axworthy in reforming Canada's resettlement system, responding to the plight of the refugees, and inspiring Canadians to participate in the new private refugee sponsorship program deserve to be recognized and remembered. It is of note that these contributions came from both the Liberal and Conservative parties while in government. Since World War II, support for refugee resettlement, especially in circumstances where the international community identifies a major refugee crisis, typically attracts the support of all parties (Molloy et al. 2017).

Scholarship on the Southeast Asian Refugee Movement to Canada

The definitive reference on refugee movements to third countries of resettlement from Southeast Asia is W. Courtland Robinson's *Terms of Refuge: The Indochinese Exodus and the International Response* which devotes a few pages to the Canadian program (Robinson 1998). Otherwise, the movement of Vietnamese, Cambodian, and Laotian refugees to Canada following the ending of the Indochinese (French colonial territories of Vietnam, Laos, and Cambodia) wars is scantily covered in the academic literature. Feng Hou of Statistics Canada describes the experience of Vietnamese refugees who arrived in Canada as adults or children in 1979 and 1980 and over a period of thirty years, and compares them with similar Canadian-born and immigrant cohorts (Hou 2021). Hou's statistical analysis is covered in the chapter of this book titled "Conclusions and Reflections." As well, there are a few research articles and a few books published about specific aspects of the Canadian Vietnamese, Canadian Cambodian, and Canadian Laotian diasporas and their experiences in Canada. However, a national study based on the personal experiences of Southeast Asian refugees in their homelands and during their escapes as well as on their settlement experiences in all of Canada over more than four decades has not yet been attempted. This book begins to fill the void.

The stories of Vietnamese, Laotian, and Cambodian refugees are dealt with separately, in parts 2 to 5 of the book. An effort has been made to present analyses of their escapes and Canadian settlement using all the interviews. Twenty more comprehensive individual narratives have been highlighted to present, in-depth, the Vietnamese, Cambodian, and Laotian refugee flight from Southeast Asia, as well as the Canadian settlement experience of each national group. It was difficult to choose which stories to highlight; all the interviews are deeply moving and compelling. Space limitations forced the authors to make some hard choices. The authors were able to draw on the thoughtful advice of the interviewing team members in making those choices.

The Structure of This Book

Part 1, consisting of chapter 1, provides a short discussion of the historical roots of the refugee movement. It describes the context for the refugee interviews on which the rest of the book is based.

In parts 2, 3, 4, and 5, the stories of Vietnamese, Cambodian, and Laotian refugees are dealt with separately. Analyses of their escapes and Canadian settlement are presented using all the refugee interviews. We gave a great deal of thought to the order in which the accounts of the three communities should be presented. Since the Vietnamese were by far the largest group admitted to Canada, it seemed reasonable that they should be placed first. As the Cambodians were the second largest group brought to Canada and because of the sheer magnitude of the catastrophe that befell the Cambodian people, they were placed next, followed by the Laotians. That said, conditions in Laos were so dire that 10 per cent of the population decided to flee.

Part 2 (chapters 2–4) and part 3 (chapters 5–8) deal with the Vietnamese refugees, estimated at 80 per cent of the overall Southeast Asian refugee movement to Canada. For this reason, they are also the majority of the HOF refugee interviewees: eighty-seven Vietnamese interviews versus thirty Cambodian and twenty-eight Laotian interviews (see appendix 2).

The experiences of the Vietnamese who fled in April 1975 as Communist forces closed in on Saigon are distinct from the later movement of boat people who escaped after having suffered under the North Vietnamese–imposed communist regime. For the purposes of this book, we refer to them as "war refugees." They merit separate treatment in part 2 (chapters 2, 3, and 4.)

Chapter 2 recounts the experiences of the Vietnamese war refugees' escapes during the war's last days and their stays in US military bases that had been designated as refugee reception centres, as well as in Hong Kong. These refugees fled Vietnam before the North Vietnamese could fully occupy the South. They were mainly military officers, government officials of the South Vietnamese government, and businesspeople who had cooperated with the Americans. The North Vietnamese blamed them for the war's enormous destruction. Immediately after the fall of Saigon on 30 April 1975, the new Communist government started to severely persecute and imprison people like them as "American puppets."

The war refugee interviewees recall the communist victory as a tragedy, and the majority remain convinced anticommunists but, at the same time, patriotic Vietnamese to this day. Their escape stories are deeply touching. They include a woman giving birth on board a sinking refugee ship before being rescued by a passing Danish freighter, and the loss of a young child who fell into the sea while boarding a refugee ship. However, compared to later refugee departures, the war refugees' escapes were quite rapid. Some fled on large naval or commercial ships, and others by air. Their accommodations in Guam or in military camps on the US mainland were relatively good, and those wishing to come to Canada were accepted rapidly.

Chapter 3 covers the arrival, adaptation, and lives in Canada of the war refugees. The majority, especially those who resettled in Quebec, were well educated and spoke French or English quite well. The private sponsorship program that was introduced through the 1976 Immigration Act did not yet exist. When arriving in Canada, they were assisted by Manpower and Immigration Canada and Quebec Immigration. In general, their adaptation and integration into the Canadian labour market was rapid and, in their view, successful. They pioneered the establishment of Vietnamese community institutions which served as important social anchors for their boat people compatriots who started arriving in Canada a few years later. Having said this, they faced cultural adaptation challenges, especially at the start of their lives in Canada.

Chapter 4 provides narrative descriptions of three war refugee interviews, detailing the war refugee experience from the chaotic escapes from Vietnam to the successful resettlement in Canada.

Part 3 (chapters 5–8) is devoted to the ethnic Vietnamese and Chinese Vietnamese boat people, a few Vietnamese refugees who escaped overland to Thailand, and others who fled from North Vietnam. These chapters recount the interviewees' lives in Vietnam after 1975, their escapes, and the refugee camp experiences.

The boat people movement started as a trickle in 1976, reached its peak in 1979 and 1980, and continued intermittently into the 1990s. Many perished on the high seas, and almost all went through terrifying experiences before reaching land in Malaysia, Thailand, Indonesia, Hong Kong, Macau, Philippines, and Singapore.

The boat people phenomenon began in earnest with the expulsion of the Chinese minority, considered by the Communist Vietnamese government as "businesspeople" to be class enemies. Historically, the Chinese minority in South Vietnam, the Hoa, were the commercial middle class of the country. The Communist Vietnamese government nationalized Chinese-owned businesses, leaving the cities dependent on the black market and inefficient government suppliers. The Hoa lost their livelihoods. Then the government forced them to leave Vietnam while also extracting payments of large sums in gold from them. Initially, they departed on large commercial ships. Their semi-official departures were organized by Hong Kong syndicates with the tacit participation of the Vietnamese government. With economic, social, and political conditions in Vietnam deteriorating rapidly – not only for the Chinese minority but all of the middle class – ethnic Vietnamese people rapidly joined the exodus, usually using small, overloaded, unseaworthy fishing boats, hence the term "boat people." By late 1979, most boat people were ethnic Vietnamese.

Chapter 5 starts by describing life under the post-1975 Communist government. There was repression, chaos, and corruption. Class enemies (i.e., middle-class people), including many HOF interviewees, were sent to re-education camps that were in fact concentration camps where labour was hard, treatment was harsh, food was scarce, and medical services essentially nonexistent. Once released, these interviewees saw little choice but to risk mortal dangers on the high seas in the attempt to escape what they describe as the hell of their lives in Vietnam. Those who survived pirate attacks, storms, shipwrecks, and being pushed out to sea by coast guard or naval vessels often owed their lives to rescues at sea by cruising rescue vessels, oil rig platform supply ships, and commercial ships that encountered them by chance. Once ashore, they could spend months, sometimes years, in refugee camps in neighbouring countries. The worst of these camps, rife with disease and death, were on isolated jungle islands visited intermittently by United Nations High Commissioner for Refugees (UNHCR) Red Cross workers, and occasionally Canadian and other immigration officials. The majority, however, were accommodated in camps regularly serviced by immigration officers of Western countries. The interviewees consider themselves lucky to have been accepted for resettlement by Canada.

Chapter 6 relates four in-depth individual stories of the escape and refugee camp experiences of the boat people in moving detail. They include descriptions of small, dangerously overloaded fishing boats, repeated attacks by pirates, the traumatic abandonment of a young child, and boats being deliberately broken up in sight of land by the refugees to prevent their being towed out to sea off the coasts of Singapore and Malaysia. They highlight high sea rescues by a German rescue ship and an Australian yacht. They also describe conditions endured by the individual boat people in refugee camps.

Chapter 7 presents descriptions of the lives of boat people from their arrival in Canada until the present day and highlights different aspects of the refugee resettlement experience over three to four decades. With the implementation of the 1976 Immigration Act at the beginning of 1979, the institutional framework for their reception and integration fell under three categories: some were sponsored by groups of private citizens, some were assisted by the Canadian government, and still others were sponsored by family members already residing in Canada. The refugees' memories of resettlement and integration in Canada under these categories form a central part of their Canadian stories. The interviewees describe many initial difficulties, but almost all of them reported having achieved what they describe as successful and satisfactory lives by the end of their first decade in Canada. Much initially depended on their relationships with Canadians who welcomed them, whether these were private sponsors, volunteers, or government officials. Generally, the personal aspects of private sponsorships provided a more lasting foundation for the interviewees' lives than more official interactions with government officials. The rapid adaptation of those sponsored by family members – themselves former refugees – demonstrates the effectiveness of family reunification within the context of larger refugee movements.

Chapter 8 concentrates on the detailed life experiences of seven individual interviewees under the above three scenarios. It shows how the relationships established between private Canadian sponsors – often from faith-based organizations – could last a lifetime. These detailed accounts reflect the immediacy of the interviewees' feelings as they describe their lives. Several of these interviewees were children when they arrived in Canada. They see their lives as stories of passage between cultures.

Part 4 (chapters 9–11) deals with the escape from Cambodia and the resettlement in Canada of the Cambodian interviewees. This movement remained relatively small until the end of 1980, but became significant afterward, with 75 per cent of Cambodian refugees arriving in Canada starting in 1981. Before the end of 1980, approximately twice as many Laotians arrived in Canada than Cambodians. However, starting in 1980, the total number of Cambodian refugees resettling in Canada surpassed the Laotian resettlement figures.

The Khmer Rouge communist regime brought the most extreme form of murderous dictatorship to Cambodia. Cities were emptied; columns of urban residents, who had never lived as farmers, were driven into the countryside. People, including many children, lost their families and often would never see them again. The Khmer Rouge's nearly four-year-long reign of terror, now recognized as genocide, was one of the worst in the twentieth century.

Chapter 9 presents their accounts of their lives in Cambodia and the narratives of their escapes. From one interview to the next, the details may vary, but the essence remains the same: life under the Khmer Rouge was a period of intense physical and psychological suffering for all the interviewees. Stories of the escapes through the jungles to Thailand and the often hostile reception by Thai authorities are also similar. They include the terrible tale of Royal Thai Army soldiers rounding up roughly 40,000 refugees, taking them to the border by bus to the top of a steep mountain, Preah Vihear, whose slopes were covered by landmines, and making them descend on foot back to Cambodia. Interviewees describe Khao I Dang, the largest Thai refugee camp, which held over 130,000 people in 1980. It was an enormous prison surrounded by barbed wire, with limited drinking water and toilet facilities and cruel but bribable Thai guards.

Chapter 10 recounts the profound culture shock that characterized the arrival experience of Cambodian refugees in Canada. Language, climate, and strange foods combined to cause initial problems. Yet it speaks volumes for the resiliency and willpower of these interviewees that after terrible and traumatic experiences in their homelands, they were able to build what they describe as successful lives in Canada for their families and their community, often with the help of the Canadians who had sponsored them.

Chapter 11's three in-depth individual Cambodian interviews are difficult to listen to in a single sitting because of the acute human suffering they depict. These three were children under the Khmer Rouge dictatorship. They went through terrible experiences between the ages of eleven and sixteen. Losing most of their families, they saw and experienced violent death and torture inside Cambodia over and over again. Several times, they barely managed to survive. Two of the three interviewees recounted their experiences of Preah Vihear, the Ghost Mountain. They describe hellish scenes with mangled corpses covering the mountainside. More than 10,000 people died on that mountain. These interviewees still carry those memories.

Part 5 (chapters 12–14) deals with the Laotian refugees who fled the aftermath of the Lao Secret War and the victory of the communist Pathet Lao on 2 December 1975. The Laotian refugee movement began before Canadian teams were able to gain access to the Cambodian refugee population. Before the end of 1980, approximately twice as many Laotians had arrived in Canada as Cambodians due to the larger number of Laotians available for resettlement in refugee camps in Thailand.

Chapter 12 describes the escape, refugee camp, and Canadian resettlement experience of the Laotian interviewees. For some, crossing the Mekong River into Thailand was relatively easy; others crossed under gunfire, and still others had to swim. As with the Vietnamese refugees, there are no reliable estimates regarding the number who perished during their escape journeys. Being in Thailand did not necessarily mean safety; some refugees were kept in detention, waiting to have their fate decided by Thai officials. A few of the Thai refugee camps were quite good with apartment-like accommodations and refugees could work and visit neighbouring towns. But most camps housing Laotians in Thailand were overcrowded, with poor accommodations, food, and hygienic conditions. Some refugees had to build their own huts from trees in the thick forests, close to the camps.

As chapter 13 demonstrates, the majority of Laotian interviewees arrived in Canada in 1979–80. Most faced culture shock. Laotian refugees recognize and express their gratitude for the help they received from the Canadian government and private Canadians. At the same time, an important aspect of their integration journey was the creation of their community associations. As was the case with the Vietnamese refugees, the sense of belonging to their own ethnic cultural group has smoothed the Laotians' way to becoming Canadians.

Chapter 14 narrates the full escape stories of three representative Laotian refugees. One was a member of an ethnic minority Hmong family who, fearing communist revenge for the Hmong support of the US Central Intelligence Agency (CIA), fled immediately after the communist Pathet Lao conquest. They walked through thick jungle to reach the border, where Thai border guards considered pushing them back into Laos. The other two stories tell of escapes on tiny boats across the Mekong River. One of the boats had a smooth crossing while the other faced gunfire from troops on the shore. All three families eventually made it to refugee camps in Thailand. The Hmong family settled in Kitchener, Ontario, helping to establish the only large Hmong community in Canada. One government-assisted family was directed to Ottawa where they still live. The other was sponsored by a private group in small-town Quebec.

The Appendices

For the first time, statistical information has been collected and compiled on the entire Southeast Asian refugee movement to Canada from 1975 to 1997, the year Canada ended its Indochinese Refugee Program.

Appendix 1 provides a statistical analysis of the refugee movement. This has proven to be a major undertaking requiring critical comparative analysis since statistical sources are found in different archival locations and are occasionally inconsistent with each other.

Appendix 2 draws a statistical profile of the HOF interviewees. The statistics aim to place the Southeast Asian refugee movement within Canada's demographic and immigration history.

Appendix 3 contains brief summaries of the twenty-eight HOF interviews with Canadian political leaders, former officials, faith community leaders, community coordinators, and sponsors. These interviews fall outside the scope of this book, but together they cover a broad spectrum of government and civil society action on behalf of the Southeast Asian refugees.

Appendix 4 provides a list of the people and organizations that funded, supported, or participated in the HOF project.

TIMELINE

The following is an overview of key events in the history of the Southeast Asian refugee movement to Canada that are critical to the stories discussed in this book:

APRIL–DECEMBER 1975
Communist forces begin takeover of Southeast Asian countries: Cambodia on 17 April, South Vietnam on 30 April, and Laos on 2 December.

1 MAY 1975
Canada decides to resettle all refugees with relatives, plus 3,000 without relatives, in Canada.

MAY 1975–76
Canadian teams in Hong Kong, Guam, Wake Island, and the United States accept over 6,000 Vietnamese refugees.

MAY 1975–DECEMBER 1980
Vietnamese government deports over 750,000 "class enemies" to New Economic Zones in the wilderness.

2 DECEMBER 1975
The capital of Laos, Vientiane, falls to the communist Pathet Lao (officially the Lao People's Liberation Army) who proclaim the Lao People's Democratic Republic. King Sisavang Vatthana agrees to abdicate, and the

prime minister resigns. Repression and the establishment of political re-education camps, called *semina* in Lao, cause 10 per cent of the population to flee to Thailand.

DECEMBER 1977
Fighting begins between Vietnam and Cambodia leading to the expulsion of 150,000 ethnic Vietnamese from Cambodia to Vietnam.

13 JANUARY 1978
Canada agrees to accept fifty Small Boat Escapees families per month.

25 JANUARY 1978
Canada approves the Private Refugee Sponsorship Program.

APRIL–DECEMBER 1978
Approximately 200,000 ethnic Chinese from northern Vietnam are expelled to China.

20 JULY 1978
Canada launches the Thailand Overland Refugee Program for Lao and Cambodian refugees.

NOVEMBER 1978
Media attention increases when the freighter *Hai Hong* arrives off the coast of Malaysia from Vietnam with 2,500 mostly ethnic Chinese refugees. Canada and Quebec agree to accept 600 refugees.

7 DECEMBER 1978
Canadian government approves the Indochinese Designated Class regulations that streamline refugee processing by immigration agents on site in the refugee camps.

11–12 DECEMBER 1978
UNHCR holds a consultation on the refugee crisis and calls for nations to resettle more Indochinese refugees.

20 DECEMBER 1978
Canada agrees to admit 5,000 Vietnamese, Lao, and Cambodian refugees in 1979.

DECEMBER 1978
Vietnamese forces invade Cambodia, overthrowing Pol Pot's Khmer Rouge regime.

FEBRUARY 1979
During the destructive Sino-Vietnamese War, Vietnam expels tens of thousands of additional ethnic Chinese residents.

5 MARCH 1979
The Mennonite Central Committee Canada (MCCC) signs the first sponsorship Master Agreement with Immigration Canada.

APRIL–JUNE 1979
There is a dramatic increase in Vietnamese refugee boats landing in neighbouring Southeast Asian countries: 26,602 in April; 51,139 in May; and 56,941 in June.

MAY 1979
The UNHCR brokers the Orderly Departure Program (ODP) for refugees who are family members of Vietnamese refugees resettled abroad.
The Matching Centre is established in Ottawa to match arriving refugees with sponsors.

18 JUNE 1979
In Canada, the newly elected Conservative government led by Joe Clark increases the target to 8,000 refugees and asks civil society to provide an additional 4,000 private sponsorships.

24 JUNE 1979
In Canada, Howard Adelman of Toronto establishes Operation Lifeline to promote private sponsorship by community groups.

27 JUNE 1979
In Canada, Ottawa's mayor Marion Dewar decides to sponsor half of the government's 8,000 refugees and launches Project 4000.

20–21 JULY 1979
At the UN Conference in Geneva, Canada agrees to accept 50,000 additional Vietnamese, Laotian, and Cambodian refugees in 1979–80.

8 AND 14 AUGUST 1979
The first two of what will be a total of 181 refugee charter flights from Vietnam arrive at Immigration Canada reception centres in Montreal and Edmonton.

SEPTEMBER 1979
In Canada, a new simplified document (IMM1314) is introduced which reduces resettlement paper burden for immigration officials by 60 per cent.

OCTOBER–NOVEMBER 1979
An estimated 600,000 to 800,000 starving Cambodians arrive at the Thai border.

FEBRUARY 1980
In a general election in Canada, the Liberal Party led by Pierre Trudeau defeats the Conservative Party led by Joe Clark.

2 APRIL 1980
The new Liberal government continues the resettlement efforts of the previous government, and Canada announces that it will accept an additional 10,000 government-assisted refugees, raising the target of total refugees to 60,000.

8 DECEMBER 1980
The last of Canada's refugee charter flights arrives in Montreal, carrying the last of the 60,049 refugees accepted to that date.

1981–97
Canada's Resettlement Program continues at the approximate rate of 6,000 refugees per year. The number of Cambodians increases, and the number of family reunifications through the ODP also increases.

13–14 JUNE 1989
The UN approves the Comprehensive Plan of Action (CPA), which means that the existing populations in refugee camps will be resettled. New arrivals to refugee camps are screened; those who fit the definition of "refugee" from the 1951 Refugee Convention will be resettled, while the remainder must return home.

1990–97
Canada resettles 16,990 refugees under the CPA.

1997
Canada closes the Indochinese Refugee Program.

Conclusion

The general outcome of this historical chapter in Canadian history is that in the period between 1975 and 1997, Canada resettled 145,125 refugees and reunited 64,955 people with their families, for a combined total of 210,080 individuals (see appendix 1). It is the life experiences of the Southeast Asian refugees who resettled in Canada during this period that are at the core of this book. They are a testament to the courage, the resilience, and the steadfastness of the refugees and of their Canadian facilitators.

PART ONE

Southeast Asia: Wars, Oppression, and Refugees

1

The Southeast Asian Refugee Movement: Its Root Causes and History

There is a voluminous body of literature about the history of the Indochinese wars and the Southeast Asian refugee movement. This chapter means to provide the historical background to the refugee interviews that are the main constituents of this book, but can provide only a restricted choice of hundreds of reference works that may have a bearing on presenting the historical context for the oral history interviews (Owen 2005; Tarling 1993; Goscha 2016).

The Colonial Period

The five constituent protectorates of French Indochina were Cochin China, Annam, Tonkin, Cambodia, and Laos. The first three were administrative divisions of Vietnam. All five were conquered in stages by France in the latter half of the nineteenth century, starting in the 1850s. The French introduced French language and culture to the urban and intellectual elites, divided the agricultural lands into large estates held by French colonists and landlords loyal to the colonial overlords, introduced French education for the elites, and converted a minority of the population to Roman Catholicism. During their domination by colonial masters, the French protectorates of Southeast Asia became deeply fragmented politically and socially (Owen 2005; Tarling 1993; Goscha 2016).

The root causes of the refugee movement lie in the history of Southeast Asia, especially the four decades between Japan's invasion of French Indochina consisting of Vietnam, Cambodia, and Laos in 1940, and the peak of the Vietnamese boat people movement from 1978 to 1980. Phases of this long period of conflict are reflected in the personal experiences of the HOF interviewees, providing a human face to violence, atrocities, and the escape to freedom in Canada (Owen 2005).

During World War II, the French colonial administration was maintained in Indochina under the Japanese occupiers. Vietnamese guerillas, members of the largest of the three historic nations of the French colonial empire in Southeast Asia, fought the colonial masters in an attempt to establish an independent Vietnamese nation-state. In the Viet Minh guerilla army, communists and nationalists joined in the anticolonial struggle (Goscha 2022).

After the defeat of the Japanese in 1945, there was a scramble for dominance in French Indochina. In the First Indochina War, the French attempted to regain control of their colonies against the Viet Minh. The latter, under communist leadership and with the support of the USSR, sidelined the Vietnamese nationalists and assumed the leading role in the fight for Vietnamese independence. While there were Viet Minh incursions into Laos and Cambodia during the war, the two smaller states as well as South Vietnam remained French protectorates until 1954 (Goscha 2022). The Viet Minh, with weapons supplied by the USSR and China and using the tested methods of Maoist peasant revolutionary war, defeated the French in 1954 (Holcombe 2020, 159–78; Davidson 1991).

Vietnam Divided

Following communist victory in North Vietnam, Hanoi's authoritarian government immediately started to persecute its former nationalist allies as well as any class enemies, meaning especially landholders in North Vietnam. Historians estimate that up to 200,000 people were executed in an anti-landlord, anticapitalist campaign during the early years of communist rule, including several of the most important nationalist leaders of the anticolonial struggle (Davidson 1991).

The Geneva Peace Accords, signed in 1954, called for a ceasefire line to divide North and South Vietnam and for communist troops and guerrillas to evacuate Laos and Cambodia. The communist conquest was initially limited to North Vietnam, and under the Accords, Vietnam was supposed to be united through elections between July 1955 and July 1956.

However, even as the French withdrew from their former colonies, the United States took over as the main supporter of the anticommunist forces, providing aid to the new conservative nationalist government of South Vietnam against communist conquest and ensuring that in the newly independent countries of Cambodia and Laos noncommunist governments came to power (Holcombe 2020, 211–18).

The first major population displacement in former French Indochina took place legally in 1954 in accordance with the Geneva Peace Accords. For three months, the populations of both Vietnams could choose where they wished to live; 100,000 South Vietnamese moved north, and 900,000 North Vietnamese chose to move south. This represented 7 per cent of North Vietnam's population, including many middle-class people, relatively well-to-do peasants, and members of the Catholic minority (Holcombe 2020, 220–38). Having experienced communism, they made their choice with their feet. The families of a number of the HOF interviewees moved south at this time.

The government of South Vietnam emerged as a fully independent state based on conservative nationalist principles. It continued to be supported by the US, which, after the communist victory in China, aimed to stop the progress of communism in Southeast Asia at any cost. Many of the 1954 refugees from North Vietnam received dominant positions in the South Vietnamese government, resulting in feelings of resentment and protests against the government by a large part of South Vietnam's population. With some communist cadres still ensconced in rural areas of South Vietnam and Ho Chi Minh's communist government exercising extreme authoritarian control in North Vietnam, the national election mandated by the Geneva Accords was feared by South Vietnam and the US. The election was never held (Singh 2015, 620–9).

The Vietnamese/American War Begins

North Vietnam regarded South Vietnam's refusal to hold the election as justification for restarting the war. The first major step was to retrain communist Viet Minh cadres who had left South Vietnam in 1954 in military and propaganda methods and send them back to South Vietnam to reinforce the communists still operating in the South. The communist cadres, renamed the Viet Cong, were able to exercise influence over ever larger areas of South Vietnam as rural guerillas.

At the same time, a network of trails, together known as the Ho Chi Minh Trail was built in the jungles of Laos and Cambodia. Along this trail, North Vietnam supplied the Viet Cong with fighting men and military equipment. Gradually, the distinction between the North Vietnamese Army and the Viet Cong became moot. Both operated following the orders of North Vietnamese military planners. Despite intense efforts by the US and South Vietnam to destroy it, the Ho Chi Minh Trail remained North Vietnam's lifeline to the south until South Vietnam's defeat sixteen years later (Dommen 1972).

Laos and Cambodia Dragged In: The Ho Chi Minh Trail

The Ho Chi Minh Trail was essential to North Vietnam's ability to pursue the war. To keep the trail operational, North Vietnamese troops disregarded Laotian or Cambodian sovereignty and operated freely in both countries. Fearing North Vietnam, in Laos and Cambodia the governments adopted neutral attitudes to the de facto occupation of part of their territories by the North Vietnamese army (Dommen 1972). But in northeastern Laos, the Hmong minority, encouraged and supported by the CIA, reacted to the constant North Vietnamese incursions by fighting a guerilla war against North Vietnam and its Laotian proxy, the Pathet Lao (Paul et al. 2013, 147–56).

The war in Vietnam, variously referred to as the Second Indochina War, the Vietnam War, or the American War in Vietnam, raged back and forth. However, North Vietnam's extreme authoritarian control of its armed forces combined with capable military leadership, as well as constant propaganda referring to the difficult social conditions of the South Vietnamese peasantry and the use of terror in southern villages by the Viet Cong favoured North Vietnam (Opper 2020, 205–33). By 1965, the Americans concluded that the war could not be won unless substantial US forces were sent to fight in Vietnam. For the next eight years, the war became an American-directed and heavily American-fought conflict. However, right from the beginning, there was a high level of opposition in the US to sending troops into an Asian guerilla war. The US was fighting a war on unfamiliar terrain, surrounded by culturally and linguistically distant rural people, often under the control of enemy guerillas who blended seamlessly into the rural population (Opper 2020, 205–33; Paul et al. 2013, 177–97).

Also, it is not an exaggeration to say that while the North Vietnamese soldiers knew what they were fighting for – the reunification of "their" country – South Vietnamese soldiers fought to prevent a communist takeover. American soldiers were often uncertain as to why they were there. The Americans attempted to balance these disadvantages by using extremely destructive military measures like napalm and Agent Orange in South Vietnam's Mekong Delta, and carpet bombing the Ho Chi Minh Trail in Laos and Cambodia. The destruction in Cambodia and Laos was catastrophic. Entire villages were obliterated, while up to 1 million civilians, mostly poor farmers and their families were killed. Although the Geneva Agreements of 1962 declared neutrality in Laos, between 1964 and 1973 the US, in a secret war, dropped over 2 million tons of bombs over Laos, making it the most heavily bombed country per capita in the history of warfare. Yet the passage of North Vietnamese forces and equipment to the south continued. The destruction alienated rural populations, turning many of them into communist supporters (Stuart-Fox 1997).

At the same time, most South Vietnamese soldiers remained committed Vietnamese nationalists who considered the North Vietnamese and the Viet Cong guerillas to be traitors, fighting in the service of international communism, an ideology foreign to the Vietnamese nation. South Vietnam suffered extremely high casualties; five times more South Vietnamese soldiers died in the war than US soldiers. But the casualties suffered by South Vietnam paled in comparison to North Vietnamese losses of human lives. The communist leaders of North Vietnam believed that victory was worth the mass sacrifice. With the extreme murderous violence and cruelty of the war, enmity between the two Vietnams ran very deep (Duong 2008, Rummel 1997).

During the war's last years, most of Vietnam's rural areas became unlivable for middle-class civilians. HOF interviewees describe living in a state of fear and incidents of terror by the Viet Cong. In consequence, the cities, especially Saigon, were flooded with refugees from the countryside. Also, some US soldiers, brutalized by the war's savagery, committed savage acts themselves. The March 1968 My Lai massacre of unarmed villagers by American soldiers, two months after the North Vietnamese Army's Tet massacres, received wide media coverage and turned ever larger segments of American and Canadian public opinion against the war. In Canada, networks to support young American draft resisters and deserters were organized. There were antiwar demonstrations throughout North America (Borch 2018; Hammond 2009; Elliott 2010, 285–348).

The essential appeal of the Viet Cong to landless peasant populations was the promise of land reform. As scholarly analyses have observed, this was South Vietnam's key social problem, the Achilles heel of the South Vietnamese government. Yet, until 1970, no South Vietnamese government could impose serious land reform, as the influential large landlords were determined to hold on to their properties. However, in 1970, largely under pressure by the US, a major effort at land reform was instituted through the "Land to the Tiller" program. Ironically, as the military situation continued to deteriorate, in theory South Vietnam managed to institute important social change by ending the old land tenancy system. On paper, by 1973, 40 per cent of agricultural land was in the hands of private farmers. In fact, much of the most productive agricultural land in the Mekong delta was, by this time, controlled by the Viet Cong. As well, much of this land had been severely damaged through the war especially through the use of American napalm and Agent Orange (Opper 2020, 205–33; Elliott 2003, 372–74).

The US Withdraws

By 1973, the US was ready to call an end to its Southeast Asian war adventure. Through the Paris Peace Accords, all US forces were withdrawn, and peace was declared. North Vietnam never respected the Peace Accords. Fierce fighting continued on the ground between North and South Vietnamese forces. The South Vietnamese forces were seriously impacted by the US phasing out of military equipment supplies to South Vietnam. With the pullout of the Americans, the fates of South Vietnam, Laos, and Cambodia were sealed (Fifield 1997, 864–5).

Communist Victory

The Second Indochina War was simultaneously lost by pro-American regimes in Cambodia, South Vietnam, and Laos between April and December 1975. The first refugees, leaving immediately before the war's loss, were South Vietnamese military men, government functionaries, businesspeople, and their families, as well as members of the Hmong guerilla army (that fought with the support of the CIA) and their families from Laos. All these refugees had actively fought against or strongly opposed the communist takeovers in Vietnam and Laos and feared severe reprisals by the North Vietnamese authorities and the Pathet Lao. As well, a few people managed to escape from communist Cambodia, even as the Khmer Rouge closed Cambodia's borders and rapidly established its bloody reign of terror (Molloy et al. 2017, 22–4).

Most refugees who left during the war's last days had good reasons to fear the new communist governments. But many people in South Vietnam, Cambodia, and Laos also hoped for national reconciliation following the communist conquests. Instead of reconciliation, however, the next several years brought severe persecution against urban and educated people, professionals, the Chinese minority, and anybody whom the new governments defined as class enemies (Molloy et al. 2017, 22–4).

In Laos, after a short period of coalition government dominated by the communist Pathet Lao, King Sisavang Vatthana, the last king of the Kingdom of Laos, was forced to abdicate and sent to a re-education camp, never to be seen again. On 2 December 1975, Laos became a People's Republic, a client state of North Vietnam, with North Vietnamese troops stationed in the country and North Vietnamese advisors active in the Lao government (Stuart-Fox 1997).

The new rulers of South Vietnam and Laos imposed a range of draconian measures on commercial classes, professionals, property holders, former government officials, and anybody who had anything to do with the pre-communist governments. These included the imposition of communist re-education on class enemies, meaning any middle-class people. For young people, much of the education in schools and universities became communist indoctrination. For adults, communist re-education meant incarceration in prison camps or being sent to New Economic Zones in jungle areas where the inmates attended lengthy indoctrination sessions at night following long days of physical labour on inadequate and nutrition-poor food. Depending on the physical health and strength of inmates and the length of time spent in re-education camps or the New Economic Zones, their incarceration resulted in severe health deterioration and even death for many inmates. Only the physically and mentally strong survived. Many were also tortured and executed in the re-education camps. Meanwhile, with the nationalization of private enterprise, devaluation of the currency, climate catastrophes, and government spies reporting on all aspects of the lives of ordinary people, life in South Vietnam and Laos became extremely difficult, especially for women with families whose husbands had been taken away for re-education (Duiker 1985; Nguyen 1983).

The promise of land reform, the main instrument for getting South Vietnamese agricultural labourers and tenant farmers to support the Viet Cong during the war, turned out to be illusory. In both South Vietnam and Laos, the new communist authorities rapidly proceeded to collectivize agriculture. As a result, agricultural production stagnated and in many regions it declined. By 1978, there were food shortages in South Vietnam, Laos, and Cambodia (Bredo 1970).

The Cambodian Genocide

However severe they were, measures against class enemies in Vietnam and Laos, including the Chinese minority in Vietnam and the Hmong minority in Laos, paled in comparison with the ruthless, murderous terror imposed by the Khmer Rouge in Cambodia against urban dwellers, the middle class, and the educated. During the three years of Khmer Rouge rule, to be a literate urban dweller in Cambodia was in many cases a death sentence. The Khmer peasantry did not fare much better. They were herded into enormous collective farms, their personal property was seized, and they were forced to labour on a starvation diet. The Khmer Rouge turned a large part of Cambodia's population into defenceless slaves and murdered one-quarter to one-third of the Khmer people (Hinton 2005).

After the fall of Saigon, economic aid to Vietnam from China dried up. Following the death of Mao Zedong in 1976, the Chinese communists, under the leadership of Deng Xiaoping, adopted capitalistic economic reforms and more open governance structures. They no longer supported their Vietnamese comrades, who had remained doctrinaire Maoists and who, following their military victories, appeared to be an aggressive military power intent on taking over the former French Indochina (Path 2012).

Expulsion of Vietnam's Chinese Minority

Although there were sporadic refugee boat departures from South Vietnam before 1978, the boat people phenomenon expanded dramatically with the expulsion of the Chinese minority – the Hoa. The Hoa were the bulk of the capitalist commercial class of South Vietnam, controlling a large part of South Vietnam's economy before North Vietnam's military victory. With the anticapitalist policies of the new government, including the nationalization of Hoa businesses, workshops, stores, and family homes, the Hoa lost their economic roles and livelihoods and were on the road to personal and family destitution. At the same time, many of the formerly wealthy Hoa managed to hide some personal wealth in the form of gold. In the midst of severe economic decline in South Vietnam, largely due to communist economic policies, the authorities wanted to take possession of the wealth remaining in Hoa hands (Amer 1996).

In mid- to late 1978, formerly wealthy Hoa in South Vietnam were given a choice: go to the New Economic Zones to do hard labour in jungle areas or leave Vietnam. A semi-legal procedure was organized through the "Cong An" or Public Service Bureau which allowed Chinese people to leave by boat, organized through private middlemen, against the payment of 4 to 12 taels of gold per adult and half that amount per child (1 tael = 1.22 ounces). This was the choice preferred by many Hoa and was the beginning of large-scale refugee departures by boat (i.e., the boat people movement). At the same time, the Hanoi government expanded its anti-Chinese campaign to North Vietnam and expelled some 200,000 Chinese from the North, across the land border to China (Robinson 1998, 31).

The Chinese response to the expulsion of the Chinese minority from northern Vietnam to China was a short but intensely destructive war against Vietnam in early 1979. Many Vietnamese villages were destroyed and the Chinese-Vietnamese expellees were sent back to Vietnam, only to be re-expelled to China by the Vietnamese (Robinson 1998, 39, 42). Thus, the expulsion of large parts of the Chinese-Vietnamese minority both from North and South Vietnam, starting in late 1977, rapidly increasing in 1978 and reaching its peak in 1979, was the beginning of the major refugee movement from Vietnam that continued through the 1980s and only came to an end in the 1990s.

The Boat People

Starting in mid-1978, clandestine boat departures from Vietnam increased rapidly month after month. In 1978, 85,000 boat refugees arrived in first countries of asylum, most in Association of Southeast Asian Nations (ASEAN) member states around the South China Sea. During the first six months of 1979, the total was 161,000. In 1978, the boat departures were still mainly quasi-legal, mostly by ethnic Chinese nationals in large freighters organized by Hong Kong syndicates. Losses of life on the high seas were still relatively low. However, the possibility of leaving Vietnam attracted the ethnic Vietnamese middle classes suffering under communist rule. By mid-1979, the refugees clandestinely leaving Vietnam were mostly ethnic Vietnamese middle-class people, using small, barely seaworthy vessels, prey to pirates and weather, and were often pushed out to sea by armed forces in the states where they attempted to land (Robinson 1998, 39–44).

Meanwhile, conditions in the Vietnamese Cambodian border regions deteriorated with serious fighting between the Vietnamese People's Army and the Khmer Rouge. During its three-year reign of terror, the Khmer Rouge attempted to either assimilate or liquidate the country's minorities including the Chinese and the Vietnamese. They murdered many Vietnamese minority people and undertook violent incursions across the border into Vietnam, wiping out several Vietnamese villages. Most of the remaining Cambodian Vietnamese escaped to the Mekong Delta region of Vietnam where they formed a large refugee population of 130,000, a major burden in a country suffering from severe economic problems (Robinson 1998, 32–3; Hinton 2005).

Vietnam Invades Cambodia

In December 1978, the Vietnamese responded by invading Cambodia. By January 1979, Phnom Penh fell to the Vietnamese Army. But this was not the end of the Khmer Rouge, who withdrew into the western jungle areas of Cambodia close to the Thai border, and regularly crossed into a no-man's land located in the jungle on the Thai side of the border. Supported by China, the Khmer Rouge remained active until the early 1990s. Cambodia continued as a state where violence often erupted during this long period, with incipient fighting in different regions of the country and frequent changes of government (Robinson 2000, 32–3; Southgate 2009).

After the fall of Phnom Penh to the Vietnamese in early 1979, Cambodians were caught between the Khmer Rouge and the Vietnamese invaders. Many Cambodians headed west into the jungles on the Thai border. As several Cambodian HOF interviewees describe, their journeys were extremely difficult and dangerous. In addition to the natural dangers of the jungle environment, they had to avoid the Khmer Rouge who were also heading west to their jungle strongholds. Once the refugees reached no-man's land across the border, but not yet formally in Thailand, they built makeshift camps in jungle clearings. Thai military security, afraid of Khmer Rouge infiltration, wanted no Cambodians in Thailand. In a notorious incident, described in harrowing detail by two interviewees, the Thai army rounded up over 40,000 refugees and sent them back to Cambodia. Ten thousand perished in minefields on the border at Preah Vihear. Partly because of the outcry over this incident,

Thai authorities became less brutal with the Cambodian refugees and allowed them into supervised camps surrounded by barbed wire, still near the border (Robinson 1998, 45–50).

By the end of 1978, the international community recognized that the refugee crisis originating in the countries of the former French Indochina presented a dangerous challenge to the relatively recently established and still delicate international order of Southeast Asia. With the exception of Thailand, which had avoided colonization, the countries of the region had attained independence after long periods of colonial domination by European powers and Japanese occupation during World War II. All the newly independent countries continued to be unstable. In each former colony, meaning the three countries of former French Indochina plus Malaysia and Indonesia, there were powerful communist movements in the immediate post–World War II period, with the communists emerging victorious in Vietnam, Cambodia and Laos. None of the noncommunist countries of the region had ratified the 1951 UN Refugee Convention and they were not in a position to easily accommodate major refugee movements from the communist countries of former French Indochina. Developed countries, including Canada, searched for solutions that would stop the instability caused by the rapidly growing refugee outflow and would maintain international order in Southeast Asia (Robinson 1998, 20–33).

The International Response

Following a UNHCR consultation in December 1978, Canada, along with other Western countries, made commitments to accept Indochinese (as they were called at the time) refugees. But the number of boat people in Malaysia, Indonesia, and Thailand, as well as the overland Laotian and Cambodian refugees in Thailand, continued to grow exponentially, and the commitments made in December 1978 rapidly proved to be insufficient. The expulsion of refugees by Vietnam combined with the unwillingness of first countries of asylum to bear the burden of the refugees by themselves created a crisis (Robinson 1998, 32–3).

In July 1979, nations involved with the Southeast Asian refugee crisis met at a formal UN conference in Geneva. Developed countries agreed to resettle all the refugees in the region, countries of first asylum agreed to house the refugees in the camps until they could travel to their final resettlement destination, and Vietnam agreed to stop expelling people from Vietnam.

The Canadian Response

Canada offered to resettle 50,000 refugees before the end of 1980, which was an enormous undertaking. This number was increased to 60,000 in early 1980. A unique aspect of Canada's undertaking was the sharing of responsibility for the initial settlement of the refugees between the Canadian government and the people of Canada through the new innovative private sponsorship program (Molloy et al. 2017, 112–21). In his interview Joe Clark, Canada's prime minister at the time, describes the complex political decision to accept the refugees, the superhuman efforts of Canadian officials to assess the refugees and send them to Canada and, especially, the generosity of Canadian communities to welcome the refugees and help them in their new lives in Canada (Interview HOF173 2021).

The Orderly Departure Program

On 30 May 1979, at a meeting in Indonesia, the UNHCR and Vietnam signed an agreement on orderly departures. This agreement enabled people to leave Vietnam in a legal manner. It applied to humanitarian cases and family reunification. Vietnam appears to have agreed to this arrangement since it allowed people who were family members of refugees resettled in developed countries to leave Vietnam, thereby lifting a burden off the Vietnamese state. Family reunification under the Orderly Departure Program (ODP) became a major element of the Vietnamese movement to Canada in the 1980s (Kumin 2008; Bersma 2024).

The years with the highest Southeast Asian refugee movement to Canada were 1979 and 1980. However, the refugee movement continued throughout the 1980s and into the 1990s. Refugee boats continued to leave Vietnam and, following the fall of the Khmer Rouge government, Cambodians left Cambodia in greater numbers. In the late 1980s, economic and social conditions in the former French Indochina improved considerably. In Vietnam, internal travel controls were relaxed, and many long-term internees were released, leading to an increase in boats arriving in neighbouring nations in 1989. At the same time, there was a growing perception among international and national officials (and even some faith-based organizations) that the nature of the refugee movement from Vietnam was changing: more of those arriving by boat appeared to be motivated by economic aspirations rather than experiences of oppression.

The Comprehensive Plan of Action

In response, UNHCR oversaw the negotiation of the Comprehensive Plan of Action (CPA) of 1989 to manage down the refugee movement. Under the CPA it was agreed that those already in the camps would be resettled. On the other hand, those arriving after a cut-off date would be screened to determine whether they met the definition of "refugee" under the UN Refugee Convention. Those recognized as Convention refugees would also be resettled. Those found not to be Convention refugees would have to return home. The UNHCR would monitor those returned to ensure their safety. This marked the beginning of the end of one of the major refugee movements of the twentieth century. For most of those individuals who were screened out, the results were devastating. One HOF interviewee describes the desperation of refugees in a Thai camp in the early 1990s with scant hope for third-country resettlement. However, once word of the screening reached Vietnam, boat departures abruptly stopped. Right to the end, Canada continued to participate in an international effort to clear the camps and accepted over 15,000 refugees for resettlement between 1990 and 1997 (Robinson 1998, 187–230; Hathaway 1993).

PART TWO

Vietnamese War Refugees

2

Escaping Vietnam: The War Refugees of 1975

The Historical Context and a General Description of the Interviewees

During the last days of April 1975, the decades-long Vietnam War ended in victory for North Vietnam. This led to the mass evacuation of residual United States military personnel and civilians, the escape of large numbers of South Vietnamese military and their families and many middle-class Vietnamese civilians. As a group, the refugees who left immediately following the war's end were mainly government, military, or businesspeople and their families who participated in or supported South Vietnam's war effort and were strongly anticommunist.

For the purposes of this book they are referred to as "war refugees" to distinguish them from the "boat people" who experienced life under the communist regime and fled later. All feared the North Vietnamese armed forces and the establishment of a communist government. The historical, journalistic, and literary sources on the war's end are voluminous and represent many points of view that often contradict each other (Appy 2003; Brune 1992). Yet the voices of refugees who escaped during the fall of Saigon and created new lives in Canada for themselves and their families have been curiously silent, until now.

Before the fall of Saigon, most South Vietnamese military as well as business owners, professionals, government officials, and any others who were afraid of the North Vietnamese were at a loss regarding what to do with no obvious means of escape. They had deep fears for the future, and the experience of the next few years in South Vietnam would confirm that their fears were well founded. Most were unprepared for the extremely rapid North Vietnamese victory.

The majority of those who made it out acted very quickly, often based on sketchy ad hoc knowledge of the escape routes. Virtually all interviewees agree that luck played a major role in enabling them to leave Vietnam at the very end of April and the beginning of May 1975.

Most of the war refugees interviewed in the project escaped Vietnam by sea. Some escaped on Vietnamese Navy vessels; others on the *Clara Maersk*, a Danish container ship that ferried almost 4,000 refugees to Hong Kong after rescuing them from the sinking Vietnamese freighter *Truong Xuan* (Molloy et al. 2017, 49–52).

Still others left on private vessels and were picked up either by one of the twenty-nine ships of the US Seventh Fleet or by the many commercial vessels leased and crewed by the US Navy waiting forty miles from shore in international waters. Two escaped in helicopters, one from the roof of the US embassy; the other, a helicopter pilot, flew his chopper to a US aircraft carrier.

Who were the refugees? In our sample of nineteen interviews, thirteen were military (including husbands or fathers of female interviewees) and six were civilians. With the single exception of a highly trained Special Forces combatant who became a naval officer, military personnel were either sailors or airmen. Our sample includes a few ordinary enlisted men. Of our military interviewees two were naval conscripts; the others were officers, including two doctors. The remainder were landowners, factory owners, professionals (an engineer, a dentist, and a pharmacist), and academics. In a poor, largely agrarian country, they were members of the relatively wealthy middle class. Some of them had connections that facilitated their departures. One of the interviewees managed to escape with his three sons through Operation Frequent Wind, the helicopter airlift from the US embassy, presented in some American accounts as a heroic rescue operation.

For most Vietnamese involved, it was not very heroic. One interviewee and his children managed to get on a US helicopter through a stroke of incredible luck, leaving behind thousands of panic-stricken Vietnamese, desperate to get into the grounds of the US embassy. Nine of the nineteen interviewees were of North Vietnamese origin. They or their parents or other family members came to the south in 1954–55 during the 300-day period of free movement agreed to in the 1954 Geneva Accords, when approximately 900,000 North Vietnamese moved to South Vietnam (Frankum 2007). Two more interviewees originated in Hué, the old imperial capital, and one came from the Vietnamese minority in Cambodia. The interviews do not reveal the origins of the remainder.

The Escapes

During April 1975, the Second Indochina War's last month, North Vietnamese forces rapidly gained ground in all parts of South Vietnam. Small boats filled with escaping soldiers and civilian refugees were already leaving for Saigon and other points south, launching from the long coast between the borders of the two Vietnams in the north and the Mekong River delta in the south.

As the war was being lost, South Vietnamese naval captain Ha Phu Cuong (Interview HOF076 2019) was dispatched by his government to central Vietnam, close to the city of Da Nang. With North Vietnamese troops advancing toward the seacoast, he captained a civilian ship rescuing people. Sailing south along the coast, "I can remember soldiers fleeing, some joined my boat to get to Saigon. [Other refugees on board] were civilians." Arriving in Saigon, the boat was moored at the Saigon naval base. On the last day of the war, with North Vietnamese troops already entering Saigon, Captain Ha decided to steer his boat down the river, escaping to the open sea. "I am a naval officer, [but] approaching April 30, [the last day of the war], the government [still] did not allow our ship to flee." There was chaos at the harbour: "I could not select who came on board, people just jumped on." Then as he saw the South Vietnamese navy leaving, he followed. There were five hundred to six hundred people packed like sardines on his ship, naval officers and sailors with their families as well as civilian refugees. "Food and water were limited, normal food supply was for the ship's crew of thirty-one, not five hundred people."

Captain Ha's ship left at the last possible moment as Saigon fell. Once at sea a US naval ship provided some food, water, and fuel. Initially the ship proceeded to Singapore where authorities refused to allow it to land. Then it sailed to the US naval base in Subic Bay, Philippines, where they stayed for twenty-four hours. From there it was directed to the refugee camp at the US naval base on the distant Pacific island of Guam. The high seas odyssey in a terribly overcrowded and undersupplied ship lasted almost two weeks.

Nguyen Trung Thu (Interview HOF075 2019), Nguyen Van Ba (Interview HOF111 2019), Bui Van Hai (Interview HOF156 2020), and Nguyen Xuan Thach (Interview HOF147 2020) were among the many refugees who, like Captain Ha, took the route down the Saigon River to the open sea. Helicopter pilot Linh Minh Ho (Interview HOF162 2020) joined the exodus. As he states, "All the helicopters were broken. On the way home, I saw a lot of commercial ships at the seaport. My wife said, 'I'm ready to go right now.'" In the chaos of the war's second-last day, with his wife and two daughters they managed to board a Vietnamese commercial ship. The next morning, "the ship left at nine o'clock, communists came at ten o'clock. On the ship, two thousand people total. On the way, pick up more and more people from small boats. Went to Guam from Vietnam, seventeen days."

Some refugees in small river vessels that could not manage in the open sea were fortunate to be picked up by more seaworthy vessels like ships of the US Seventh Fleet or commercial ships. Nobody knows how many small vessels were never rescued and were lost at sea.

Other refugees, including eight-year-old Vu Thanh Uyen Tanya (Interview HOF143 2020), left with their families on the ships of the South Vietnamese naval squadron headed for the Philippines from the Saigon naval base. Le Van Chau (Interview HOF044 2019), a medical doctor in the South Vietnamese Army, describes extreme scenes of chaos at the naval base. Initially only naval personnel and their families were allowed on the naval vessels; soldiers with guns kept civilians away from the ships. In Le's words, "there are too many people. They [the South-Vietnamese soldiers] discharged their weapons because there are too many people. I saw that this was Saigon's agony." Then, under pressure from crowds of panicked people who broke through barriers, civilians and non-navy military personnel were also allowed to board the ships. "We somehow managed to get inside," close to the naval boats.

"There are already three hundred to four hundred persons on that boat ... To get on the boat there is a plank. People walked single file on the plank. In front of me there is a young woman with a baby on her back, she is holding the hand of a little boy, maybe five years old. Me, I had my baby in my right arm and a pack on my back. A person coming off the ship on the plank in the opposite direction somehow pushed [the mother in front of me]; she let go of the little boy and he fell in the water. His mother stopped and cried, 'Save my son, save my son,' but nobody could help, we were far above the water. Behind me my wife was being pushed by the people behind her. 'Move, move.' We had to move, or it would be death for us as well. No choice, we had to push the screaming mother who lost her son onto the boat." With tears in his eyes, Le states, "This image comes back to me every year" on the anniversary of their escape from Vietnam. It haunts his memories to this day.

The family of Nguyen Luan Van Phung (Interview HOF015 2019), including her bomber pilot husband and her two young sons, also left with the naval flotilla. On 28 April, a few weeks after a miscarriage and a life-threatening operation at the small Pleiku Air Force Base hospital, Nguyen and her small family waited at Tan Son Nhut Airport for a plane to take them out of Vietnam. But it was too late: the airport runways were destroyed by North Vietnamese shelling. The family managed to make it to the naval base and were among the last to climb onto a ship. Their odyssey through the chaos of Saigon to the totally chaotic naval base – people and luggage falling into the water, soldiers with guns attempting to push back the crowds – is described in vivid detail by Nguyen.

The voyage to Hong Kong of the large commercial ship *Truong Xuan* was particularly dramatic. Pham Thu Giang (Interview HOF070 2019), daughter of Captain Pham Ngoc Luy, was on that ship along with her extended family. Pham provides a full version of the *Truong Xuan*'s voyage under her father's captainship and its rescue by the Danish freighter *Clara Maersk*. Because its departure was delayed by serious mechanical problems, the *Truong Xuan* was the third large freighter to leave Saigon Harbour. The other two ships that left before it were both ambushed by the North Vietnamese. The *Truong Xuan* was fortunate to be number three. As Pham relates, "My father [Captain Pham] accept everyone who wanted to go, as well as people along the ship route to the ocean, more than 3,600 [on board the ship], people just came, people just ran. As the ship move toward the ocean, a lot of small boats follow. My father just throw them rope; people just pulled them in. [They were] army officer, soldier, lawyer, doctor, even Buddhist monk, Catholic priest, famous singer, and writer and, of course, ordinary people with children. They just sit side by side, had no room at all."

On the way to the open sea the *Truong Xuan* ran into serious mechanical problems but had to keep going since the only other choice was to return to Vietnam and arrest by the communists. There were food and water shortages. "People start to fight over water … Two suicides took place on deck … The [ship's] engine stops once, then starts, then stops because water start to get into the engine room." The boat started to sink and Captain Luy sent out repeated mayday calls. The pleas for help were ignored by two passing ships before the *Clara Maersk* came to their assistance. Pham insists that the refugees on the *Truong Xuan* were indeed extremely lucky; they were rescued by the *Clara Maersk* from the sinking *Truong Xuan*.

Most refugees left Saigon by sea at the last possible moment with little preparation or supplies. But there were some who had the means and the foresight to prepare in advance, including the family of Dr Tran Van Dung (Interview HOF054 2019). This medical doctor's departure was planned by a businessman uncle who bought a medium-size seagoing vessel, sold places on the boat, bought supplies, and obtained permits to allow the refugee boat to leave from Vung Tau harbour, about eighty kilometres from Saigon. This boat left South Vietnam on 26 April, four days before the fall of Saigon, with 150 to 180 people on board.

Already in international waters, Tran's boat ran into serious mechanical problems, with water inundating the vessel's lower levels and pumping being insufficient to clear the ship of water. As this was happening, the boat met a line of commercial ships in the international zone crewed and captained by US military. As Tran relates, "The captain asked help from the American ship to repair the pumping system. The Americans told him to wait. [But meanwhile] the problem worsened; the ship was in danger of shipwreck, [the people on board] were in mortal danger. The captain had no choice, he decided to sail back to Vung Tau … As they sailed, they were followed by an American ship that notified them that it had received permission to help them." The US commercial vessel took the ship's crew and the refugees on board, eventually taking them to Subic Bay. Tran considers himself very fortunate to have survived a possible shipwreck.

Another refugee who left well prepared on a private vessel was Vu Van Thai (Interview HOF046 2019), owner, along with his extended family, of a ten-boat fishing fleet registered in Japan. Several of his large, highly mechanized but empty fishing boats with their Japanese sailors (Vu speaks Japanese well) were in Saigon harbour at the end of April. After misadventures with one boat, Vu and his family, his sister and her family, and one more couple left for the sea on another boat on 30 April. There were ten people and the Japanese crew on a large, almost empty vessel. As they reached the sea, the crew of a South Vietnamese naval river boat accosted them, boarded with their weapons, and then sank their own river boat. Later, another empty fishing boat of the Vu fishing company joined them, and the two ships headed for Singapore. The Singapore authorities refused to allow them to stay in Singapore, instead making them take on additional refugees and telling them to sail to the Philippines. The two large fishing vessels arrived in Subic Bay eleven days later.

There were air force pilots who escaped by helicopter with their families. Among them was Nguyen Huyen Chau (Interview HOF047 2019), the wife of a helicopter pilot and part of a prominent South Vietnamese family (her father was the head of the State Treasury). They left at the last possible moment from a flat roof beside her father's house, with her parents waving a tearful goodbye. To this day she treasures a memento, a contemporary edition of *Newsweek* magazine whose cover page records their arrival on the US aircraft carrier *Hancock*. An alert news photographer managed to get a photo of their helicopter being dumped into the sea to make room for more refugees on board. Other helicopters were also pushed overboard after unloading their passengers. This picture has become a symbol of the 1975 refugee exodus from South Vietnam.

One of the easiest of escapes is described by Ton Nu Thuy Lan (Interview HOF019 2019), a high-school girl in early 1975. Both of Ton Nu's parents were prominent anticommunist intellectuals who had studied in France and England and served as international bureaucrats. At one point her father was a minister of the South Vietnamese government. In April 1975, when he was dean of social sciences at Saigon University, German journalists befriended her family, and on 24 April managed to get them on one of the last regular scheduled flights from Saigon to Bangkok. From there they flew to Germany, crossed into France, and were sponsored by Ton Nu's uncle and aunt, professors in Montreal.

Another relatively easy escape was that of the family of fourteen-year-old Le Tien Dung (Interview HOF042 2019). His parents were prosperous businesspeople, a factory owner and a store owner, who had American connections. They were able to arrange a flight from Tan Son Nhut Airport that took them directly to Clark Air Force Base in the Philippines on 27 April – one of the last flights of any sort out of Saigon. They stayed at the US base only four hours. From there the Americans flew them to the US army base on Wake Island which had been turned into a refugee camp (Molloy et al. 2017, 48–9).

The above escape narratives are of middle-class or upper-middle-class people, military officers, professionals, businesspeople, and intellectuals, with the armed forces personnel being the single largest group. Most of the military are officers, including some senior officers. But among the interviewees are two conscripts of working-class social background, serving as skilled specialists in the navy. They are Tri Duc Pham (Interview HOF164 2020) and Bui Van Hai (Interview HOF156 2020).

Tri Duc was a mechanic on a naval oil tanker that supplied fuel for other South Vietnamese navy ships. In the last days of the war his ship was near the coast to the north of the Mekong Delta supplying South Vietnamese war ships with fuel. As his ship proceeded south along the coast, he witnessed small boats heading out to sea. As Pham says, "Civilians and army were leaving the coast and asked to be taken on our boat. Some of them, if they wore South Vietnamese army uniforms, were allowed to board." Others, including all civilians, were not. "We only take army guys; we don't take civilians … There were so many people, we cannot take all, we only take so much." They reached Saigon under severe war conditions and on the last day of the war they were moored on the river at Saigon naval base. What happened next confirms Le Van Chau's (Interview HOF044 2019) description above: people, including civilians, military, and their families, broke into the naval base and climbed onto naval ships, which became severely overcrowded. Then, Pham's tanker proceeded to the Philippines along with the South Vietnamese naval convoy, picking up many refugees – "men, women, children" – as they sailed down the Saigon River and then on to Subic Bay in the Philippines. Pham became a refugee despite himself, simply by being on his ship. He describes deep feelings of loss as he left Vietnam: "I did not want to leave, I wanted to fight." Pham's description of loss is among the most poignant of all the interviews. With tears in his eyes, he relates that in Subic Bay, "we lowered our flag and put the American flag up, which I regret all my life … I still want to fight for freedom of South Vietnam."

Bui was a welder at the Saigon naval workshops. On 30 April 1975, Bui still wanted to go to work, but there was nobody there. He met only one of his fellow workers, a friend who was also wandering around the city. The friend was married with a child and said he wanted to leave. Bui, who was single, simply decided on the spur of the moment to go with his friend. Along with the friend's family, they went to a private boat moorage and "liberated" a small, abandoned yacht that had belonged to a US embassy official. With no knowledge of navigation, with no supplies (they had some bottled water but nothing else), they steered the small boat down the river, picking up two more families along the way to the sea, eighty kilometres away. It was a miracle that they survived. On the open sea they were picked up by a US ship and were later transferred to a South Vietnamese naval vessel which took them to Subic Bay. Bui's sense of loneliness and intense personal loss after leaving Vietnam and realizing that he was alone in a completely unfamiliar world are the most striking elements of his interview. They characterize his experiences in the camps until his arrival in Canada.

The Camps

Except for the family of Le Tien Dung (Interview HOF042 2019), who went by commercial flights to Europe, most war refugees escaped by sea. The Danish freighter *Clara Maersk* carried Pham Thu Giang (Interview HOF070 2019) and Nguyen Bui Thi Mui (Interview HOF055 2019) to Hong Kong, where they spent a short time before being interviewed by

Canadian visa officers and proceeding to Canada. Most of the war refugee interviewees passed through the Philippines – Subic Bay or Clark Air Force Base – on their way to American refugee camps in Guam or on Wake Island.

All agree that life in the refugee camps in Guam; Wake Island; Camp Pendleton, California; and Indiantown Gap, Pennsylvania, was bearable and could even be pleasant. There were movies provided by the camp authorities. The refugee children – two in Guam, one on Wake Island – enjoyed the Pacific beaches. Their parents were full of worries, concerned about what their futures would bring. However, because of the impending monsoon season, most of the interviewees were transferred by the Americans to camps on the US mainland after a few weeks on the Pacific islands. The food was quite good.

Le Van's Chau's (Interview HOF044 2019) immigration interview was somewhat frightening because, according to his recollection, the visa officer initially told him that since he was a medical doctor, Canada might not accept him. However, all the other interviewees agreed that the Canadian officials who interviewed them were polite, friendly, and helpful. The refugees decided to choose Canada for a variety of reasons. Many already had family members living in Canada. Many could speak French; some could speak English. Reestablishing contacts with their families in Vietnam was important and they felt that this would be easier from Canada than from the US. And some refused to stay in the US, a country they blamed for the war's loss. Generally, the refugees knew little about Canada before arriving, but some made serious efforts to learn about the country through the use of camp libraries.

While some expressed preferences about their Canadian destinations, most were content to go wherever they were sent, if they could start their new lives as soon as possible. This applied to all the educated middle-class people. The two former enlisted naval men felt so lost and missed their homelands so much that they appear to have been somewhat lethargic about final immigration to Canada. Yet they, too, wanted to go somewhere where they could establish a new life. This applies especially to Bui Van Hai (Interview HOF156 2020), who missed working very much and wanted to go a place where he could quickly start working again.

Refugee Impressions

Several interviewees commented that the US was prepared well ahead of the fall of Saigon for the loss of the war and the flight of over 100,000 refugees. Otherwise, why set up large refugee facilities at a few US military bases around the Pacific Ocean months ahead of the war's end? The experience of three Vietnamese vessels that arrived in Singapore being redirected to sail to Subic Bay in the Philippines confirms that Singapore authorities took advantage of the assumed US policy. Two of the boats arrived in Singapore empty but were forced to transport many refugees being expelled by the Singapore authorities to Subic Bay.

The Hong Kong experience reinforces this impression. When the *Clara Maersk* arrived in Hong Kong there were no US refugee processing facilities in the British Crown colony, implying that the Americans concentrated their initial refugee reception and processing at Subic Bay for ships and Clark Air Force Base for aircraft. In contrast, the Canadian immigration staff in Hong Kong started processing the *Clara Maersk* refugees interested in coming to Canada before the Hong Kong authorities could even register them (Molloy et al. 2017, 49–52).

These refugees had to leave South Vietnam. They would almost certainly have been severely persecuted by the new Communist government had they stayed. Yet many of their families refused to join them in leaving, and many of those who stayed behind were later severely persecuted. Leaving the country of their birth meant leaving large parts of their identities behind. As chapter 3 will show, their lives in Canada would become a steady, challenging effort to fit into a new culture, yet preserve the old identities tying them to their country of birth.

3

The Vietnamese War Refugees' Lives in Canada

Background

The 1952 Immigration Act was still in effect in 1975. But its discriminatory regulations favouring European immigrants and refugees had been removed in the 1960s. By the early 1970s refugee protection and resettlement measures could be applied to non-Europeans including the Vietnamese war refugees. This facilitated the resettlement in Canada of just under 9,000 Vietnamese, Laotians, and Cambodians between 1975 and 1978.

In reviewing the resettlement experiences of these refugees, it is important to note that Canada's private sponsorship program that played such an important role with subsequent waves of refugees from Southeast Asia was authorized by the 1976 Immigration Act and only came into effect in late 1978. While some 1975–76 Vietnamese refugees recall being befriended and assisted by "church ladies" and other Canadians, none were formally sponsored by private groups. The Canadian government was responsible for their initial resettlement in Canada, and most of them were expected to start working soon after arrival. Story after story mentions the extensive help they received from kind individual Canadians who were often affiliated with faith-based groups.

Integration Experience of Refugees and Families after Arrival

As Saigon was falling, there were strong representations by family members in Canada, including a demonstration in Ottawa by the tiny Vietnamese student community of Montreal. These actions had a major effect on the Canadian government's humanitarian decision to accept sponsored family members and 3,000 additional refugees (Molloy et al. 2017, 29). Nineteen interviewees who left Vietnam immediately before or very shortly after the fall of Saigon were resettled in Canada rapidly, arriving during the spring, summer, and early fall of 1975.

All refugees and their families were welcomed in English Canada by Canadian government officials from Manpower and Immigration Canada. In Quebec, officials of the Quebec Immigration Ministry welcomed the refugees. The officials arranged hotel or apartment rental accommodations and provided or helped to shop for clothes (usually from second-hand stores). They provided cash funds to enable the refugees to buy food, and helped them find their first jobs. The refugees could enroll in government-sponsored language classes but based on the refugees' stories, language classes were not always available in all parts of the country.

Early Years of Settlement Experience in Quebec

While there is some overlap between the social and educational characteristics of the interviewees who started their Canadian lives in Quebec and those who arrived in English Canada, the two groups are quite distinct. Unlike most refugees destined for English Canada, the Quebec-bound refugees were either university-trained professionals and academics, or business families (or the children of such families). As well, the professionals were able to become active in their professions relatively rapidly. No unmarried refugees arrived in Quebec; they all arrived as families.

Eight interviewees were directed to Quebec, including six to Montreal, one to Quebec City, and one to Sept-Îles. They included two medical doctors, a teenage child of a business family, another teenage child of an academic family, an electrical engineer, the former part-owner of a fishing company, a naval captain with extensive experience as a merchant marine captain, and a pharmacist. Most of them of them spoke fluent French and some English. In pre-1975 Vietnam, French knowledge went along with higher social status and educational achievement. Those refugees who spoke French were generally destined for Quebec. Some of these refugees, and especially their families, did take French classes offered to them at provincial training centres, in part because they found spoken Quebec French difficult to understand on arrival. Seven out of the eight had family already living in Quebec.

All these refugees expressed their gratitude to Canada and Quebec for providing a chance for a new life. Their first impressions of Quebec were of friendly officials and friendly people. Some of the earliest arrivals in May 1975 were surprised by cool temperatures and the traces of snow. But most arrived during warm summer weather and remained unaware of the extreme Canadian winter until late October 1975, when the unaccustomed cold temperatures caused serious hardships for them during their first winter in Canada.

Another difficulty mentioned by most interviewees was the unavailability of Vietnamese foods in Canada. Once they discovered Montreal's Chinatown, which was still tiny in 1975, they could get some of the foods they were used to, but this remained a problem for several years.

In 1975 there were few Vietnamese living in Quebec. A major initial hardship for the newly arrived refugees was being alone in a foreign environment out of contact with their families in Vietnam. As Ton Nu Thuy Lan (Interview HOF019 2019), a teenager when she arrived in Quebec, states, "Changes are hard for a teenager. I was unable to say goodbye to anybody ... We had no news at all, I didn't know what happened to our family in Vietnam. So, the first few months were hard." Ton Nu's father maintained his ties to Vietnamese culture by working on Vietnamese national causes throughout his life in Canada. "He wanted to devote his life to Vietnam. [He had a piece of soil], he said this is soil I brought from Vietnam, to show the love for my country." Ton Nu's integration process was relatively smooth. Coming from a prosperous intellectual family, language was no problem for her since she went to a French lycée (secondary education) in Vietnam and was able to continue in a lycée in Montreal. Ton Nu eventually got a university education and is now a bilingual human resources specialist working for Canada's federal government.

For Le Tien Dung (Interview HOF042 2019), another teenager, language was initially a problem. He now speaks impeccable French, but on arrival in Montreal, he says, "I could barely speak French. I had to relearn [the language]. The Quebec accent was difficult, it took some time to get used to it." He also mentions that food was an issue where his family lived: "There was no Asian food in Brossard. Every three days we had to make an expedition to get our kind of food." And for his parents, winter "was a very difficult period psychologically. They were isolated; they could not leave their house" because of the extreme cold. He emphasizes the psychological difficulty of being separated from their families left behind in Vietnam: "During the first year … we had very little information about our friends, our families in Vietnam. Are they persecuted? Are they in the camps? … We had absolutely no news." The first three years were hard: "We had a sense of isolation." Yet Le's family arrived with some resources and had Vietnamese contacts in the Montreal region. As he states, his parents wanted "to get close to family and friends, some of whom already lived on Montreal's South Shore." Family, uncles, and aunts offered them help. "We stayed in Montreal until we could buy a house in Brossard. … We arrived in Brossard on July 1, 1975." Le eventually obtained a master's degree in business administration and is now a senior executive working for the City of Montreal.

Often, Vietnamese teenagers who entered school classes were the only Vietnamese students and had to become accustomed rapidly to a significantly different cultural ambience. Initially, the refugees were welcomed by the Montreal Vietnamese Students Association. But it does not appear to have played a major role in the refugees' early settlement experience.

Families already established in Quebec often helped the newly arrived refugees. Ton Nu's uncle and aunt were university professors in Montreal and helped her parents find initial jobs. Nguyen Trung Thu (Interview HOF075 2019) presents the opposite, very brave approach by a newly arrived refugee. He was an engineer with considerable experience in Vietnam. His wife had an uncle in distant Sept-Îles. So "I was directed for initial settlement in Sept-Îles. There I was offered a job as a technician. My uncle said, 'Take it, it has a very good salary' … But if I take that job, I get stuck [working as a technician] … So, I did not take that job." He decided that as a highly trained engineer he did not want to do a lower-level technician's job for years. Instead, he made an application to get a master of engineering degree in Montreal. With the help of Manpower Canada, he managed to get his degree. Then, relatively quickly, he found a position as an engineer in Trois-Rivières, which was the beginning of a successful engineering career that took him from Quebec to Ontario and eventually to many places around the world.

All Quebec-bound interviewees eventually resettled successfully. The refugees state that luck played a major role in how they managed to restart their lives in Quebec. Yet listening to their stories, it is evident that, especially at the beginning, a powerful work ethic, perseverance, and in some cases extraordinary self-confidence were key to their success. Thus, initially, the only health sector–related jobs the two medical doctors, Le Van Chau (Interview HOF044 2019) and Tran Van Dung (Interview HOF054 2019), could get through the federal Department of Manpower and Immigration were as orderlies earning minimum wage on the graveyard shift at the St Jean de Dieu hospital for the mentally ill in the far eastern end of Montreal. As Le narrates, "It was a part-time job, at minimum wage, two or three nights a week … Meanwhile, my wife got a job as a hairdresser's apprentice … We were ten Vietnamese doctors who worked there … The director of the hospital tried to help us, raising our status to nurse's helpers with a higher wage of four dollars per hour. But the nurse's union refused." They had no money to buy cars and endured long public transit commutes in all types of weather to work through the night taking care of patients. After two years, the Quebec College of Physicians and Surgeons allowed Vietnamese doctors to take a short medical upgrading course and compete for rotating internships. Our two interviewees passed the upgrading course (only a minority of Vietnamese physicians did the first time), managed to obtain rotating internships (again only a minority of Vietnamese physicians did), and three years after arriving in Quebec, they were on their way to successful Canadian medical careers.

The merchant marine captain Ha Phu Cuong (Interview HOF076 2019) had a story that required daring and initiative in a new, still unknown country. Soon after gaining a rudimentary acquaintance with the city, he headed down to Montreal harbour, where "the shipping master gave me a list of seven companies. I interview every seven of them, people liked me talk about my last job, every one of them, [but he got no job offer], then I see office of shipping agent and shoved letter of job inquiry [under his door] … Then I had very interesting interview." He was hired on the spot and shipped off to Taragona, Spain, while his wife stayed for six months in an east-end Montreal apartment. His career eventually took him to Toronto and Great Lakes shipping and from there to long-distance ocean merchant shipping. The former fishing company owner Vu Van Thai (Interview HOF046 2019), penniless on arrival in Montreal, eventually after years of study qualified as a geophysicist.

The initial settlement of this group of the Quebec-bound interviewees took between three and five years. Of course, as the above demonstrates, this was an exceptional group of people. And we must not forget the early experiences of many of their spouses, working for minimum wage in Montreal sweatshops. The question of when the refugees started truly to feel at home in Canada is a more complex one and will be treated later in this chapter.

Early Years of Settlement Experience in English Canada

The eleven war refugees bound for English Canada arrived with much weaker language skills than those destined for Quebec and several never learned to speak English well. Partly because of this, the initial settlement experience of most of these refugees was quite difficult. Like their Quebec-bound compatriots, they found the first winter and the lack of familiar foods in Canada hard. Most took some English language courses, although some preferred to cut these courses short and start working as soon as possible. Their two main difficulties were the cultural milieu and finding good jobs.

Getting used to Canadian culture was especially hard for refugees who arrived alone, without families. Four of the interviewees, including two naval conscripts and two naval officers, arrived as single men.

One naval officer, Nguyen Van Ba (Interview HOF111 2019), had left his wife and three children behind in Vietnam and was never reunited with them. During his forty-five years in Winnipeg, he could only get low-paying jobs and could not save enough money to sponsor his family; he still speaks slow, rudimentary English. Another naval officer, Nguyen Xuan Thach (Interview HOF147 2020), left his parents and siblings in Vietnam. In the early years he took labour jobs and sponsored his brothers and their families to come to Canada as soon as he could. Eventually, after taking an electronics course, he got much better jobs, although, as he says, "I am homesick for my beautiful Vietnam to this day."

The two naval conscripts, Bui Van Hai (Interview HOF156 2020) and Pham Duc (Interview HOF139 2020), arrived in Montreal after a flight from Pennsylvania along with 250 other single former sailors and soldiers. From there they were sent by bus to Toronto, where a Canada Manpower official took charge of them. Bui continues his story: "[The officer] said that London [Ontario] would take us all. In London we stayed in the YMCA hotel for almost a week while Manpower found apartments for us. After that, we lived in an apartment building. There were three groups in three apartments. All were men, eighteen men, all soldiers … except for three or four who were students … The *London Free Press* … posted an article about us … A few Canadian people in London came to visit … They befriended us." Three-bedroom apartments accommodated six Vietnamese refugees, two men per bedroom.

The newly arrived young men, without any resources, were provided the customary government settlement assistance, including second-hand clothes, English courses, a small money grant to live on, and help in finding their first jobs. All of this they appreciated and continue to appreciate. Yet, they describe their early Canadian experience as one of profound culture shock. Pham continues, "Six guys crammed into a three-bedroom apartment, two guys in a bedroom, we shared everything together." Groups of young Vietnamese men wandered the streets of London, attempting to buy supplies in strange stores without speaking the language. They had a sense of being lost, of loneliness and abandonment. Pham describes, "I bought a roll of salami without knowing what it was and devoured the entire roll in one sitting." Two of their apartment mates were desperately thinking of suicide and had to be talked out of it. "We were lonely, we were scared."

Their salvation came from Canadians who sought them out, invited them to their homes, and helped them in any way possible. Formal private sponsorship did not exist at the time, and people did this on their own initiative. As Bui tells the story, "When I first arrived, maybe it was the coordinator, a volunteer, who called about us, so a few Canadian people in London came to visit. They were the adopted parents of Vietnamese children whose flight crashed a few months ago." These children had come to Canada as orphans on a baby flight in April 1975. "They shared us among themselves, with each of them taking us to visit his or her home. For myself, I met Mr and Mrs Wolsey ... Mrs Donna was very dear to me." To this day, Pham Duc and Bui Van Hai (Interview HOF156 2020) consider these Canadians to be their saviours.

As a result of these early experiences, they think highly of all Canadians. Eventually both found steady work as a welder and a mechanic millwright, respectively, and both married and had children. Again, as with most other Vietnamese refugees, their work ethic accounts for much of their success.

On arrival in Toronto, Pham Thu Giang (Interview HOF070 2019) was an unmarried young woman. Yet there were major differences in her preparedness for her new life. She was a professional, had finished dental training, and had already practised dentistry in Vietnam. She already knew English and only required a short course to upgrade her language skills, enabling her to find a job as a bank teller. Importantly, she arrived with two young adult brothers and the three of them lived together in a three-bedroom apartment. After three years in Toronto, newly married with a newborn baby, she passed her Canadian dentistry exam and started to practice as a dentist.

Of the military pilots who came to English Canada, only one, helicopter pilot Linh Minh Ho (Interview HOF162 2020), was able to obtain, after three years in Canada and a year of study, a Canadian pilot's licence and resume his career. Later he became a skilful Arctic pilot based in Vancouver but spending most of the short Arctic summers in Canada's Far North. (Picture a pilot from tropical Vietnam flying in Canada's extreme north and camping in tents on one of the northernmost Arctic islands near the North Pole! Ho has the photographic record to demonstrate his unusual experience.) The other helicopter pilot, husband of Nguyen Huyen Chau (Interview HOF047 2019), studying while working as a janitor in Calgary, managed to retrain as a geophysicist and eventually obtained a master's degree. A fixed wing aircraft pilot, husband of Luan Van Phung (Interview HOF015 2019), retrained as a machinist.

For refugees with families, the early years in Canada meant living very frugally in a new language in reduced economic and social circumstances. Nguyen Ba Trieu's (Interview HOF002 2019) wife and six children, left behind in Vietnam, were sponsored after five years of extremely hard work by the father, who speaks only rudimentary English and French to this day.

The stories of two families of former naval officers, told by their children Le Thuan Kien (see his individual story in chapter 4) and Vu Thanh Uyen Tanya (Interview HOF143 2020), were typical. They appear to have managed their challenges well. Tanya Vu was a little girl in 1975. She recalls, "We were the first bunch of refugees that arrived in Edmonton … We were in a hotel downtown … They [Canada Manpower] helped us find work. There was no organized program to help us learn English … My father found work after two days. He worked in a metal shop. He started with two dollars and fifty cents an hour." Tanya Vu remembers her father working at low-paying jobs in Edmonton for the rest of his life. He found it hard to come to terms with this. Her mother, also working in low-paying jobs, became the family's core in Canada. Tanya Vu had a happy, if quite poor childhood and does not recall special hardships in her life in Canada. She credits her happy childhood to a loving extended family, including an aunt who took care of her while her mother worked.

4

The War Refugees: Three Stories

The recollections in this chapter are those of Nguyen Ba Trieu, Nguyen Bui Thi Mui, and Le Thuan Kien, who describe their experiences during the last days of April 1975 as they escaped the advancing North Vietnamese army into South Vietnam and the challenges that they faced as they fled from their homeland to make Canada their home.

Nguyen Ba Trieu

The quotes in this story are from an interview (Interview HOF002 2019).

Nguyen Ba Trieu is a vigorous elderly gentleman well into his nineties. He is sharp and remembers the story of his long life well. He was accompanied by his third-oldest son, Nguyen Duong, who is in his late fifties and was nine years old in April 1975. The elder Nguyen speaks broken French, and his son speaks fluent English but no French. Throughout the interview he often required the help of his son to translate from Vietnamese into English. His son added his own recollections in English, so this was a trilingual interview. If anything, this made the story more gripping as deep feelings were expressed in the exchanges between father and son.

The interview's main theme, perhaps the abiding theme of Nguyen's life, is his hatred of communism. As he passionately insisted several times throughout the interview, the only thing that would make him leave Canada would be if Canada turned communist. But he obviously considers this notion absurd, adding with a smile that this could never happen.

Nguyen was born in North Vietnam and spent his childhood and early youth there. As he states, "I left North Vietnam in 1954, to go to South Vietnam. My father was a landlord, he was condemned to death." He is convinced that had his father stayed in North Vietnam he would have been killed. "My uncle, who was a major landowner, but stayed in the North, was killed by the communists, he was stoned to death." As his son summed it up, "They were farmers, they owned land. All who owned land were persecuted." Nguyen continued, "With my parents and siblings, along with many other people from the North, I sailed on a ship for the south from Haiphong harbour." This was during the three-hundred-day period of free movement between South and North Vietnam in 1954–55. Settling in Saigon, he lived there as a prosperous man, owner of a small bakery workshop manufacturing Vietnamese pastries, until his escape in late April 1975.

Father and son describe their last days in Saigon as a time of utter confusion, the city filled with a panicked population. By this time, Nguyen was married with nine children, ranging in age from twelve to two years old. His son recalls spending the evening of 28 April on the roof of their house watching the destruction of the runways at Tan Son Nhut Airport by North Vietnamese shelling. "I was young, I saw planes flying, we went up to the roof to watch the fireworks." For the Nguyen children these were exciting fireworks. Not so for their parents.

The next day, Nguyen decided to leave before the North Vietnamese, the communists whom he feared, marched in. As he says, "I know the communists, I cannot live with the communists." He had no idea how he would leave but the family lived not far from the United States embassy. He headed on foot with his three oldest boys, aged nine to twelve, to the embassy. His son explains, "The oldest of his children was twelve, the youngest was two, there was no way to take nine kids with him, he took the oldest three." The rest of the children were too young to risk a dangerous escape and they stayed behind with their mother. They did not know it at the time but for the next five years the Nguyen family would be separated.

At the US embassy, Nguyen and his boys became part of the enormous crowd attempting to get into the building. His son continues: "We saw helicopters on top of the US embassy … It was chaos, we saw people climbing fences ... thousands and thousands of people ... pushing against the embassy gates." But the front gate was barred shut, and US marines were guarding it. Then they headed for the side gate, arriving just as the gate opened for less than a minute to allow a US official – according to the Nguyens, the ambassador – to enter from the outside. "When people realized the gate was open, they were rushing through. We were lucky enough that we were close to the front ... As they shut the gate maybe fifteen, twenty people got in ... My father, there is a big marine pushing him, my father yelled 'crawl' ... We were little kids, we crawled under the closing gate." It was a miracle that they were not trampled by the crowds pressing behind them and an even greater miracle that they got inside at all since the building's perimeter, especially the gates, was guarded by marines. They were the last non-VIP Vietnamese to get inside the embassy. The Nguyen family was immortalized on the cover page of *Newsweek*, a magazine cover that they guard to this day as a memento of their escape from Saigon under siege.

Nguyen's son continues, "From the embassy roof we were helicoptered to a US battleship ... Helicopters were coming and going, dropping people off. The deck got so full, the helicopters can't land any more. The helicopters landed, then were pushed overboard to make space for more people ... We were on that battleship only that evening, then they transferred us to a cargo ship."

There was a large open space in the hull of the cargo ship where the crowds of refugees stayed cheek by jowl during the nine-day-long sea voyage to the US military base on Guam. "We were given water ... A food was basically army reserves food ... In terms of bathrooms, there was no bathroom space on the cargo ship, so they created a platform over the edge of the ship," with open-air toilet facilities exposed to the winds.

The base in Guam was turned into an enormous refugee camp. By the time Nguyen and his sons arrived on the island the camp was full of refugees, many looking for family members. Handwritten signs were posted all over the camp. The Nguyens, who stayed in Guam for two months, wanted to go to Canada, but the refugees accepted to go to Canada were limited to 1,500 and they were not accepted. From Guam they were transferred to Camp Pendleton in California where they were rapidly accepted and flown to Ottawa after two weeks, arriving in Canada in July.

Why go to Canada and why to Ottawa? Nguyen states, "I would not go to the USA." The US bears responsibility for the loss of his country. "I will go anywhere in Canada if there are no communists there … The Canadian immigration officer in Guam suggested Ottawa as the destination." His son adds that the choice of Ottawa was conditioned by the facts that they already had some family in Ottawa, and that Ottawa was on the linguistic frontier between English- and French-speaking Canada. A few years later Nguyen was able to sponsor his wife and children still in Vietnam before his friends in the US could sponsor their families, demonstrating to him that coming to Canada was the right decision.

Nguyen arrived in Ottawa in July 1975 with his three young sons. Nguyen Duong, nine years old at the time, remembers being told that Canada is a cold country, but it was not at all cold, it was warm. Of course, when winter arrived, they realized that it got very cold. "Ladies from a church were very nice, very helpful, they really helped us at the beginning … We're very grateful for their help. These ladies went out of their way to help us. Whatever we need, food, clothing … One lady, Mme Louis, she was very nice to us. She has passed away now, but we kept in contact with her [over the years] … The ladies from the church were the people who helped us the most." Both father and son remember with gratitude the positive help they received from individual Canadians.

Nguyen is a man of energy and determination. As he says, "After one month, I got a job with R.L. Crain paper company in Ottawa, I kept it for seventeen years, until retirement." His son adds, "He was doing other jobs too, like cooking. He worked so hard that we [the children] never saw him. He was sending money to the family [his wife and six other children] back home." Later, "he got another job as a short order cook at the downtown Holiday Inn." He worked hard to save money so that he could sponsor his wife and children to come to Canada as soon as possible. For years he was working at two or more jobs. Throughout his long life in Ottawa, he worked hard at several jobs in English. His son states, "My dad was able to understand English, but because his pronunciation, because he felt he can't speak it, he was not confident in speaking English … It's still not his preference, but he picked up English as well."

Nguyen instilled a profound work ethic and a sense of independence in his boys. They had to be the best at whatever they did. Within a few months his sons learned English and became excellent students at the Lord Elgin Public School. For several years, the boys won scholarships offered by Nguyen's employer for children of the company's employees. "The president of R.L. Crain congratulated my father, since he's never seen children of the same family win the scholarships year after year." The boys also became athletes, champion members of an Ottawa judo club. Since their father was working all the time his sons mostly accomplished this independently. "This is a sense of pride for my dad."

By 1977, Nguyen was able to sponsor his wife and six remaining children to come to Canada. As he says, after "four years, I sponsored my family. It took the sponsorship eleven months to come through." His family arrived in Ottawa in January 1980. Nguyen insists that Immigration Canada processed the applications rapidly, and the delay was entirely the fault of the Vietnamese authorities.

During the late seventies, the fate of family members left behind in Vietnam was the opposite of the family in Canada. Based on his mother's account of their lives, Nguyen Duong tells a story of terrible privation, famine-like conditions. This average family's day-to-day lives in Vietnam – even outside the re-education camps – explain the individual human experiences leading to the mass exodus beginning in 1978.

Once Nguyen's wife and the six youngest children arrived in Canada, the family was very poor. "We were crammed into a three-bedroom apartment, eleven of us. It was basically a subsidized housing unit … Eventually they found a second apartment for us, so we had two apartments side by side." But during their entire forty-year Canadian experience they continued to believe that in this country any person can accomplish anything if she or he works hard enough. And they did: all nine children graduated from university and have lives as successful Canadians.

Nguyen claims not to have had any integration problems. This, despite his broken French and his almost nonexistent English. For him, from the moment of arrival, the conditions of his family's life in Canada were preferable to life in Vietnam under a Communist government. His central message to his children is that they must be loyal Canadians, grateful for the opportunities this country has provided them.

According to Nguyen Duong, for the children integration in Canada was, at times, a more difficult problem. He recalls that he has been on occasion reminded that he is not "a real Canadian … I find it very hurtful when they say, 'You Chink, go home'" – even though he speaks perfect English and is completely at home in Canada. For him, the correct reaction to this type of abuse is to demonstrate his Canadian identity by doing better than his ignorant name-callers.

This family has proudly maintained its Vietnamese identity to this day. In the late 1970s Nguyen established the Vietnamese Community Association of Ottawa and was its first president. At the time there were only four hundred Vietnamese people living in Ottawa. At his modest apartment, Nguyen had a virtual open house for any Vietnamese. The young Nguyen remembers his dad "hosting a lot of people … [He established] some sort of Vietnamese community, because there was none … At the same time finding Asian food was difficult … My dad was probably the first to make pho [Vietnamese soup] and he was inviting a lot of people to come around. I remember people coming, dropping by, just to have pho with us."

In retirement, Nguyen has written and privately published several books in Vietnamese describing his life's lessons for his family and for future generations. At the same time, the family is enormously proud of its Canadian identity.

Nguyen Bui Thi Mui

The quotes in this story are translated from an interview (Interview HOF055 2019).

Nguyen Bui Thi Mui is a well-spoken woman in her early seventies. The interview was in French, a language she speaks very well. She also speaks English well. Nguyen Bui recounts hair-raising events in a calm manner but at times, recalling terrible memories, is overcome by emotions. She is a pharmacist who had completed her professional training in Vietnam. At the time of the fall of Saigon, she was married, had a two-year-old son, and was nine months pregnant, on the verge of giving birth.

Nguyen Bui describes the last days of April 1975 as "total chaos. Every day, we witnessed bombs falling. People who worked for the South Vietnamese government wanted to leave." Nguyen Bui's husband, now deceased, was an agricultural engineer from a family in central Vietnam who eventually became a South Vietnamese government official. He had studied in France where he had been a member of an anticommunist student group. "My husband, an ardent opponent of communism, wanted to leave at all costs." He always remembered his own family's experience under the communists in the 1950s, when "his landowner father was buried alive by the communists."

She states, "I was married, pregnant and in hospital awaiting my child's birth. I left the hospital, risking hemorrhage or giving birth on the bare earth." Her husband told her, "We need to go to the French embassy to ask for asylum." But by that time the French embassy had been evacuated. Then, the family went to the US embassy to await evacuation by helicopter from the embassy's roof. "But the last US helicopter had left and our family, including our two-year-old child, was stranded at the US embassy as North Vietnamese soldiers entered the building."

She continues: "We hid in a clothes-closet while the North Vietnamese performed a superficial inspection. We were not found." Eventually they slipped out of the building unnoticed. On the day of the fall of Saigon, the two of them walked the streets of the city amidst the scars of war and human and vehicular chaos, carrying their child.

They headed for Saigon harbour, as their last possible hope of finding an escape route. They paid a barge to take them to the freighter *Truong Xuan*, the last oceangoing vessel still in the harbour. Nguyen Bui describes "climbing on board the ship on a rope ladder, nine months pregnant. I was expecting to give birth at any moment, with my husband behind me carrying our toddler son on his shoulder." There were close to 4,000 refugees on board the vessel, all available space filled with people.

The ship, normally used for metal transport, had returned empty to its Saigon base. Seeing the mob of people desperate to escape, Captain Pham Ngoc Luy allowed them all to board while sorely needed mechanical repairs were carried out. This was the major reason why the *Truong Xuan* was still in the harbour when Nguyen Bui, her husband, and her child arrived, a stroke of luck for this family.

When it was hastily repaired – as it turned out, not fully repaired – the ship headed out to the open sea. Nguyen Bui recalls a terrible incident when a man "jumped overboard to commit suicide. The Captain, Pham

Ngoc Luy, turned the ship around to save him. He succeeded. They found him and brought him on board … These images have stayed with me forever."

They remained on board the *Truong Xuan* from midday on 30 April until the afternoon of 2 May. Nguyen Bui gave birth to a baby girl with the help of a refugee doctor at about three or four in the morning on 2 May on the ship's bridge, the only somewhat private space on the ship. "People called a doctor. One was found on board … There were no medical supplies. A woman found a pair of scissors to assist with the birth." Nguyen Bui was parched. When asked what she felt, she replied that "it was an extreme moment. At that time I was beyond fear. I felt nothing, I could do nothing." She just allowed things to happen to her.

In the afternoon of 2 May, the refugees were transferred from the *Truong Xuan*, which was dangerously taking on water and close to sinking, to the *Clara Maersk*, a passing Danish container ship that answered the Vietnamese vessel's distress call. "I was too weak to transfer to the *Clara Maersk* unaided. I and the baby were carried on a stretcher by four young refugees on a rope bridge between the two ships."

The *Clara Maersk* headed for Hong Kong. Escorted by a British naval vessel, it entered Hong Kong harbour on 4 May 1975. Nguyen Bui recalls: "My newborn daughter and two-year-old son were airlifted by military helicopter to a British military hospital." At the time of her arrival in Hong Kong, Queen Elizabeth II had also just arrived in the crown colony for a royal visit. To this day Nguyen Bui believes that the refugees were given temporary asylum in Hong Kong by the queen herself. Indeed, British authorities had honoured the request of Captain Luy not to send the Vietnamese back to their homeland, now under North Vietnamese control.

After ten days in the hospital Nguyen Bui was moved to a refugee camp where the family was together again. Within a couple of days, they were contacted by Canadian immigration officers who said that with a newborn baby she should not be staying in a refugee camp and offered to resettle her family in Canada as quickly as possible. The family knew virtually nothing about Canada, only that Canada was cold and French was one of Canada's languages. Since the Canadian officers were nice and cared about them and her husband spoke excellent French, they accepted

Canada's offer. Within a week, on 23 May, the family was on a plane to Vancouver, British Columbia.

After changing planes in Vancouver, Nguyen Bui and her husband, small son, and newborn baby girl were among the first Vietnamese refugees to reach their Canadian destination. As she states, "We landed in Vancouver on 23 May, made a stop in Montreal where we went through immigration formalities and were greeted by a Quebec immigration officer who took us to Quebec City and put us up at the Hotel Hélène. We stayed in that hotel for one month. My husband chose Quebec City as our destination because he spoke French and thought that he could find a job more easily in Quebec."

Her first impression was of a cold place. "I saw snowflakes … We have never [before] seen this … Even though it was May 23, it was very cold … and then later, in December, I put on boots and couldn't walk, I wasn't used to boots."

Yet the "extraordinary warmth" of the welcome compensated for the cold climate. "We received a great deal of help from the Quebec government." While they stayed in the hotel, Quebec provincial officials accompanied them to search for an apartment, buy food and clothes, and help them with all their immediate needs, and they found a first job for her as a hotel receptionist. Very rapidly, she passed her initial pharmacist examination. Because her daughter had been born just before her rescue by the *Clara Maersk*, a Danish ship, "my daughter had a Danish passport … Thanks to the Danish consul in Quebec City I was sent to Saint Jacques de Beauce, a small town south of Quebec City, to do an internship" to qualify for her professional licence in Quebec.

Nguyen Bui found the people of small-town Quebec welcoming and friendly. "They took care of me … My work was appreciated. After six or seven months I was able to work as a pharmacist's assistant. In 1977, less than two years after my arrival in Canada, I had my professional qualification." She was now a fully licensed pharmacist.

Still living in small-town Beauce, "I received a phone call from my friends in Montreal, calling me to come to Montreal to buy a pharmacy … I only had $2,000, but I received a loan of $5,000 from my cousin." With this, she opened her first two pharmacies in Montreal in 1977. Her husband could not requalify as an engineer in Canada, so "he stayed with me as an administrator in the pharmacies." She emphasizes that she worked extremely hard. "When I opened the pharmacies, I worked without relaxing ... I did my best to give back to society what I have received." But she also emphasizes that if you work hard in Canada, you can achieve anything.

Within three years of arrival in Canada Nguyen Bui and her family felt fully at home. She had her own pharmacies where she took care of the professional side of the business, while her husband took care of the administration. At the same time, with sadness and feelings of nostalgia, she came to terms with not being able to return to Vietnam. But she maintained her contacts with Vietnam. Over the years, "I helped the family in Vietnam, I sponsored about forty relatives, and I helped the community."

Today, Nguyen Bui strongly feels that people who have come to Canada as refugees must pay back this country's generosity. She herself has done her best by engaging in community service for decades, mentoring in her profession hundreds of newly arrived refugees and immigrants from all parts of the world. She is proud that her efforts have been recognized. "This is why I have received first the Hygeia Award of the Association québécoise des pharmaciens propriétaires, and later the Governor General's Caring Canadian Award." Both were awarded for outstanding community service.

Finally, Nguyen Bui feels gratitude that Canada has enabled her to educate her two children to become successful professionals. They are both cosmopolitans: one has a successful fashion design firm in California; the other is a business executive in Singapore. Both have sent special messages for the Hearts of Freedom interview, emphasizing their pride in being Canadian. For Nguyen Bui and her family, Canada has truly become their new homeland.

Le Thuan Kien

The quotes in this story are from an interview (Interview HOF071 2019).

Le Thuan Kien is a man in his late fifties. He is highly articulate and recounted his experiences in a well-organized manner in unaccented Canadian English. When Saigon fell, Le was twelve years old.

He states, "My parents were from North Vietnam. They left for the south in the 1954 population exchange, met in Saigon, and were married." He is the oldest of four sons, and went to St Paul's Catholic School in Saigon until the family's departure in 1975. As a child in Vietnam, he lived with his parents and members of their extended family in comfortable circumstances on the Saigon naval base. "My dad was in the navy, he was a high-ranking officer, we lived in a naval compound. My childhood was unremarkable." Until the very end of the war, he experienced few hardships.

Le states that in late April 1975, as Saigon was close to falling, his extended family "left along with other officers and their families … My dad was able to get my maternal grandparents, my maternal uncle and aunts, as well as my paternal grandmother. We were one of the lucky ones, we were grateful for that." Naval personnel at the base, along with their families, boarded naval ships and the whole flotilla left Saigon naval base on 29 April under the command of Le's father, who was the chief officer of the fleet.

A child at the time, he remembers: "We left on a Vietnamese battleship in a fleet, with the understanding from my dad's point of view that the navy would gather on a coastal island, Con Son Island, and the navy would return to fight." However, the South Vietnamese government surrendered to North Vietnam the next day and "there was no reason for us to return any more and we kept on to the Philippines." The South Vietnamese naval ships continued to cross the South China Sea to the US naval base at Subic Bay. The voyage to Subic Bay was uneventful. He does not remember facing hardships, although the ships were overcrowded. "Imagine a huge battleship, people were everywhere" with numerous civilian family members of naval personnel, as well as some other civilian refugees. Some basic supplies, such as milk for the baby of one of Le's aunts, were difficult to obtain during the voyage. "It was quite traumatic for the adults, but we were just little kids."

"Next day, at Subic Bay, we basically became stateless, we lost the war … It was quite an ordeal … to enter the Philippines." The South Vietnamese naval officers, with US officers acting as intermediaries, had to negotiate with Philippine authorities before being allowed to land. "All the ships had to remove the yellow [South Vietnamese] flag" and the ships were transferred to the Americans and entered the harbour under

US flags. With the loss of their country, the South Vietnamese sailors and their families became refugees.

In Subic Bay, "All those people [the refugees] had to be transferred to several tankers, if you can imagine huge tankers carrying many people … From Subic Bay we left for the American islands of Wake and Guam." The tanker that transferred them to Guam was extremely overcrowded. "Family after family would be lining up to each other on the deck inside the hull. There were people everywhere … There were no mattresses, we were sleeping on simple paper-thin coverage … Food was scarce for all these people … cans, dehydrated."

On Guam, he recalls, "We left the ships and entered … American Army camps. There we would stay for two months." He remembers his stay in Guam as an unstressed, peaceful time. It was sunny summer weather; the Vietnamese children like himself played on the beaches. "There was little to do so we watched lots of movies presented by the camp authorities."

After two months, they were moved to the US army base in Pendleton, California. "It might have been easy for my father in the US … [He knew the country,] having spent time there as an officer … but my dad decided to move forward to Toronto, Canada." Why? As a military man who had just come from a losing war, he did not want to expose his four young boys to conscription. As well, the maternal side of Le's family spoke French and they preferred to go to Quebec. Finally, there was an uncle who was a student in Toronto and stayed in Canada after the loss of his homeland. The decision to choose Toronto was also influenced by the fact that Toronto was English-speaking and his father believed that there would be a better future in an English-speaking place. Canada accepted the family in Camp Pendleton and they flew to Toronto two weeks later.

Le arrived in Toronto in July 1975 as a twelve-year-old with his parents and three brothers. He recalls feeling strange during the first weeks. In Vietnam and in the camps, white people were the rare exception. "In Toronto, I saw crowds of non-Vietnamese people for the first time." He was part of a minority, surrounded by strange white people who were visibly different than himself. In the hotel where they were lodged, "I was first exposed to blond people … We became friends with a family of blond people who worked in the hotel."

He continues, "We were staying in a hotel for several weeks. We were close to Chinatown; I remember eating Chinese chicken wings … Then we were moved to a different hotel and my parents would have to find housing … We were left without any financial assets, we left everything back in Saigon, we were given stipends … My mom looked for rental housing … For my parents it was traumatic."

During his first summer in Toronto, he went to English language school. "I spoke not a word of English back then." His parents went as well, and the family got a permanent home. At the same time, his parents went to courses to be retrained for jobs in Canada. "My mother was a teacher back home, in the Vietnamese school," but she spoke no English and retrained as a hairdresser in Canada. His father, a high-ranking naval officer in Vietnam, "had courses as a [stationary] engineer … looking after furnaces … He decided to have quick training to put food on the table" and eventually worked in the hospital system. Once trained, both parents got jobs that they kept till the end of their working lives.

Le entered grade 7 at Neil McNeil Catholic High School. "I struggled with English for a year, maybe a year and a half before I felt comfortable … By the time I reached the end of grade 8 my English was quite functional." Then he became a good student, finding high school relatively easy. With only a few Vietnamese students at his school, he became more proficient in English than in Vietnamese. In high school he had good friends; most were non-European immigrants from all parts of the world, but he also had a good friend who was white, who remains his friend to this day.

A shy boy, he never talked about his school accomplishments with his parents. "My parents looked quite surprised when they came to my graduation … seeing my name on the honour roll. I did not think it was such a big deal for them, but they told me [how proud they were]. I was quite touched to be able to make them proud."

Unlike many other Vietnamese students at the University of Toronto, Le did not know what he wanted to do in life and entered Arts and Science. He did well in his math and computer courses, but he wanted something else. "So, I applied to the U of T medical school after two years." He was accepted, but his family had no money to finance his medical education. In the mid-1980s medical school was still relatively inexpensive compared to today, so he was able to finance his education through student loans. After four years of medical school, "I worked as a family doctor for a year ... While working as a family doctor I applied to ear, nose, and throat [ENT] surgery. The school here in Toronto sent me to UCLA in Los Angeles" to start training as a specialist. Following this, he came back to the University of Toronto to finish his specialist training. He has been an ENT surgical specialist for several decades. It is noteworthy that Le and a friend graduated together from the University of Toronto as the third and fourth Vietnamese graduates of the medical school.

During his high school years Le wanted to fit in so much that by the time he graduated he was seriously thinking of changing his strange-sounding (in English) Vietnamese name to a more Canadian-sounding name. But as an undergraduate at the University of Toronto he became aware of the Vietnamese Student Association, was strongly attracted to it, and was a regular at the association's Friday evening meetings. At the association he recovered his original cultural and ethnic identity which he had been close to abandoning. Eventually, he became the student association's president. As he expresses it: "Despite adapting to a Canadian way of life, I suddenly felt more Vietnamese. Even now I feel more Vietnamese, yet I am a proud Canadian."

During the busy years of his medical specialist training, Le had little time to spend on Vietnamese community activities. But once he was established with a solid professional practice, a wife, and two children, he could again concentrate on the interests of Canada's Vietnamese community. He played an important role in establishing Toronto's Golden Age Village for the Elderly, the first Vietnamese old-age home in Canada. He became active in the Toronto Vietnamese Association and later was a board member of the Canadian National Vietnamese Association, eventually becoming the association's president.

After years of lobbying efforts by the association and Senator Thanh Hai Ngo, the government agreed that the yellow-red striped flag of the Republic of Vietnam could be raised in Canada's public spaces, including Parliament and Toronto City Hall. For Le this is a major achievement, demonstrating that Canadians of Vietnamese ethnicity could be proud Canadians while maintaining their Vietnamese identity and continue to hope for a better future for Vietnam.

Conclusion to Part Two

Life in Canada: Family, Culture, Integration, Identity

The group of Vietnamese refugees that arrived in Canada following the fall of Saigon in 1975 have certain common characteristics. Almost all were middle class in Vietnam and had a strong work ethic and a sense of ambition for their own and their children's future lives. Most started to work in low-paying jobs considerably below their qualifications soon after arriving, often before completing their language courses.

They are strongly family oriented and made enormous efforts to bring family members, including spouses and children, but also parents and siblings to Canada. Even when living in poor, often hand-to-mouth circumstances, they made great efforts to inculcate in their children the values of hard work and education. It is remarkable that most children of these refugees have university educations and are successful professionals, businesspeople, or public servants in Canada.

At the time these refugees arrived, there were only a few Vietnamese people living in Canada. Most were French-speaking university students temporarily in Canada with limited resources, concentrated in Montreal. These students could not return to Vietnam after the fall of Saigon and were given the opportunity by the Canadian government to become permanent residents.

As mentioned previously, the 1975 refugees did not have private sponsors. By contrast, more than half of the much larger number of Vietnamese boat people who came to Canada after 1978 had the benefit of the private sponsorship system. Nor did the 1975 cohort have the support of a large segment of the Canadian public which followed the broad media coverage of the boat people phenomenon in 1978–79 (Molloy et al. 2017, 98–9; Pappone 1982).

To be sure, the spontaneous help of individual Canadians not affiliated with institutions was important to the 1975 arrivals and for some single refugee men it was the difference between despair and hope for the future. This help and the assistance provided by some government officials conditioned most refugees to consider Canadians to be good people.

An important element of the early Vietnamese refugee experience was the rapid formation of ethnic cultural associations across Canada. Strong community spirit was already present among the newly arrived refugees when a few of them first got together in Nguyen Ba Trieu's kitchen in Ottawa in 1975 to eat pho soup. It continues today, over forty years later, as witnessed through the elaborate Vietnamese New Year celebrations supported by ethnic associations in Canadian cities. Thousands of Vietnamese Canadians show up to have fun, listen to music, look at elaborate art and culture displays, buy goods offered at business booths set up by Vietnamese shops, meet their friends and relatives, and eat and drink wonderful Vietnamese specialties provided by scores of Vietnamese restaurants (Dorais et al. 1988; Dorais 1991, 2010; Bun and Dorais 1998).

Two things should be noted about the settlement and integration of the war refugees who came to Canada in 1975–76. First, the people of this relatively small movement established the ethnic community infrastructures that were able to help the large number of boat people who started to arrive in Canada in 1979. Several of the interviewees state that it was important to help the later arrivals and that they did so. Second, some of the important leaders of the Canadian Vietnamese ethnic communities were part of the earlier 1975 movement, including Nguyen Ba Trieu, the first president of the Ottawa Vietnamese Association, and Le Thuan Kien, the former president of Canada's National Vietnamese Association (Dorais et al. 1988; Dorais 1991, 2010; Bun and Dorais 1998).

For the university-trained professionals and former military officers who were able to resume their specialized high-skill occupations (helicopter pilot, ship's captain) in Canada, the initial integration period is not hard to define. Relatively soon after they had Canadian professional licences and could work in their fields – a period of three to seven years – they felt at home in Canada. Today, some see themselves as completely "Canadianized" – for example, one is a manager with the City of Montreal, another is a federal public servant – but at the same time they continue to identify with their Vietnamese roots.

An anecdote related by engineer Nguyen Trung Thu (Interview HOF75 2019) demonstrates the latter point. In the 1990s, Nguyen was working on a project in Burkina Faso for SNC Lavalin, a Montreal engineering firm. At a social event, a French colleague asked him to demonstrate the Vietnamese language by translating a simple French phrase into Vietnamese. Nguyen had difficulty doing this and suddenly realized, in the middle of Africa, that he was more Canadian than Vietnamese. Another, somewhat similar experience was recounted by Tanya Vu, who arrived in Canada as a young child and had all her schooling in English. Years later, when visiting Vietnam as an adult, she realized that she spoke English better than Vietnamese and was regarded as Canadian in her country of birth.

The above interviewees feel themselves to be both Vietnamese and Canadian and are proud of both identities. As Le Thuan Kien (Interview HOF071 2019) has expressed, "As I grew older, I became a prouder Vietnamese person, more passionate about Vietnamese goals … Here in Canada, I have done well, we were given a chance [to succeed], to live a free life … It takes a refugee to appreciate this … We owe it to future generations to open [Canada's] doors to new refugees." Nguyen Bui Thi Mui (Interview HOF055 2019), who was granted the Governor General's Award "in recognition of your selfless contribution to your community and to Canada," is one of many Vietnamese war refugees who have repaid Canada as well as their own community. This demonstrates that after forty-five years, identity may be a fluid concept. In Canada, we can live with and celebrate fluid identities. Our Vietnamese Canadian interviewees feel this deeply and are profoundly grateful for this.

The identity of nonprofessional refugees engaged in trade occupations or low-wage work presents a more nuanced case. They consider Canada to be generous for having given them a second chance at a peaceful and free life. While some say that they have not had major difficulties in Canada, and they consider themselves to be well integrated in this country, they obviously have had difficulties which some describe in graphic detail. Even after forty-five years, some suffer from homesickness and dream of returning to Vietnam. But most would not consider returning or even visiting Vietnam while the present government is in power. The refugees' nostalgia for their place of birth, their original culture, is deep. But so is their feeling for their new homeland, which has given them freedoms and opportunities that they could not have had in Vietnam. Their nostalgia is balanced by the knowledge that their children have achieved more than they ever could have in Vietnam, and for this their love for Canada is very deep.

PART THREE

Vietnamese Boat People

5

The Boat People: Escape from Vietnam

This chapter describes and analyzes the experiences of twenty-six interviewees who left Vietnam between 1977 and 1989. It examines their lives during the final years of the war, the post-unification years after 1975, their difficult lives in communist-dominated Vietnam, the perils of their escape on the high seas, and their lives in the refugee camps before departing for Canada.

The War's Last Years

Decades of war had sharpened the ideological differences between the opposing sides in the Vietnam War. North Vietnam had the goal of establishing a unified communist country while South Vietnam wanted to prevent a communist victory at all costs. Both sides were deeply committed, but the country's geographic and social conditions favoured the North. Years after the French colonists had left, the system of large estates owned by absentee landlords and farmed by landless tenant farmers was still in place in the small, difficult to approach or to control villages and hamlets of the South. With a poverty-stricken peasantry, cadres (organizers) of the communist Viet Cong controlled regions where most of South Vietnam's population lived. The years between 1965 and the end of 1975 saw terribly destructive warfare. Despite major advantages in terms of firepower and the "body count" of battlefield casualties, United States and South Vietnamese forces were unable to defeat the Viet Cong supported and directed by the North Vietnamese communists. Even where government forces were in control in the daytime, the Viet Cong ruled the night.

As Le Tuyet (Interview HOF102 2019) explained, "We ran away before the war ended. We were afraid that the communists would take over our city [Dalat] ... [but] we did not even think that the [whole] country would collapse. The cities surrounding Dalat already fell to the communists ... The whole [area] was in hands of the communists ... My sister in Saigon sold her house" and sent the money from the sale, "so that we could fly to Saigon ... We would be safer in Saigon." Nguyen Tam (Interview HOF108 2019) confirmed that in the central coast farming area around Quang Ngai, not far from the infamous hamlet of My Lai where in March 1968 there was a massacre of South Vietnamese villagers by American soldiers, there was constant violence. "I born in that village, between government and communists, back and forth ... One quarter of the people join the communists at night ... We were poor, we had nothing ... There was big fight, what can you do, we run away from the fight." Nguyen witnessed shootings and executions by both sides.

The Tet Offensive was a surprise attack launched on 30–31 January 1968 throughout South Vietnam by the 80,000 troops of the North Vietnamese Army and the Viet Cong, who struck more than one hundred towns and villages. The attack was repulsed by American and South Vietnamese forces with great losses for the attackers. But the enormous brutality of the communist offensive imprinted itself on the consciousness of the South Vietnamese middle class and contributed to the fear felt by them at the prospect of communist rule in a united Vietnam (Elliott 2010). Several of our interviewees, including Ton Nu Thuy Lan (Interview HOF019 2019), Chu Trong Huyen (Interview HOF068 2019), Le Tuyet (Interview HOF102 2019), and Nguyen Quyen (Interview HOF130 2020), have commented on the brutality of the North Vietnamese Army and the Viet Cong during the Tet Offensive. Nguyen Ngoc Duy (Interview HOF072 2019) calls it the "Tet Massacre" and describes the situation in Quang Ngai during the Tet Offensive: "We were lucky to survive. My dad went into a sugarcane farm which was large, bushy, so he managed to hide in there for three days, otherwise I believe that he would have been killed ... The whole family was lucky enough to survive that event." The Tet Offensive was a turning point in the war, despite the high cost to the North Vietnamese and the Viet Cong. It was the beginning of the end of the US commitment to South Vietnam.

By the early 1970s, war in Vietnam had become increasingly unpopular, sparking mass domestic and international protests. The US military and government came to see the Vietnam War as unwinnable, moving it to bring a negotiated end to the war with the signing of the Paris Peace Accord in January 1973. The US began pulling its forces out of Vietnam in early 1969 and following the signing of the Paris Peace Accord in January 1973 removed its remaining troops. With this, the fate of South Vietnam was sealed. Many of the interviewees, including Nguyen Duc Hieu (Interview HOF069 2019) and Hoang Chinh (Interview HOF081 2019), consider the American decision to withdraw from their homeland a betrayal and have little love or respect for the US.

The essential element to retain from the last ten years of the Vietnam War is that in the vicious battle of two opposing ideologies, it was the ordinary people of South Vietnam who suffered. Starting April–May 1975, once the Communist forces marched in, they would face many more years of extreme suffering. Their suffering was compounded by the destruction of so much agricultural land by napalm and by the extensive US bombing that had taken place during the war.

Life in South Vietnam Following the North's Victory

All the interviewees agree that the immediate aftermath of North Vietnam's victory in South Vietnam was chaos. This is understandable following an enormously destructive military campaign. But the sense of chaos lasted in South Vietnam for years, arguably until the late 1980s. Chaos was accompanied by despotism at both the state level and the local level. Authority was feared. People did not know what to expect or what might happen to them in their daily lives. Denunciations were commonplace; people had to watch everything they said. This aspect of the new political regime is emphasized by most interviewees. It was referred to as "hell" or an "unlivable life." Huynh Min Truc (Interview HOF004 2019) described his life as "living in a big jail. I had to be careful about my language, with friends, because can be persecuted by police, government official, if I say something they don't like ... If I talk to a friend, he can report it to the police ... They encourage people to denounce their friend."

Local policemen could do whatever they wanted. Nguyen Quyen confirms that

> after the time the communists took over, the majority of us are persecuted ... Everybody so afraid of each other because at that time you, any member of your family talk about the communists, anything bad, they encourage anybody in the house that they bring you in to the government authority ... Everybody live in fear, afraid of each other. For us, it was the same thing. I remember I was reading the book *1984*, after when I came to Canada, *1984* by George Orwell, and what it described ... I was having the same memory of what they have done in Vietnam. (Interview HOF130 2020)

Wholesale arrests and incarceration in re-education camps or prisons were applied not only to former military officers but to "bourgeois elements," meaning any people or families who were middle-class urban dwellers under the previous regime, whether they were professionals, government officials, merchants, or artisans. Most of our interviewees – or their family members – had spent time in re-education camps or in the labour camps of the New Economic Zones. Among them are Tran Le Hong Phuc (Interview HOF010 2019), Nguyen Hong Nhung (Interview HOF034 2019), Tran Quoc Tuy (Interview HOF064 2019), and Pham Thi Anh (Interview HOF066 2019). Based on these testimonies, perhaps the best way to describe the essence of post-1975 South Vietnam would be as "lawless arbitrary despotism."

Re-education Camps and New Economic Zones

According to North Vietnamese propaganda, the re-education camps and the New Economic Zone camps, routinely referred to as concentration camps by the interviewees, were institutions established to transform bourgeois mentalities into socialist ones. In fact, they were places where prisoners performed heavy physical labour, mostly in isolated regions far removed from the cities. After a day's labour, there were nightly propaganda sessions for the exhausted men. Inmates like Nguyen Duc Hieu (Interview HOF069 2019) were given three scant meals per day, consisting of "some tapioca in the morning, three spoon of salt water and one spoon of rice, sand and earth, at noon and in evening, every day like that … We try to survive. When we go to field, we eat frog … In morning, small bowl of rice, in afternoon, small bowl of rice." Nguyen, a big man whose body needed nutrition, describes constant hunger as the most unbearable element of his six years in a camp.

Officially, camps were educational, not penal institutions. Therefore, incarceration in them was not part of a judicial process. People were forcibly incarcerated in them by the state if it was felt that they needed to have their mindset changed and were released by the state when their mindset was considered to have changed. Some camps were better, others were worse. In one camp, a family member like Nguyen Hong Nhung (Interview HOF034 2019) could bring food to her father. Mai Liem (Interview HOF074 2019) was in an ill-supervised camp from which he would escape. Other inmates were never heard from during the entire period of their incarceration. There do not appear to have been hard and fast rules, but inmates were often moved from camp to camp. Some prisoners were moved to camps in North Vietnam.

A typical example of the irrationality of the re-education camp system emerged during the interview of medical doctor Truong Huu Do (Interview HOF146 2020). His wife, Truong Lam Lieu Kim, is also a medical doctor. Like most other South Vietnamese doctors, he was in a re-education camp between 1975 and 1977. "At that time, we were severely short of doctors because of the doctors in the South, about 3,500 of us at the time, the majority of the male doctors who served in the military along with those who served in the Ministry of Health were all herded into the re-education camps. The remaining female doctors, only just over five hundred of them had to take care of 17 million people so it was very difficult." Eventually, after repeated appeals by his wife, Truong was released, on condition that both he and his wife would serve as doctors in a rural district, which they did until their escape from Vietnam.

Societal Impact

With many men in the camps lacking a source of steady income, women, often with large families, had to earn a living, leaving children and adolescents without supervision. Families, like that of Mai Liem (Interview HOF074 2019), were often divided with a part of the family, without previous farm experience, working in the rice fields. Daily hunger became a routine part of life for many people, especially in the famine year 1977. After two major currency devaluations, paper money had little value, so people hid gold and jewelry to provide their families with some security. Some men, like Chu Trong Huyen (Interview HOF068 2019), refused to be conscripted to fight in Cambodia and went into hiding in rural areas. Others, like Nguyen Tam (Interview HOF108 2019), escaped from the army and got lost in Saigon's urban jungle. Phan Ni Tan (Interview HOF086 2019) perhaps provides the best summary of conditions after South Vietnam's defeat: "We were sad, but we were also full of hope. We wanted to cooperate to rebuild the country. [But] the communists were specialists in revenge, in retaliation. They drove people into the forest with wild animals and no source of water. They sent students for three weeks here and three weeks there [with no rhyme or reason]. I don't know how people coped."

Escaping from Vietnam

After the fall of Saigon, the average quality of life in South Vietnam deteriorated, and daily life became arbitrary, dangerous, and poverty-stricken. A large proportion of South Vietnam's middle-class population wanted to escape from the country, even at a high risk to their lives. However, following the initial refugee outflow during and immediately after the fall of Saigon (see chapter 2), escaping the country became extremely difficult and there were few escape attempts between May 1975 and mid-1977, mostly by fishermen with easy access to boats and knowledge of the seacoast.

Larger numbers of Vietnamese refugee boats again started to arrive in countries around the South China Sea in mid-1977. Their numbers dramatically increased through 1978, reached high levels by the end of the year, and became catastrophically high through 1979. The new refugee outflow did not take place in a vacuum. Government actions against the Chinese minority, the Hoa, became visible to observers in March 1978 when independent businesses – almost all in Chinese hands – were terminated and government raids attempted to confiscate any gold or US dollars possessed by the Hoa. By this time, the government was also providing the Sino-Vietnamese with the possibility of departure in return for gold and their properties.

The departure of Hoa refugees was semi-legal. In 1978, it was still taking place, organized through a Hong Kong syndicate with the connivance of the Vietnamese government. The *Hai Hong* was a freighter filled with thousands of Sino-Vietnamese refugees, each of whom paid up to 12 taels (50 grams) of gold for their journey to freedom; this was a typical human trafficking operation through which both the syndicate and the Vietnamese government made a great deal of money. However, the *Hai Hong* ran into serious difficulties, which became a highly publicized incident through international media, and its human cargo were regarded as refugees by the UNHCR as well as by resettlement countries like Canada (Pappone 2015; Molloy et al. 2017, 95–103). By mid-1979, the large semi-official freighters were abandoned, and smaller boats were taking their place in a semi-official, semi-clandestine manner, organized inside Vietnam, passing through several intermediary stages before a percentage of the fees paid by the escapees (usually about 50 per cent) reached Vietnam's central government.

The escape mechanisms, like virtually all aspects of life in South Vietnam, were arbitrary. In the interviews, each story of preparations for the outgoing boat trip was somewhat different. However, the stories had several things in common. Preparations had to be made in secrecy with as much discretion as possible. But discretion was not always maintained; members of the extended family and friends knew when people were leaving. Arrangements were usually made through organizers who often dealt with the authorities and arranged for the boats. Payments were made to the organizer in gold and the escapees had no insight regarding the ultimate destination of the payments. There was corruption at every level.

While the boat departures remained semi-legal, by 1979 they were also clandestine, quite dangerous, and usually took place at night. Even after having paid for their journey in gold, if the escapees were caught, they were handled as illegal emigrants and were accordingly penalized or not. Again, this was arbitrary and depended on the attitude of local officials and police, many of whom could be bribed. Pham Eric Phong (Interview HOF008 2019) was a Vietnamese Chinese refugee who escaped as a teenager with his parents. His parents, he recalls, "told me that they had to pay gold to the Vietnamese official so we can purchase a place in the small boat. Another way to say this is that we had to bribe the local official to secure the boat that we can escape from Vietnam." Pham approaches the complex issue of the Hoa boat departures by stating that Vietnamese government sanctioning was "directly no, [but] indirectly yes. What happened at the time is that in 1979 there was a war between Vietnam and China, so the Communist government wanted all the Chinese-Vietnamese to leave Vietnam as soon as possible. So, they make the arrangement with the [local town officials to force the Chinese to] escape Vietnam ... That's how we got to the boat." In response to Vietnam's invasion of Cambodia in 1978, China launched a punitive invasion of Vietnam along its norther border in February and March 1979.

Extreme danger is described in the narrative of Chu Trong Huyen (Interview HOF068 2019), when the small boat he was in was caught in crossfire on the Saigon River between police on the shore and a military vessel on the water. Being Chinese and part of an organized departure helped to mitigate danger, but it did not ensure a secure departure, as the story of Judy Trinh (Interview HOF029 2019) demonstrates. Trinh's "family was a family of means. We were able to liquidate our assets ... We had the equivalent of thirty pieces of gold ... in shape of a credit card ... We would use those pieces to bribe officials to let us out of the country ... There was a very long bus ride ... My father had to leave the bus for hours at a time ... to avoid checkpoints ... he basically walked around the military checkpoints" during the bus trip to the seashore. And most successful escapes, whether Hoa or not, were usually preceded by one or more failed escape attempts as in the case of the Truong family (Interview HOF146 2020).

The escape of Lam Dat Minh (Interview HOF145 2020), a poor Sino-Vietnamese man in hiding, illustrates the disorganization and corruption of communist officialdom. Lam's first attempt to escape failed. Along with the rest of his group, he was arrested by the police of Rach Gia, his escape boat's harbour town. Most of his group was released after paying a bribe. But he remained incarcerated since he had no money. The next day, he simply walked off as he was performing some street repair work for the police. He made it back to Cholon, some sixty miles away, and his next escape attempt was successful.

To escape in 1979, it was still an advantage to be Chinese. Several ethnic Vietnamese interviewees pretended to be Hoa to get on Chinese boats, including Pham Eric Phong (Interview HOF008 2019), Tham Le Kim Thu (Interview HOF020 2019), Nguyen Mai Chi (Interview HOF053 2019), and Ho Cong Thanh (Interview HOF133 2020). Tham Le Kim Thu had her name altered and paid a large sum of money in gold to get on a "good" boat as a pretend Chinese person. Nguyen Mai Chi bought a false Chinese ID and changed her appearance by having her hair styled in a Chinese manner.

Ho Cong Thanh (Interview HOF133 2020) was a young Vietnamese man when he escaped with his wife and child in May 1979 on a Hoa boat. His story contains a detailed account of how the system functioned. It is a tale of extreme callousness, inhumanity, and greed. He states that he, as a "true Vietnamese, got the paperwork [by bribery] to show that I'm Chinese … The same for my wife … After many delays, a semi-official trip was organized … The two of us paid twelve ounces of gold each … That's what we paid the organizer. Some of the local police didn't get paid, didn't let us depart. So, it's chaos. For the Chinese people, business-people, they don't really care, but for us we're Vietnamese they did not let us go … But then, later, they probably bribed some officer and they let us go." But this was not the end of their odyssey. In the severely overloaded boat, still in Vietnamese waters, they were robbed by heavily armed Vietnamese fishermen turned pirates, before being allowed to depart on a dangerously stormy sea.

Altogether, approximately 75,000 Hoa left Vietnam by boat (Amer 1996, 77–9, 87). In the course of 1979, the proportion of ethnic Vietnamese boat people increased rapidly and through the 1980s the overwhelming majority of the boat people were ethnic Vietnamese. The system established during the early period of the refugee boats remained in place. People left by paying organizers in gold. The organizers obtained the boats and the supplies and paid the bribes to various local authorities and police. Some of the money made its way through the system to the central government. A relatively small minority of refugees had the expertise to build their own boats, but this had to be done very carefully in great secrecy. By the end of the movement, about 1 million boat people managed to reach refugee camps in countries of first asylum.

Vietnamese Refugees at Sea

There are hundreds of first-person accounts describing the high seas experiences of the boat people. Each is special and stands on its own. Together, these stories can serve as the basis for examining the principal elements of this very important part of the Vietnamese refugee experience.

The interviews are deeply moving for both the interviewee and the listener. From the moment they left Vietnam until their arrival somewhere on the littoral of the South China Sea, their sea journeys contained the extremes of human experience. These included death and disease, hunger and thirst, storms and calm. Most of their boats were barely seaworthy and were enormously overloaded. (Overloaded because of the greed of the organizers who squeezed the maximum amount of gold out of the departing refugees.) Many were captained by incompetent individuals, some of whom had never navigated a ship beyond coastal waters. Many had faulty equipment and experienced frequent breakdowns. They were often lost at sea. Survival depended on luck or chance or perhaps divine providence.

Listening to the boat people's experiences, there are elements of unimaginable evil and selfless heroic goodness. Emergencies like the boat people crisis appear to bring out the worst as well as the best in people. There were experiences that showed the evil side of individuals. Piracy in the Gulf of Thailand became a cottage industry when Thai fishermen realized in late 1978 that the boat people, despite being stripped of valuables in Vietnam on their way to their boats, still were able to hide objects of value – gold and jewelry – on their persons. Some refugees were attacked by pirates repeatedly. Among these were Pham Thi Anh Quan Lisa (Interview HOF066 2019), Chu Trong Huyen (Interview HOF068 2019), and Pham Thi Duyen (Interview HOF073 2019). Others, like Pham Eric Phong (Interview HOF008 2019) and Nguyen Mai Chi (Interview HOF053 2019), were lucky and escaped pirate attacks.

After the first pirate attack there was usually little to rob. So, subsequent pirates, in their anger at not finding booty, took the women on board their boat and sexually violated them. But even this was not enough. To ensure that the refugee boat would float helplessly without reaching land they often stripped boats of their engines and other equipment and took the boat's food and water supply.

As a helpless refugee on an overloaded boat, Tran Quoc Tuy (Interview HOF064 2019) witnessed terrible pirate attacks. "The day after leaving, as the sun was rising, we gained a little bit more confidence. Then we turned south, we turned in a southern direction. Then we met a large Thai fishing boat. Unfortunately, they were [fishermen turned] pirates. They gathered everything of value and left. Next day, another pirate boat found us. This time they were professionals. They came, they gathered valuables, but we had already lost everything. They thought that we could have hidden something in a corner of the boat, they started to tear up the boat. They broke our motor. We had nothing left … [Then] they pushed a person into the sea, this person fell into the sea."

He continued: "The person who fell into the sea, my wife found a piece of wood and threw it to him, he accepted it … The pirate boat was like a large trailer truck that would break our small boat into pieces. They tried to take some young girls to the other boat, but when they saw the person still in the sea, they attached our boat to theirs, and started to drag our boat in circles to make us lose our orientation, we no longer had a compass. As we were dragged, we saw the person in the water in the distance on the piece of wood." When the pirates saw the person sink, they left the refugee boat without a functioning motor or compass. Tran's boat eventually drifted close to an oil drilling platform and was saved by an Australian refugee rescue boat.

A particularly vicious episode of murder, rape, and abduction took place on Pham Thi Duyen's boat (Interview HOF073 2019). The pirates murdered one young girl and took five girls from the refugee boat and transferred them to their fishing boat; they were never returned to the refugee boat. This was not an isolated incident. Two girls were also abducted by pirates from Lam Dat Minh's (Interview HOF145 2020) boat and two more girls were abducted from Le Tuyet's boat (Interview HOF102 2019).

On a refugee website, the Koh Kra refugee camp is described as "Hell on Earth." Koh Kra is a tiny, deserted island of rock and jungle in the Gulf of Thailand that was used by the Thai pirates as a prison for Vietnamese refugees and a depository for refugee women and girls, who were kept there to be sexually assaulted. The Vietnamese Heritage Museum notes: "By October 1980, 160 refugees are known to have died on [Koh Kra]. The total no doubt was far higher before a detail of six or eight marines was stationed on the island in the spring of 1981 and halted the carnage."[1] The girls abducted by pirates from the three refugee boats of the interviewees probably ended up on Koh Kra. A UNHCR field officer, Theodore Schweitzer, with the help of Thai police, managed to rescue 1,250 refugees from Koh Kra.

And yet, as the story of Buchan Tho Trong (Interview HOF018 2019) in chapter 6 shows, pirates occasionally showed some spark of human feeling toward an individual refugee. Also, very importantly, as described by several interviewees, including Tran Quoc Tuy (Interview HOF064 2019) and Buchan, several ships representing private humanitarian organizations or private individuals cruised the South China Sea looking for lost refugee boats, boats in danger of breaking up, and boat people needing medical care.

The German rescue and medical assistance ship *Cap Anamur* was perhaps the best known. A second ship was the *L'Île de Lumière*, a hospital ship of the Médecins sans frontières organization, which along with the *Cap Anamur* provided medical care for over 35,000 boat people. This

1 A comprehensive description of living conditions is available at Vietnamese Heritage Museum, 2024, "Koh Kra – Hell on Earth," accessed 29 July 2024, https://vietnamesemuseum.org/our-roots/refugee-camps/thailand/koh-kra/.

medical care was badly needed; without it many of the severely ill and weak refugees would have perished. A third such ship was the SS *Akuna*, which rescued the refugees from Tran Quoc Tuy's severely battered vessel anchored near an Indonesian oil drilling rig and took them to Singapore; Singaporean authorities only allowed the SS *Akuna* to deposit the refugees in Singapore after the ship's owner, Col Jack Bailey, a retired US Air Force fighter pilot, paid a hefty fine, and the UNHCR in Singapore guaranteed that the refugees would be resettled in a third country. The fourth ship was the *Tug Challenge*, a motor supply vessel captained by Jay K. Elder, supplying oil drilling rigs in the South China Sea. During the summer of 1979, the *Tug Challenge* rescued 2,700 refugees and transported them to Pulau Tengah refugee camp. Among them was Pham Thi Duyen (Interview HOF073 2019), whose boat was waiting for rescue near an oil drilling rig.[2]

In addition to the above rescue ships, many passing ships also picked up refugees from boats in trouble. Le Thi Kim Yen and Dao Thi Kim Quyen (Interview HOF052 2019) were picked up by a British oil tanker. They were fortunate: the tanker took them to Japan. Phan Ni Tan (Interview HOF086 2019) was picked up by the oil rig supply ship SS *Panama* and taken to Pulau Bidong refugee camp. Some passing ships did not even acknowledge the overloaded, decrepit refugee boats. Thus, Pham Thi Anh Quân Lisa's (Interview HOF066 2019) boat was ignored by three separate passing ships. The opposite happened to Le Tuyet's boat (Interview HOF102 2019). After being robbed and stripped by one pirate boat, which also abducted two girls, a second pirate boat – it should probably be called a Thai fishing boat – rescued the refugees.

For those fortunate refugee boats that were rescued, and others that arrived on a Malaysian or Thai beach, on an Indonesian island, or near an oil drilling rig without incident, being on land again was the end of their sea journeys. But for other refugees, sighting land was the beginning of another stage of their suffering. Following sea journeys of between

2 For extensive information on all aspects of the boat people exodus and the stories of *Cap Anamur*, SS *Akuna*, and *Tug Challenge*, see Refugee Camps.info, 2018, https://refugeecamps.net/. For the story of *L'Île de Lumière* see Institut National de l'Audiovisuel, 2010, "Ile de lumière: navire hôpital," accessed 21 August 2024, https://dai.ly/xfd63h.

two days and two weeks, often after being robbed and violated by pirates, squeezed like sardines in the bottoms of fishing boats without food or fresh water, and surrounded by human waste and disease, the refugees thought that they had arrived at their goal. However, before the international community agreed to mass third-country refugee resettlement, Malaysia frequently refused to allow refugee boats to land for fear of encouraging the arrival of more refugees (Lipman 2020, 52–89).

As a result, boat people arriving in Malaysia during the first half of 1979, and hoping to be allowed to stay there, often destroyed their boats near the shore and swam to the beach. This was the solution chosen by the captains of the boats on which Nguyen Hong Nhung (Interview HOF034 2019) and Do Nghia (Interview HOF103 2019) arrived. In the case of Pham Thi Anh Quân Lisa (Interview HOF066 2019), she was too weak to attempt to swim to the shore and was carried on the back of another refugee. It is impossible to guess how many refugees perished attempting to swim to shore from sinking boats. Some refugees, including Tran Phuong Thu (Interview HOF027 2019), were robbed of all their remaining possessions on a Malaysian beach. Often, those refugees with intact vessels were forced back to sea by the Malaysian coast guard or navy.

A story which demonstrates how boat departures were handled by the Vietnamese authorities provides an appropriate ending to this section. Tran Le Hong Phuc (Interview HOF010 2019) was a teenage boy in 1979. His family had already suffered a great deal. His father had been killed and his mother remarried. They wanted to leave Vietnam at all costs. His mother handed over 20 taels of gold to two men who came to their house. On 15 June 1979, he, his mother with a baby in her arms, his sister, and his stepfather, along with 250 other people, were herded onto a large fishing boat by Vietnamese police. They had no captain, so a fisherman who knew little about navigation steered the boat. They immediately hit a very bad storm that lasted for five days. Tran and his family thought that they were going to die.

Tran continues the story: "Luckily in the morning the storm calmed down. After six days we were desperate, all we want is to go back to the shore … Two children died, we have no more food, no more water … Then an [oil exploration] supply boat came … They say follow us, then we just follow that boat. In the morning around 7 a.m., I saw a big boat [an enormous oil exploration vessel] … from the European country mostly from Germany and Holland … They were looking for oil in Vietnamese territorial waters. They ask us, 'Did you come from Vietnam?' 'Yes, yes!' … We had no communication. We threw up written paper messages [the refugee boat was far below the deck of the larger vessel] … We explained our situation … Can you bring us up to your boat? … They say, 'We can give you food and water and show you the direction to the open sea,' but we say we don't trust our pilot [captain] any more … We want to stay here, you let us in … We wait 'til the afternoon, they give us bread and water, then the captain of the boat decided to take us in." But there were Vietnamese police, officials, on the boat, which was still in international waters, so the transfer was politically sensitive and accompanied by serious set-tos between the Europeans and the Vietnamese officials.

As the refugees were being transferred to the oil drilling boat, their fishing boat capsized, and many people perished, including Tran's sister and baby brother. Tran has deeply traumatic memories of their drowning. Then, more Vietnamese authorities arrived and attempted, without success, to entice the refugees back to Vietnam. Finally, the Vietnamese officials agreed with the Dutch and German management of the oil drilling boat to allow the refugees to leave Vietnam. After a period, the Europeans bought the refugees an expensive new boat. Led by two supply boats, and followed by Vietnamese gun boats, the new boat with the surviving refugees on board set off.

Then the refugee boat was attacked by four Vietnamese gun boats in international waters and was forced to sail back to Vietnam. The two supply boats accompanied the small flotilla and filmed the entire incident. Back in Vietnam, the refugees were taken to prison. But six weeks later, they were told that they would be leaving Vietnam. They received new IDs and passports and left on regular airplane flights for the Netherlands and Germany.

As Tran understands it, on learning of the incident with the oil drilling boat, Chancellor Helmut Schmidt of Germany threatened to cut off all aid and break diplomatic relations with Vietnam. Soon after, the refugees were on their way to Europe.

The Refugee Camps

After arriving in neighbouring countries, the interviewees lived through a range of camp experiences. For all of them, it was important to be in an "official" refugee camp visited by representatives of resettlement countries like Canada.

A few, like Tran Quoc Tuy (Interview HOF064 2019) and the couple Tran Thi Duc and Tran Anh Kiet (Interview HOF050 2019), ended up in Singapore after difficult and painful voyages. They were special cases as Singapore refused to allow any refugee boats inside its territorial waters (Yuen 1990). The refugees inside its single camp entered the city state after being picked up by rescue ships. The camp in Singapore contained only one thousand refugees, who were well treated and made it rapidly to Western resettlement countries like Canada. The family of Le Thi Kim Yen (Interview HOF052 2019) was fortunate to be rescued and taken to Japan where there were very few refugees. In Japan, they were well treated and spent a short time in a comfortable non-camp-like facility before leaving for Canada. Other fortunate refugees ended up in Palawan camp in the Philippines, where conditions were very good.

Even though Hong Kong became a major Vietnamese refugee resettlement centre with numerous camps that accommodated many refugees bound for Canada, relatively few of the Hearts of Freedom interviewees passed through it. Conditions in most of the Hong Kong camps were relatively good if terribly crowded, as confirmed by Canadian visa officers who selected refugees for Canadian resettlement from the Hong Kong camps (Molloy et al. 2017, 329–38). However, in February 1979, being allowed to land in Hong Kong by the authorities was still a lottery for the refugees. The freighter *Skyluck* waited four and a half months in Hong Kong harbour with over three thousand refugees on board, before the refugees scuttled the boat and were allowed ashore in June 1979.[3] Huynh Chau and Huynh Hieu (Interview HOF173 2020), a Hoa couple, spent a short time in Hong Kong where the husband was able to work before leaving for Canada. Ethnic Vietnamese refugee Tham Le Kim Thu (Inter-

3 For media coverage of the journey aboard the *Skyluck*, see "Viets Storm Hong Kong," *Toronto Star*, 30 June 1979.

view HOF020 2019) arrived with her husband in Hong Kong in April 1979 as a "pretend" Hoa on one of the last large "Chinese" boats with 1,200 other refugees on board. She was housed in a restrictive and regimented former Royal Air Force facility.

But the worst refugee camp in Hong Kong was Chi Ma Won on Hei Ling Chau Island, a former leper colony. Nguyen Quyen (Interview HOF130 2020) and his older brother spent three months in this camp. He describes conditions in the camp as horrible, with small portions of bad food and very hot dilapidated living facilities. Nguyen was constantly hungry in Hong Kong and wondered whether it was worth leaving Vietnam, given the conditions in which he found himself.

Most of the interviewees headed south from Vietnam, toward Malaysia and Indonesia. If they were lucky, they arrived relatively rapidly in one of the UNHCR camps after landing on Malaysian beaches or Indonesian islands. The main UNHCR refugee camps were Pulau Galang in Indonesia, Pulau Bidong and Pulau Tengah in Malaysia, and Songkhla in Thailand. Before being transported by Malaysian police buses and/or by boat to the nearest camp, the refugees often spent days on the beaches, exposed to the elements. Do Nghia (Interview HOF103 2019) came ashore on a Malaysian beach in July 1979 and was taken by boat to the enormously crowded refugee camp of Bidong Island (Pulau Bidong). He describes camp conditions: "At that time four hundred people come every day, [there were] thirty or thirty-five thousand, and many people come … [in the camp] every day, men in the family coming down to get water, collect some food, go up to the hill, chop some wood, bring it down … use wood for cooking."

Some refugee boats, often crippled but still somewhat seaworthy, were pushed out to sea by Malaysian coast guard or navy vessels, to land on one of the tiny, rocky, usually uninhabited Anambas islands of the Indonesian Riau archipelago. Some of the refugee boats landed directly on these islets or were directed there from oil drilling platforms.

Several interviewees describe the "camps" on these islands. On arrival, the refugees were left to their own devices. They had to construct crude living facilities, simple huts built of wood and palm leaf covers. They needed to find a source of fresh water. The islands were visited by Indonesian Red Crescent and UNHCR boats bringing food supplies. Some of the islands were visited by Indonesian fishermen; others had tiny fishing villages on them. Fish, caught by the refugees themselves, were an important food source.

According to Nguyen Mai Chi, camp conditions on the Anambas Islands were terrible, with rampant disease and high mortality. She describes these rudimentary island camps:

> They took us to Araya Island where there were already twenty thousand refugees, but where there was nothing, just bare ground, forest, and huts that the refugees themselves built. We slept on the ground for a few days, and then the men went into the forest to cut wood and the women gathered [palm] leaves for the roofs. Camp Araya was a makeshift camp, very unhealthy. There was a creek where everybody washed themselves; we had to go higher and higher because the water became dirty. There were septic tanks, but the septic tanks filled up very quickly; there were many ten-year-old children who died because of this. I was on Araya Island between May and October and between October and December on Galang Island … It was very hard, the life of refugees in the camp, so I volunteered to work in the Indonesian dispensary on another island called Leton. The dispensary was for Indonesians, but since there were so many refugees with health problems, rapes, cases of violence, they had to be treated, so I volunteered. I stayed six days per week in the dispensary to help Vietnamese refugees from six o'clock in the morning to six o'clock in the evening. We treated about four hundred refugees every day. There were cases of rape; young women fifteen to eighteen years old full of infections, gonorrhea, syphilis. You had to treat them. Many were pregnant; you had to treat them or perform abortions. There were many cases of infection … My role was to open files, do interviews and do triage of the refugees, and then pass the files to the nurses and doctors. I also had to assist in treating the refugees. I received some summary training from the doctors and nurses … Our camp wasn't really a camp, it was an island. We could go wherever we wanted … There were several very basic camps on different islands. (Interview HOF053 2019)

She continues, describing the refugee camp on Pulau Galang: "The UNHCR paid the Indonesians to build barracks on Galang Island. There was running water, it was rudimentary, but it was more comfortable. There was an aluminum roof; there were two rows of wooden beds for fifty people in each row; the barracks were very long. The UNHCR gathered us there, so that we could be interviewed by refugee-receiving countries. They didn't have to travel to all the small islands."

Canadian immigration officials did have lists of names based on sponsorships from Canada which were passed on to UNHCR officials who frequently visited the islands. As well, Canadian visa officers from Singapore did visit the difficult-to-reach Anambas Islands camps several times and selected refugees directly from the islands, arranging their transport to Galang with the UNHCR (Molloy et al. 2017, 237–45, 257).

In the main UNHCR refugee camps, the refugees generally consider conditions to have been adequate with enough food and acceptable sleeping accommodations. Having said this, they all wanted to leave the camps and proceed as soon as possible to their new homes in the West. For those with family in Canada, it was the obvious primary resettlement choice. For the rest, most knew nothing of Canada, and they chose resettlement in Canada because it offered to resettle them first.

A touching episode was recounted by Tran Phuong Thu (Interview HOF027 2019), a very well-educated older woman. On Pulau Bidong, she acted as the translator for Ian Hamilton, Canada's chief immigration official in Singapore responsible for refugee selection from 1977 to 1979. She did not consider it to be her preferred destination, but Hamilton convinced her to choose Canada. A few months later, when Hamilton returned to work from sick leave, she again hesitated, but he again convinced her to choose Canada. She is happy that she made this choice and remembers Hamilton with affection.

Conclusion

It was both very expensive and extremely dangerous to set to sea in small, unseaworthy, overloaded boats, often under the command of incompetent captains. The interviewees' stories demonstrate that this was well known in Vietnam. Yet many people took the chance and left for the possibility of better lives far from their ancestral homes and their culture. Was their motivation economic? Their comments indicate that to a small extent it was. But their more important motivation was the fact that since the beginning of May 1975, it had become virtually impossible to lead a normal human existence in South Vietnam, especially for urban middle-class people, including the Hoa. The interviewees constantly repeat that life in South Vietnam had become hell and they had fled to freedom.

The communist cadres spoke frequently of freeing the Vietnamese people from colonialism and exploitation. But their talk, repeated as dogma in schools, universities, workplaces, and especially re-education camps, was contradicted by the realities of people's daily lives. There was little food, paper money had little value; it was dangerous to talk openly. The North Vietnamese victory in the war, which was supposed to unite Vietnam, instead directed revenge against the South Vietnamese urban and middle classes. Average urban people – not only supporters of the former regime – faced an existence where nothing was certain; where the government and the police had to be feared; where officials, policemen, and the military were corrupt. Many Vietnamese decided that facing the dangers of a terrible sea journey, the possibility of death on the high seas, and new lives in alien cultures was preferable to miserable, terrified lives in Vietnam.

6

Boat People Escapes: Four Stories

This chapter presents the full stories of an educated married couple of Vietnamese ethnicity, both of whom were middle-class professionals in Vietnam; an English language Canadian journalist of Chinese-Vietnamese (Hoa) ethnicity who was a young child when she left Vietnam with her parents and her toddler sister; and a Canadian professional who escaped as an unaccompanied eleven-year-old boy.

These stories highlight some of the most gripping aspects of the Vietnamese boat people experience. In each case the accounts attempt to present the full story from the interviews in a focused manner. Reflections on the extreme precariousness of lives in Vietnam and the boat people's journey are in the refugees' own words.

Tran Thi Duc and Tran Anh Kiet

The quotes in these two stories are translated from an interview conducted in French (Interview HOF050 2019).

Tran Thi Duc and Tran Anh Kiet are a well-dressed, well-spoken married couple. Although elderly, they appear youthful, and tell their stories in a lively, intelligent manner. Their youthful appearances and manners became especially impressive as the stories of the horrors they had experienced unfolded. Tran Thi Duc speaks French well. Tran Anh Kiet, although she understands French, prefers to express herself in Vietnamese, and her husband acted as her translator. As the interview progressed and she told her story, it became increasingly more terrifying. As witnessed through her body language and facial expressions, she exercised great self-control in telling her story, which was evidently easier in her Vietnamese mother language. At the time of their escapes and their lives in camp, both were still single. Their two separate stories follow.

When Saigon fell, Tran Thi Duc was thirty-five years old. He thought of leaving but hesitated and finally decided not to leave before 30 April 1975. Like many others, he felt that living in peace under a Communist government would not be worse than life had been during the lengthy war. After all, he was not a military man. As he explains, three weeks after the communist conquest, "I was working as a senior executive of the South Vietnam Electricity Company, a state enterprise. I was arrested and taken to prison like everybody without exception, whether engineer or official. We were taken for re-education. Really, it was forced labour. Re-education, it is brain washing." After four weeks, he was released and sent back to his place of work. Apparently, the new government needed his expertise.

Tran Thi Duc's re-education camp experience convinced him that he needed to leave Vietnam. After three to four months of preparation he managed to find a boat that was to leave from Vung Tau, the harbour city sixty miles downriver from Saigon. He describes his first escape attempt. To get to Vung Tau, "we hired a river taxi; the river taxi's owner denounced us. An armed patrol boat was waiting for us on the river and promptly arrested us."

This time, Tran Thi Duc was imprisoned for three years, spending one year in a regular prison, followed by two years in a re-education camp. He describes conditions in the prison "as hell. There they tortured people. I was not tortured myself but witnessed them torturing other prisoners. In the re-education camp there were all sorts of people, not only refugees [those who had attempted to escape]. Conditions in the re-education camp were better than in the prison; it was outdoors." The hard labour and the repeated indoctrination sessions in the camp were bad, but being outside, inmates did not have to suffer the filth and disease of the prison. After three years, he was again released and allowed to work as a scientific professional.

Out of detention again, Tran Thi Duc was convinced that he must leave. Conditions in Vietnam were "hell, it's hell over there, the state of the economy, the communists, stupid nationalization, nothing to eat with small salaries" added to "constant oppression, police surveillance." He learned of a boat that would be leaving and managed to get a place. "For my second escape attempt I had no more money. I could not come up with the funds (5 taels of gold) demanded by the trip's organizer." The organizer took pity on him and allowed him on board without demanding payment. There were sixty people pressed together on a small vessel. The boat headed out to the open sea toward Malaysia. After two days of sailing they had serious mechanical problems. As the boat started to sink near the Malaysian coast, a large yacht passed by. The yacht, privately owned by a wealthy Australian, rescued the refugees.

Once on board, the Australian yacht took the refugees to Singapore, the closest major port. Since he arrived on an Australian vessel and not a refugee boat – refugee boats were not admitted into Singapore territorial waters – Tran Thi Duc was admitted to Singapore and was placed in a former military barracks which served as a refugee camp. "The refugee camp in Singapore was the best organized. The UNHCR paid for everything" and was responsible for his maintenance and living expenses while in Singapore. Fortunately, Canadian and Quebec officers rapidly found a guarantee that had been signed in Tran Thi Duc's favour by a close friend in Montreal. Years before, he had studied in Montreal, and he still had close friends there. Within four months of arriving in Singapore, Tran was on his way to Montreal. As he observed, his survival was due to pure chance and luck. Had the Australian yacht not picked him up, he would have been lost at sea, one of the many victims of the boat people crisis.

Tran Anh Kiet is from a middle-class Catholic family and was still single at the time of her escape. She studied chemistry at the University of Saigon and was teaching at a lycée at the time of her departure from Vietnam. "Life was terribly hard in communist Vietnam. My salary had no value. Vietnam was no place to start a family, it was hell." She had tried to escape once before but failed. "The second time I succeeded, but I almost died." The interview did not indicate whether she was punished after her first escape attempt.

By early 1980, she was the last member of her immediate family in Vietnam. "My South Vietnamese soldier brother had fallen in battle. After an escape attempt by boat, my sister with three of her children perished at sea. My youngest sister managed to escape and was in Canada … I decided to escape for the second time in March 1980." She still had two nephews in Vietnam; it is unclear who her nephews' parents were or how old they were, but they were not small children. Taking her two nephews with her, she paid for places on a boat in taels of gold. They set out on the open sea in an unseaworthy vessel carrying sixteen people, including two women and some children: "I did not know the destination until we arrived near Singapore."

"The boat was in bad condition. Before we could enter Singapore territorial waters, an armed Singaporean naval vessel barred our way and made us turn around. In heavy seas, our boat started to break apart." The Singaporean vessel was still within hailing distance and made a half-hearted effort to help some of the people on the sinking refugee boat. The next hour was horrific: "First, the Singaporeans agreed to save women and children but no men, using a helicopter with a hanging ladder to airlift them on the boat; doing this, a family of four with two children would be divided. The mother of the family refused to go under these circumstances. It is unclear whether any refugees were finally rescued by the Singaporean naval boat, which eventually left, leaving refugees stranded in the water."

Wooden planks and empty barrels, the boat's wreckage, floated on the surface of the sea. Some of the refugees, including Tran Anh Kiet, had plastic floating devices around their waists. They floated in the water, battered by high waves, hanging on to the planks or to the barrels. She does not recall how many of the refugees perished, but she could see the family with the two children and witnessed the death of the mother and the younger, two-year-old child. She continues: "I remained in the sea from early morning until nightfall. I could not tell who else was floating along with me, except for one of my nephews who was relatively close to me." As she remembers, she could see many boats, but nobody picked her up. She says, "I was small in the water, they could not see me." She was convinced that she would die. As a Catholic she prayed to the Virgin Mary.

A ship passed by with lights on, the sailors could see her, she was picked up. They also picked up three other shipwrecked persons, including one of her nephews. The ship was flying a Panamanian flag but had an Indonesian crew. The crew was very considerate to the shipwrecked refugees. Eventually she ended up in the single refugee camp in Singapore (see Tran Thi Duc's story).

Tran Anh Kiet stayed in the camp where she was supported by the UNHCR for a relatively short time. She was sponsored by her sister and arrived in Montreal very rapidly. Eventually, she met Tran Thi Duc; they married, had a daughter, and had a good life in Canada. Tran Anh Kiet believes that partly luck, but mostly divine mercy, saved her when she was close to death in the South China Sea.

Judy Trinh

The quotes in this story are from an interview (Interview HOF029 2019).

Judy Trinh, born in 1974, left Vietnam as a young child and speaks expressive Canadian English with no trace of an accent. She is an Ottawa-based journalist. She only has a few memories of her family's escape from Vietnam and relies on her mother's and father's memories. Over the years, her parents have told her a great deal about their lives in Vietnam and their refugee exodus.

Trinh is from a prosperous Chinese minority family. Her parents are both educated people. In Vietnam her mother was an accountant and a Chinese-language journalist; her father worked in the family textile factory. The entire family lived together at her grandfather's large family house. But as the North Vietnamese assumed power, all of them left Vietnam. As she explains, "We were the last members of the extended family to leave, my grandparents had gone, my father's siblings had all left, the reason that we remained was because my sister – two years old at the time of their departure – was born premature and she was very ill." Her mother was fearful that she might not survive the trip.

They finally decided to leave in late 1978. "My father had served for a time with the South Vietnamese military … He was told that he would be put into a re-education camp … When he knew that he was targeted, we had to leave immediately." The family had assets that they liquidated before leaving and had in their possession 30 taels of gold and US$75.

They travelled to the seaside in a bus. Before arriving at military checkpoints, to avoid detection, her father left the bus and rejoined it later. Once on the seashore, a small boat took them to a Vietnamese island where they waited for months until a fishing boat could be found to take them to Malaysia. Eventually, their family was taken aboard a fishing boat. "It was a five-day journey in the spring of 1979, the fishing vessel was the size of a yellow school bus. They were able to fit 315 people on that boat. My mother describes it as being so cramped that if you turned your head, you would bump noses with the person next to you." During the five-day journey, her little sister had severe dysentery and they feared that she would die. Another young child did die on the boat.

Trinh continues: "On the third day, we were boarded by pirates, they were armed with guns and machetes, they wanted everyone's valuables." The Trinh family was left without any resources. On the fourth day, another group of pirates boarded the boat. Angry at finding nothing of value on board, the pirates stripped the refugees of everything, including all food and drinking water. Unless they hit land soon, "we knew that our ability to survive on that boat was very limited."

"On day five, we saw land in the distance, that was Malaysia … My dad describes it as everyone letting out a cheer when they could see land on the horizon. But that hope immediately turned into frustration." On arriving closer to land, they were met by a Malaysian naval ship and told that they would not be allowed to dock in Malaysia, since the closest refugee camp was full and could not accommodate more refugees. Their boat was directed back to international waters.

On board their boat, the captain told the refugees that they could not head back to the open sea. He had no idea where he could take them. "He said we are going to turn the boat around; we will sink the boat, and everyone will have to swim to shore. That night, we turned around and approached to within 300 or 400 metres of land." The men on board, using any available tools, proceeded to break the boat apart and set the engine on fire. "If the boat was going to sink, there was no way to turn around, we would have to be accepted into a refugee camp." The refugees had no choice. They had to make it to shore somehow. People jumped overboard, ready to swim to shore. Others grabbed anything that floated, hoping to float to shore.

> My mother tells the story that my dad jumps overboard and she's with me, she is holding on to my sister, and she is telling me to jump. But I'm scared, my dad down in the water is calling for me "jump, jump" but I don't know how to swim. My mother puts down my sister, basically grabs me and throws me overboard, hopes that my dad will find me. And then she grabs my sister and jumps overboard with my sister. But we made it, we made it to shore. When we first arrived in Canada my mother used to have nightmares, recurring nightmares of that scene, tossing me overboard.

On shore, they carried Judy's severely sick younger sister, suffering so much from dysentery that she might die at any moment. "My mother is pacing along the seashore, she is praying … My family comes from a Christian background … Then she sees something floating on the ocean and it washes ashore, and it is a glass bottle with a red cross on it." The bottle with the red cross, a gift of the sea, contained the medicine that stopped the infant's severe dysentery and saved her life.

Eventually, the family was picked up by a bus from the beach and taken to Cherating refugee camp. The only recollection Trinh has of the camp is finding a shiny penny in between the floorboards. Surviving photos show her in pink pajamas running around the camp. Key to the Trinh family's admission into Canada was a letter of guarantee written by her aunt in Alberta. The letter had survived all the family's adventures inside her father's clothes, close to his heart. Six months later the Trinh family arrived in Canada.

Buchan Tho Trong Pham

The quotes in this story are from an interview (Interview HOF018 2019).

Buchan Tho Trong is a well-spoken, youngish man, looking a decade younger than his age. He speaks colloquial Canadian English. The story of his escape provides an example of the frequent undoing of Vietnamese extended families following 1975 that resulted in many unaccompanied minor refugees. Occasionally, during the telling of this story, the interviewee's emotions came to the surface. He indicated that he chooses to be identified by the family name of his adoptive Canadian father, Buchan.

Buchan was the second-youngest of five children living in Saigon. He was six years old in 1975. "My father was working as a bank investment advisor … My mother was a homemaker, she didn't work." On 30 April 1975, his father who had also been a South Vietnamese army officer, disappeared immediately after the fall of Saigon. He showed up at home a few days later. He was sent to re-education for a year. "My mother had to find ways to support the family … My father used to be absent from his home all day trying to make a living."

He does not know where his father went or what he did, but earning a living largely became his mother's responsibility. She would leave very early in the morning and travel by bus west to the Cambodian border, a region of Vietnam she originated from and knew well, where she would buy household goods, some of which came from Thailand. The next day she sold the goods for profit in Saigon. Being a child, Buchan did not know about the details of his parents' activities. But the Trong children were left alone most of the time as their parents attempted to make a living. Buchan recalls that "in 1978 there was sort of a famine, we didn't have food to eat, I was constantly hungry during the famine year, the family had no money." He was wandering the streets of Saigon by himself as he got older.

His father escaped from Vietnam by himself in May 1980, leaving his family. He ended up in England. "A year later, during that year, when my father arrived in England, he sent a letter home to my mom, asking if we could send some of us out of Vietnam … He asked for two of us … I was the one who got along with him of all of our siblings, so he asked for me and one other," his older brother, to join him. Their mother sold all her possessions to pay for a boat trip and, acting through her sister in the countryside, bought places for her two boys ages eleven and seventeen on a boat leaving the country clandestinely.

She took the two boys to her sister's place in a rural village west of Saigon. The sister's son, Buchan's older cousin, made the arrangements for a boat. They had a plan to leave Vietnam:

> My mother, my brother, and I made the trip to my aunt's place in the countryside … It was the easiest and closest location to get a

> pilot from there … After a few days, we left one evening … We got on a power canoe. They took us to another meeting place where we got on another boat. When I got on the bigger boat, I didn't realize that I didn't have a chance to say goodbye to anybody … People were pushing us around, "Get on and keep quiet." I didn't see my mother. I didn't know that my brother didn't come with us. I was the only one.

Buchan left in pitch dark with his cousin, his cousin's wife and their three children. They boarded a fishing boat with about seventy others. His older brother remained in Vietnam and Buchan would never see him again. Later, he found out that the cousin, who organized everything, did not allow his older brother to come on the boat. "There was only enough money for one of us … I knew the real truth about my cousin."

The boat was terribly crowded. His cousin ignored him and settled down with his immediate family at the back of the boat. From this point, eleven-year-old Buchan was completely alone:

> Within the first few hours I became sick, I started to throw up. I don't remember much after that. All I knew I got so sick I was looking for a place to lie down. I went to the back of the boat, tried to find a place to lie down … My cousin's extended family [second cousin] actually kicked me out. They [had a hut] at the end of the boat, because she was trying to make room for her neighbours. After that I never spoke to them again … After that I went to the front of the boat. I sat down.

The next day, "the first day out, we were met by Thai pirates. These guys … some of them painted their faces, some carried machetes, some carried knives. We had a spare engine, they took that … They rob everything they could lay their hands on … I was terrified." Soon after the pirates left, the boat's engine died, and the refugees were left without motor power, aimlessly drifting on the South China Sea.

From the second day, a pattern was established. Every day a different Thai fishing boat came with fishermen who had become opportunistic pirates. When they saw that there was nothing left to plunder, they transferred the girls and women to the Thai fishing boat for about a half-hour.

Then they also transferred the men and the children and searched the empty refugee boat for any hidden valuables. Buchan did not witness what was done to the refugee females, but in his description, he implied the unimaginable. The pirate fishermen were not always extremely bad people. They often provided some simple food, sticky rice and boiled fish, to the refugees. Later, they transferred all the refugees back to the refugee boat.

The daily pirate attacks continued for seven days. By the fourth or fifth day, Buchan was thinking that his chances of survival on the refugee boat were decreasing, that he would somehow need to find a way to escape. On the same day, the pirates not only transferred the refugees back to their boat, but also transferred to the crippled floating vessel thirty additional Vietnamese boat people whom they were holding on their own boat. The already terribly crowded refugee boat now had one hundred people on board.

"I was thinking that if I saw an opportunity, I would try to get off our crippled boat. I didn't know what I was going to do, but I had that thought in my mind." By the seventh day, the pirate-fishermen arrived relatively late. It was already starting to get dark when they transferred the refugees to the Thai fishing boat where conditions were chaotic with refugees milling about on the boat. "Those guys were nice, they gave candies to the kids, so I thought that maybe I could carry out my plan ... In the middle of the night, they started to push people [refugees] back to our own boat." Buchan, a small, barely noticeable boy, took a chance. "I saw an opening and crept into the engine room." He found a narrow, hidden space and crept inside. Eventually, he fell asleep. He awoke the next morning but stayed hidden. About halfway through the morning, he crept out from his hiding place covered in grease and engine oil. He was found by the ship's cook, washed off, and given work clothes.

For the next week he stayed on the fishing boat. He could not communicate with the captain or the crew but tried to make himself useful by working with them. He was well fed, the cook appeared to like him. After a week, they met another fishing boat and Buchan was transferred from one Thai vessel to another. To this day he does not know why. The second fishing boat was much like the first. The captain, the crew, and especially the cook treated the small, malnourished boy relatively well; they fed him and gave him water. He worked alongside them for two weeks.

After the second week, they met a large ship, a freighter. The fishing boat hailed the freighter and pulled alongside the bigger boat. Buchan continues: "The next thing I saw was a huge ship … They came close to the ship … They signalled me to climb on to the big ship with a rope ladder, so I came up … Somebody on that ship spoke Vietnamese and he said that the ship was a German rescue ship." The Vietnamese speaking person asked details about Buchan and whether there were other refugees to rescue on the fishing boat. Before he left, the Thai boat's cook gave the young boy fried shrimp and the gift of a string of beads.

Buchan was then transferred to a German rescue ship, the *Cap Anamur*. The ship had been sailing the South China Sea, searching for boat people to rescue. Reacting to the boat people crisis on the South China Sea, a German couple, Christel and Rupert Neudeck, founded the committee Ein Schiff für Vietnam (A boat for Vietnam) in 1979. Relying on private donations, they chartered the freighter *Cap Anamur* and cruised the South China Sea. During the worst period of the boat people crisis, the *Cap Anamur* rescued more than 11,000 refugees stranded on the high seas and provided medical care to 35,000 others (Merziger 2016, Schoepfel 2019).

Buchan spent the next six weeks onboard the *Cap Anamur*, well fed and cared for. The ship kept cruising and picking up refugees. "On that ship they rescue a previous boat of twenty-nine people, I was added to that … I became friends with one of the boys on that ship and two other cousins … To this day we're still friends … one of my best friends." Eventually, having rescued 396 refugees, the German freighter, running out of supplies, headed for the Philippines.

At the end of July 1981, the refugees were unloaded from the *Cap Anamur* at the Palawan refugee camp, a large camp housing at the time almost ten thousand refugees (Lipman 2020, 201–32). Soon after his arrival, Buchan was fortunate to run into two sisters in Palawan who were good friends of his sisters back in Saigon. The sisters, eighteen and nineteen at the time, invited him to stay with them at their small temporary house, an offer he gladly accepted since the alternative was staying in large barracks. He has positive memories of the camp. Food was plentiful; there was a school, a church, and a pagoda. He still remembers his Scottish teacher, who started to teach him English and with whom he maintained contact for a few years after leaving the camp. There was a beautiful beach next to the camp where the refugee kids could swim and play. There were no movement restrictions; the refugees could freely walk to the neighbouring town.

On arrival in the Philippines, Buchan immediately wrote to his father in England; he felt that this was the most secure way to contact his family. He had memorized his father's address before leaving Vietnam. His father contacted his mother in Vietnam. After three months, this was the first sign of life his mother had of her young son.

His father wrote to him that he should ask to be resettled in Canada rather than England. According to his father, settlement conditions in England were bad; Canada was much better. Also, his father had been in contact in Canada with a potential private sponsor, Saint Matthew United Church in Richmond Hill, Ontario. Bryan Buchan, a member of the church and the young refugee's future adoptive dad in Canada, had by 1979 already adopted several underage Vietnamese refugee cousins. Now it would be Buchan's turn.

The amazing story of his adoptive Canadian father, Bryan Buchan, and the eleven Vietnamese children that Buchan sponsored, is described in chapter 8. Young Buchan Tho spent six months in Palawan camp and six more months in a Manila transit camp before arriving in Canada in June 1982.

Conclusion

These four stories demonstrate how precarious the boat peoples' experience was. Every interviewee in this chapter could easily have perished at sea. It was chance that ensured their survival. Some of their family members had perished. Southeast Asian cultures consider it very important to preserve the memories of dead family members. But family members of refugees lost on the South China Sea have no graves. As the following two chapters will show, most Vietnamese refugees were able to build successful lives in Canada despite the traumas of their escapes from Vietnam.

7

Resettling the Boat People in Canada

This chapter describes Vietnamese resettlement and integration from coast to coast during close to four decades. This is a daunting challenge, given the length of time and the variety of life stories. It examines and compares the experiences of privately sponsored and government-assisted refugees as well as some who were sponsored by their refugee families already resettled in Canada.

By late 1978, Canada's 1976 Immigration Act was implemented, and Vietnamese refugees became part of the newly created Indochinese Designated Class. They no longer had to demonstrate individually that they were fleeing persecution but were accepted as members of a designated group on humanitarian grounds. As well, the private refugee sponsorship provisions of the new Immigration Act were now in place. Starting with Canada's faith-based organizations, a range of private Canadian groups rapidly and enthusiastically began to sponsor Southeast Asian refugees. In 1979–80, Canada admitted sixty thousand of these refugees through an intense effort in a two-year period. Those sponsored by private groups outnumbered those assisted by the Canadian government. This remained a characteristic of this refugee movement until the movement's end in 1997.

The Orderly Departure Program (ODP), established under the auspices of the UNHCR, came into force in early 1979. Canadian visa officer René Bersma played a crucial role in defining how the ODP would be implemented. Eventually, following difficult negotiations with Vietnamese authorities, the ODP used Canada's regular family reunification program to allow family members left behind in Vietnam to join their families already resettled in Canada (Bersma 2024). Through the ODP, as soon as they had the financial resources to do so, many newly resettled Vietnamese refugees sponsored their family members in Vietnam. Family reunification became an important part of the Vietnamese movement to Canada through the 1980s and early 1990s (Kumin 2008). At the same time, many family-sponsored Vietnamese had already escaped from Vietnam and were living in refugee camps before being sponsored by their families in Canada.

Privately Sponsored Refugees: Initial Settlement and Integration

The personalized help and support private sponsors provided to refugees was the new private group sponsorship program's defining feature. Although the private sponsorship undertaking was for one year, many private sponsors continued to assist refugees beyond the year. For unaccompanied minor refugees adopted by Canadians through the private group sponsorship program, these personal ties often lasted for a lifetime as family ties. In some cases, however, the private sponsors only lived up to their commitments minimally. In other cases, the refugees wanted to be independent as soon as possible and did not wish to rely on assistance from sponsors.

Refugees arriving in Canada had been warned about Canada's climate, but experiencing it still came as a shock. In March 1981 in Kapuskasing, Ontario, seventeen-year-old Michael Do Duy Tien (Interview HOF021 2019) "couldn't believe how people could live in such cold." In a Southeast Asian camp, Do Thi Kim Luong (Interview HOF174 2020) had been warned that "Canada is a very cold place. People live in houses which are just like an icicle. When people walk on the street, everything is covered, just not the eye. I said I don't think I'm gonna live there, that's too cold for me." Being transferred from plane to plane in Vancouver and Edmonton airports, "I'm very curious now, I want to see the igloos … I looked outside, there are no igloos, so I said maybe this is not Canada yet." On finally arriving in Halifax in December 1979, she was cold. "People walked around in coats, lots of snow, but still no igloos."

But even in the summer, in August 1981, Tri Duc Pham (Interview HOF164 2020) felt cold in Edmonton. "In August it was very cold, it's not that cold in the sun, but the moment a cloud come(s) by you feel cold right away." The private sponsors either welcomed the refugees with clothes appropriate for Canada or took them clothes shopping. Some of these refugees received clothes through their sponsoring churches.

In the beginning, the hardest problem for most refugees was not being able to communicate. Learning English or French was the first challenge of their Canadian lives. Four of the interviewees, arriving in Canada as unaccompanied children or as very young single men, acquired language competency in fully English or French speaking environments. Three unaccompanied minor refugees, younger than eighteen, were adopted. Being young and living among non-Vietnamese speakers, they had great advantages in language acquisition and acculturation to Canadian life.

Eleven-year-old unaccompanied child Buchan Tho Trong (Interview HOF018 2019) learned English in public school and the home of his adoptive schoolteacher dad. Another unaccompanied minor, Le Hoang Chau (Interview HOF043 2019), was sixteen when he arrived in Sherbrooke, Quebec. "I was adopted. It was a family that was so good to me. My parents, I consider them as my parents ... they immediately sent me to a private school to learn French ... Next school year they sent me to (another) private school; I was the only immigrant in that school. My mother helped me. Every morning she took out a French-Vietnamese dictionary and worked with me." Eventually, he was sent to university, living with his adoptive parents. He remains very close to them. Although he now lives and works in Montreal, he visits them in Sherbrooke often. In Kapuskasing, Ontario, the third adoptive minor interviewee, seventeen-year-old Michael Do Duy Tien, learned English with the help of his English teacher adoptive father and other members of his sponsorship group.

All three adopted refugee interviewees are extremely grateful to their adoptive parents for making their early adaptation to Canada so easy. Two of the three remained with their adoptive families a long time and remain very close to their Canadian parents. The third, Michael Do Duy Tien (Interview HOF021 2019), left Kapuskasing for Toronto after one year once he turned eighteen. He wanted to be independent and Kapuskasing was far too cold and lonely. He and his Vietnamese refugee cousin were the only Vietnamese people in the small northern town. They missed their cultural community, the Asian food, and the opportunities offered by Toronto. Yet he insists that he is very grateful for the efforts made by his sponsoring group and short-term adoptive father.

Seminary student Dinh Thanh Son, known in Quebec as Jean Baptiste (Interview HOF051 2019), arrived in his early twenties and was fortunate to learn French in a completely French environment, in the Grand Séminaire de Montréal. Sponsored by the Sulpicien religious order, he was eventually ordained a priest. He was studying as a seminary student in French after nine months of French language schooling. As he says, "I had to throw myself into full studies, even if deficient in language." Despite the full immersion these four young men received, they report that it still took them two to three years to feel fully at ease in an English or French educational environment.

The experience of the other privately sponsored refugees with language acquisition was more varied. It went along with their general experience of welcome and support by the private sponsors. Sixteen-year-old Vu Thuy Alexander (Interview HOF144 2020) was privately sponsored along with his older brother. Their United Church sponsors in Edmonton provided them with all the necessities of life, including a first job for his brother, transportation to his grade 9 class, and English instruction for both. The experience of Nguyen Terry Tho (Interview HOF172 2020) and his family was also very positive. His Truro, Nova Scotia, sponsoring church welcomed them with a nice house and a fine meal. He already spoke English, so they did not need help with language acquisition, although at the beginning Terry had trouble understanding Canadian accents. The sponsors quickly found good jobs in Truro for Terry and his brother.

Nguyen Thanh Thuy's (Interview HOF085 2019) family, sponsored by a church in Windsor, Ontario, spoke relatively good English on arrival, so did not require language classes. Their sponsoring church "rent for us a beautiful town house, brand new … everything is furnished, very nice house … The first night my sponsor told us this is your home, rest and then tomorrow they will come for us … I told my husband, oh my God, we don't have any money … I am worried because nobody give you for free … I told my husband just have the blanket and we sleep on the floor." They could not believe that they would have a nice house free of charge. This family rapidly decided that they wanted Canadian qualifications and wanted to live in a larger, more business-oriented city than Windsor, close to an established Vietnamese community. Within one to two years of their arrival, both husband and wife were studying and had jobs in Toronto. Although they moved from Windsor relatively rapidly, they continue to have very positive feelings for their sponsors.

Like several other refugees, Zung Trinh (Interview HOF159 2020) of North Vietnam and her family were also sponsored by a church congregation in Summerland, a small town in the Okanagan Valley of British Columbia. This family was linguistically gifted and spoke very good English even before arrival in Canada. They remain on good terms with their sponsors who provided them with all the elements needed to start a new life in Canada, including jobs: "Then one day we visit Vancouver and as soon as I see Chinatown, I see Vietnamese food and I decided to stay, I don't want to go back at all [to Summerland]." They visit their friends in the Okanagan often, but they moved to Vancouver as soon as they could. When Zung experienced Vancouver's Chinatown for the first time, with its cosmopolitan atmosphere and its Asian gastronomy and culture, nothing could keep her in Summerland.

The early experiences of Do Thi Kim Luong (Interview HOF174 2020) were more difficult. She speaks of her sponsors in positive terms, yet in her story she describes several instances of cultural misunderstanding between her small-town sponsors and her family. Do was pregnant when she arrived with her husband and a small child in the seaside Nova Scotia village of Mahone Bay. They were sponsored by a local church. "They rented for us an apartment above a clothing store … when we arrived we didn't know it was our apartment … They didn't tell us … When we get there, our sponsor already had there a dining room table with two big turkeys [it was before Christmas] … That's the first time I ever saw a bird that big. I didn't know I had to eat them." This was culture shock. Everything was strange to them. They had no idea how to eat the strange food, they could not communicate with anybody, and there were no Vietnamese speakers in Mahone Bay. But the sponsors made every attempt to teach them English rapidly. "Six volunteers [ladies from the church] came to our house one hour [each day] to teach us English … My six teachers they are wonderful, they are so good."

The Do family received from the sponsors a stipend of $75 per week for food, which was a fortune for them. They saved $40 every week. Soon she and her husband were able to send their savings to help their parents in Vietnam. When the pastor of their sponsoring church found out about this, he berated Do, saying that she was misusing the money meant for her family. She was terribly upset, asking him in broken English, "What did we do wrong? I think he mad at us, but what did we do wrong? I don't know … Inside of me I was worried." In her culture helping her parents as soon as she could was a duty.

Later, immediately after her daughter was born, the newborn child had jaundice, was misdiagnosed by the local hospital, and was saved at the last possible moment after being rushed to a Halifax hospital. "What's going on, what's happened? … I don't know what's going on with my baby, please help me. I don't know what's going on." In recalling this, Do is in tears. Despite these negative experiences, she has only positive things to say about her sponsors. But the Do family could not stay in the small town; there were no jobs for them. To get better jobs and to be closer to other Vietnamese and some Asian food stores, they moved to Halifax within two years.

Three more privately sponsored refugees also had some negative experiences. Nguyen Son Thi's (Interview HOF169 2020) large family of ten was initially housed in a small townhouse in Vancouver with a single bathroom. Her husband was never offered English lessons but started to work as a welder within days of arrival. He continued working for decades in this occupation. She was given some help with English, but the lessons never took. To this day she speaks little English and needed her daughter's help with translation at the interview. She and her daughter recall their start in Canada as being hard. It was a Vietnamese Catholic priest who provided some help after their arrival. Her daughter insists that her mother is a tough, hard-working woman, and her strength brought the family through some difficult times. At the same time, both women insist how lucky they are to be in Canada and how grateful they are to this country for accepting them.

Tran Chi Hieu (Interview HOF149 2020) started to work immediately after arrival as a labourer. His sponsors housed his family in the basement of a large home together with the owners, a prosperous older couple. When he asked for help with language training, he was told that he already spoke English well enough and did not need more training. Proud and independent spirited, he moved out of the house after six months and found an apartment for his family. He has never stopped working since his arrival in Canada, has never again asked for help, and is proud of his independence.

On arrival in Canada, after being cleared through Griesbach military base in Edmonton, Tri Duc Pham (Interview HOF164 2020) was being sent from Edmonton to Saskatoon as a government-assisted refugee. But his understanding, through a Vietnamese friend already in Canada, was that he was being sponsored by a private group in Toronto. He let Canadian officials know this and they redirected him to Toronto instead of Saskatoon. Once in Toronto he was greeted by his friend, but no sponsors. After a few days, he got a job and his own accommodations. He never received any language training – his spoken English is very good – and was on his own from the moment of his arrival in Toronto.

The initial resettlement experience of privately sponsored Vietnamese refugees in Canada has several common elements. First, most of these refugees received some very valuable help from their sponsors, and this help made their initial language acquisition and acculturation process easier and smoother. In several cases this help lasted much longer than the single-year commitment undertaken by the sponsors. In the few cases where help from the sponsors was less effective, the refugees were able to get starting jobs on their own and rapidly became independent.

Second, the majority of the refugees appreciate the help they received, and many have maintained close friendly relations – or, in the case of the adopted unaccompanied minors, family relations – with their sponsors.

Third, many refugees sponsored by private groups already had another Vietnamese refugee in Canada – a family member or friend – who acted as their contact with the Canadian sponsoring group. Thus, refugees who had been already resettled in Canada often acted as intermediaries for the private group sponsorships.

Fourth, none of the interviewees who were sponsored by private groups in small communities, usually church congregations, stayed in those communities. For social, economic, and educational reasons, they all moved to larger centres which usually had better job and educational opportunities, as well as Vietnamese communities. The single exception to this was the family of Huynh Vinh (Interview HOF114 2019), who moved to a smaller town to start their restaurant business.

Government-Assisted Refugees: Initial Settlement and Integration

The initial settlement assistance received by government-assisted refugees and privately sponsored refugees was similar. Both groups received clothing, accommodations, food stipends, language training, and help with finding a job. Routine problems encountered on arrival in Canada, like getting used to Canada's climate and Canadian food, were also similar. The major difference between the two refugee streams was that for privately sponsored refugees most of the assistance was provided by individual members of the private group, often a church congregation, while federal government officials provided most initial settlement assistance for government-assisted refugees. In general, the close personal relationships established with the sponsors made the difficult initial adjustment to Canada easier for privately sponsored refugees, although, as the previous analysis demonstrates, several interviewees who were privately sponsored did face serious initial adjustment problems.

Most refugees wanted to start working as soon as possible at any available job, which was usually either manual labour or dishwashing, or some other low-wage factory or service job. For Vietnamese medical professionals, being a manual labourer in Canada was very difficult. Although a prominent surgeon in Vietnam, the husband of Lam Thu Van, Truong Minh Tri (Interview HOF045 2019), started in a manual labour job after arrival in Montreal and continued in manual labour jobs for the rest of his working life; he did not qualify as a doctor in Canada. She herself was also a doctor in Vietnam. But she could not work as a doctor in Canada either. She did occasional jobs and took care of her family. She emphasizes the important help provided by local volunteers in Ville Saint Laurent for her family's initial settlement. Hoang Chinh (Interview HOF081 2019) is another medical doctor who could not work in his profession in Canada. During his first years following his arrival, he worked in various manual labour jobs. "My dream was to come back to the medical field. It was difficult. It took me two years … to find out about the process … I contacted the Employment Centre in Kitchener, could you help me find a job that is related to the medical field?" He was referred to a hospital where he worked as a porter. Eventually, he passed the qualifying examination but could not get a rotating internship to qualify as a medical doctor. His attempt at retraining as a computer technician was also unsuccessful: he could not find a job in the latter field.

Huynh Hien Thanh (Interview HOF152 2020) was a veterinarian in Vietnam, but his first job was working for a lumber company; he could never qualify as a veterinarian in Canada. His wife, who had been a doctor in Vietnam, was unable to qualify as a medical doctor in Canada. But eventually, both Hien and his wife succeeded, through extreme hard work and study, to return to the medical field. After years of effort, he became the supervisor of a medical laboratory and she a nurse.

A dentist who managed to qualify in his profession in Canada was Hoang Dinh Tri (Interview HOF142 2020). While his first job was as a dishwasher, he quickly found work as a dental lab technician through the help of a Canadian dentist. "When I told him that I had the intention to come back to my profession so I could practice dentistry in Canada, I wanted to know what he thought. He said that it is impossibly difficult … [After further discussion] he granted me a tryout at his dental lab … Gradually they let me do work like repairing dentures and setting teeth for new ones. After two months … the staff there was very happy with my work, I then was hired immediately and permanently." After proving himself excellent at this job, he could save enough money to go from Alberta to Montreal and follow an upgrading course for foreign dentists at the University of Montreal. He managed to pass first the Quebec and then the national dentist qualifying exam. He went back to Edmonton and established a dental practice that, among other patients, has catered to Vietnamese refugees. He considers himself very lucky; several fortunate circumstances made possible his requalification as a dentist in Canada.

Among the post-1978 interviewees, a professional with an easy initial job experience was engineer Vu Huu Quang (Interview HOF154 2020). Along with his wife, Au Thi Minh Nguyet, he had studied in Montreal in the late 1960s and obtained Canadian qualifications. Immediately after his arrival in Montreal, Vu was hired by the Canadian multinational engineering firm Lavalin. He spent his working life as an engineer with Lavalin in Toronto and later in Calgary.

Most of the new arrivals could not speak English or French and received language training for a maximum of one year. Some interviewees, like

Nguyen Van Thoi (Interview HOF155 2020), spoke some English on arrival, but still needed some courses to expose them to Canadian English.

The story of Lu Thi Nhan (Interview HOF137 2020) highlights some of the major initial settlement problems faced by the new arrivals. She was a university student, studying math and physics in Vietnam. She had difficult escape and refugee camp experiences, and was pregnant on arrival in Edmonton. Her husband got a job in a Chinese noodle factory. Her landlady took her to the hospital to give birth. "I had my baby for about a few months. I stayed home all the time and got depressed. That winter, my husband still worked from dawn to dusk. His work needed more help, so I came to work there too … My hands were lacerated … My hands were bloody." She hadn't known that she needed gloves for the work. Then she had other factory jobs while her husband continued his long daily commute to the Chinese noodle factory. And their two very young children were babysat by an old lady. "I jumped from job to job. I worked four jobs in a year."

Nguyen Van Thoi (Interview HOF155 2020) is the type of individual who survives under any conditions and retains his optimism and good humour. When his first job as a mechanic proved to be too difficult in the dead of a cold winter in Regina, Saskatchewan, he moved to Edmonton, where he quickly got a factory job. In Edmonton, he became one of the first members of the new Edmonton Vietnamese Association and an organizer of the first Vietnamese New Year celebrations in the city. Since his still shaky English was much better than that of most newly arrived refugees, he translated for them at Manpower Canada's Edmonton office and helped them fill out forms. When, during an economic downturn in Alberta, he was laid off from his factory job, Manpower Canada hired him temporarily to travel around Alberta, visiting and interviewing recently arrived Vietnamese refugees scattered around the province. His comments about this experience shed light on the early experiences of many refugees, especially those in small towns. "Isolated in small settlements, not knowing the language or the culture, the refugees felt lost far from their homeland … were stressed and lonely, having thoughts of suicide." It is little wonder that Vietnamese refugees originally destined for small towns moved as soon as they could to larger cities where the support and companionship of their compatriots was available.

Truong Huu Do (Interview HOF146 2020) succeeded in qualifying as a medical doctor in 1986. Immediately, he became the doctor of the Calgary Vietnamese refugee community. In his interview he describes the early resettlement problems of the community observed through interaction with his patients: "Social issues were a big problem … At work they could not speak English well and became an easy target for bullying. They could not speak to protest or defend themselves. They could not share their burden with anyone and just felt sick … [they had] depression."

One of the most difficult arrival-in-Canada experiences was that of Phan Khanh Phuong (Interview HOF148 2020). He was sent alone to Grande Prairie, Alberta. On arrival, nobody greeted him at the airport. Fortunately, he spoke some English so could ask for help. An airport official phoned Canada Manpower. Phan was told to take a cab to the Manpower office where they did his paperwork and sent him off to a motel, again by cab. He was not given any money (Manpower paid for his motel and food) and saw no Canadian official for two more days. There were some other Vietnamese refugees in Grande Prairie and eventually he got to eat some noodle soup with them. To escape his circumstances, he phoned a refugee friend in Thunder Bay, Ontario, and took a bus there. Eventually, Phan made it to Toronto and has had a successful life there.

As the above demonstrates, many of our government-assisted refugee interviewees had difficult arrival and initial settlement experiences. At the same time, all of the government-assisted refugees were provided with the basics of a frugal initial life, including accommodation and financial stipends, as well as language and Canadian culture orientation (included with English as a Second Language [ESL] courses in English Canada and with Centre d'orientation et de formation des immigrants [COFI] courses in Quebec). Our interviewees recognize this and, despite their initial difficulties, appreciate Canada for enabling them to start their lives anew, away from oppression and poverty in Vietnam, the terrors of their escape voyages, and the harsh uncertainty of life in the camps.

Family-Sponsored Refugees: Initial Settlement and Integration

Several of the interviewees were sponsored by their families in Canada, Vietnamese refugees who had arrived in Canada before them and had the financial means to sign family class or assisted relative sponsorships.

Truong Van Hoan (Interview HOF041 2019) and his fourteen-year-old son were sponsored by two of his brothers living in Montreal. In escaping with his son, he had left his wife and two younger children behind in Vietnam, hoping to sponsor them as soon as he could. On arrival in Montreal, Truong's brother came to get them from the Longue-Pointe army base arrival centre and took them to their apartment. They lived with his brothers and their families for one year and, since his French was relatively good, he rapidly found a clerical job. His son went to school and after one year they rented their own house. After five years in Canada, he sponsored his family. His wife with two other children joined them rapidly, directly from Vietnam. He has spent his entire working life as a quality control specialist in a Montreal factory. Later, this family sponsored another brother and sister. With the family's help, their initial settlement and integration went smoothly.

Vu Ninh (Interview HOF082 2019) left Vietnam with a very young son and two teenage nephews and ended up in Singapore following a rescue by the German rescue ship *Cap Anamur*. His sister Nguyen Bui Thi Mui (Interview HOF055 2019), a refugee who left Vietnam in 1975, was already a well-established owner of a pharmacy in Montreal (for his sister's story see chapter 3). She sponsored him, his son, and the two nephews. On arrival in Montreal, she got him an apartment and a job in her pharmacy. After one year in Montreal, he moved to Toronto, where he had some close friends. He quickly got a job and sponsored his wife and two remaining children, who arrived in Canada directly from Vietnam in 1985.

Family sponsorships appear to have been the smoothest road to rapid and successful refugee settlement. During the 1980s, refugees already established in Canada could use family sponsorships to bring their families left behind in Vietnam to Canada. They were fortunate: their families did not have to go through the difficult, often terrible experiences of boat escapes and lives in refugee camps. With the Orderly Departure Program in place, family-sponsored immigrants were now allowed by the Vietnamese authorities to travel to Canada directly from Vietnam.

Life in Canada: Becoming Canadian, Feeling at Home in Canada

The question of when the initial settlement period of Vietnamese refugees ended and when they felt at home in Canada was posed to the interviewees. Replies varied from interview to interview and depended on age, language skills, employment situation, family situation, the type of assistance the refugees received, their families, and the type of relationships they formed over the decades. Much depended on the attitudes of the interviewees. It is virtually impossible to do a meaningful statistical analysis of the replies to this question – there are too many variables. Yet, these replies display the spectrum of interviewees' feelings toward Canada and their place in it.

At one end of the spectrum is Ho Cong Thanh (Interview HOF133 2020), a well-established Edmonton accountant. Ho states that in the refugee camp he was a stateless person, rejected by the country of his birth. He remembers the exact date Canada became his home; it was an important date in his life. He was still in the refugee camp on "May 16, 1980, when I received the piece of immigration paper … For us refugees, we don't have a state, we don't have a nationality … Canada is a home country that took me, took my family. This is home to me … Even now, when I go back to Vietnam, it has not been my home … that country … This is home, right here in Canada." He considers that the minute he received his Canadian immigration papers he became a Canadian. Yet his life since his arrival has not been easy. It required extremely hard work and perseverance.

As president of the Vietnamese Buddhist Temple in Edmonton, Ho has maintained a strong connection to Vietnamese culture, which for him is an essentially Canadian thing to do. Also, he is on the board of several nonprofits doing community work. He has taken his successful adult children to Vietnam to reconnect them with their Vietnamese roots. For him, this too is a Canadian action. He considers helping others and not judging them the Canadian way. As he says, "I can relate to the most recent Syrian people … In Edmonton we have a group organized by Nhung Tran-Davies [Interview HOF141 2020; see chapter 7]. She was a refugee in the 1980s as well … I can relate to that and hope I can make some help … because I don't judge, I was not judged when I came here … so, I don't judge [other uprooted people]."

At the spectrum's other end is Nguyen Ngoc Duy (Interview HOF072 2019), a small businessman in Toronto. For Nguyen, Canada is the country that accepted him in his need and for this he is very grateful. He calls Canada his "second country," not his home. He insists that "nothing will replace my homeland." He was married to another Vietnamese refugee in California and sponsored her to come to Canada. "In July 1985, we had our first son, and then the next year, by the end of October 8th we had our second son. And we named them Viet and Nam, so we call them together often 'Viet-Nam.'" After thirty-nine years in Canada, he still hopes that someday, once the communists are no longer in power, he will be able to return to Vietnam.

The above two gentlemen are well integrated and speak excellent English. Their different outlooks about their primary home country appear to be a function of their emotional commitment to each country. Of course, this applies to all the interviewees, and with the passage of time and new roots established in Canada, the emotional commitment to Canada of most of our interviewees continues to grow.

The other interviewees fall between the above two extremes. The interviews with the following three refugee women demonstrate how initial difficulties turned into very successful lives by the steady application of hard work during the early years, the gradual growth of solid career and employment opportunities, and the help of new Canadian friends.

After moving to Toronto from Windsor to join her husband, Nguyen Thanh Thuy's (Interview HOF085 2019) family was living in very simple circumstances, with both spouses working hard to save money. She worked in a department store and attended a course on wedding preparations, while her husband worked as a bookkeeper. "We hard working people, we try to save." Within four years of arrival, they bought a house. "We bought the house [in] 1984 only for $81,000. [In] 1987, the house jump to, increase 200, almost 300,000, so that's why we got the money." With the profits from the sale of the house, they started a brewing business that proved to be quite successful. But during these early years Nguyen felt under pressure from constant overwork and their simple lifestyle. She was very stressed and homesick. Yet she continued to work and opened her own travel agent business. "When I involved in the travel business, also I do a lot of volunteer work in the community … I work with Saigon TV as a co-anchor … People invite me to sing at their parties, I became more popular … The first few years of my life in Canada were difficult because you still homesick and you know nobody … I always want to go back, because of the communists that means I could not. But after ten years when your life is more established, and you have friends and your job is quite stable, I starting to love this country."

Pham Thi Duyen arrived in Canada completely alone, following terrible life-threatening experiences during her high seas escape. A well-educated woman who speaks good English, "in London, [Ontario], I worked at the Japanese Garden as a waitress and bartender … and then back to school … at Western University." Her life changed for the better once she got married and moved to Toronto, and she and her husband were able to sponsor both their families to come to Canada.

> Now I'm retired after twenty-eight years working for Toronto District School Board as an ESL instructor … My jobs were most helpful in my integration … It is a very multicultural society, and they give you opportunities as long as you work hard and make effort … It took me very long to feel at home in Canada, because I'm the only one, leave my family behind … Culture shock. Many times I felt like outsider and I was so lonely … It took me very long until my father and my two young sisters were united with me. (Interview HOF073 2019)

The story of Minh Karlsson (Interview HOF171 2020) highlights the importance of Canadians who were not private sponsors in helping refugees feel at home in Canada. On arrival in Canada, she was directed to Kamloops, British Columbia. "I met very nice people in Kamloops." The Canada Manpower people in Kamloops

> were very kind, supportive, helpful. I was so distraught because in the camp I was surrounded by friends, by Vietnamese people … Here in Kamloops, I was living by myself in the apartment, and it was May, but it was cold, and on the streets I saw lots of cars but nobody walking around, not a soul … like it's a ghost town to me … I'm so used to see hustle bustle of life … I cried every day. I lost

> a lot of weight. It was very stressful. But then … my English teacher … [and a whole team of new friends] they were all of them very supportive, very sympathetic … They helped me go through the transition … But still deep down I was so lonely and depressed.

Her new supportive Canadian friends helped her to make an application to Simon Fraser University and drove her to the university in Burnaby for her admission interview. Within a year she was accepted by SFU, where she studied to be a teacher. Her life changed immediately; she was now in an environment that suited her, at home in Canada. Years later she visited Vietnam with her Canadian husband. Everything was strange in her country of birth where she now felt like a stranger; she had become Canadian.

Hoang Chinh (Interview HOF081 2019) and Lu Thi Nhan (Interview HOF137 2020) are two well-educated refugees with good English skills who drifted from one short-term menial job to another during their early years in Canada. Eventually, a decade after arrival they managed to find meaningful employment, both in people-helping occupations. They are both writers, describing the refugee and immigrant experience through their stories. After often being sick and depressed through the early years, Lu emerged as one of the founders and coordinator of Edmonton's Multicultural Health Brokers in 1992. This organization helps all newcomers – not only Vietnamese – with their health needs. As she says, "I had to integrate [in Canada] in order to help newcomers." Her work with a range of local ethnic groups made her recognize the important role of cooperation among different immigrant groups.

After a long period of drifting, Hoang became an immigrant settlement worker for the YMCA for fifteen years. He was happy in this job, as it partially freed him from his feelings of guilt for not being able to qualify as a doctor, not being able to help the people who need him. With his settlement counselling work, he was in a people-helping occupation. Hoang appears disheartened that with the aging of the older generation and the inability of the young generation born in Canada to read Vietnamese, the reading audience for Vietnamese books is diminishing. He believes that he made the right choice in coming to Canada and is now happy to be Canadian.

By virtue of their religious calling, the two Catholic priests Father Thanh Son (Jean Baptiste) (interview HOF051 2019) in Montreal and Father Tran Tien (Interview HOF166 2020) in Vancouver felt at home in Canada very rapidly, although in the case of Father Tran, his religious conversion experience came after being somewhat lost, drifting in the streets of Vancouver with other young Vietnamese refugees. Both priests are intimately connected to the emotional and material needs of their Vietnamese parishioners in their respective cities. In addition, for the past several years Father Tran has established annual medical care voyages to Vietnam. He organizes and accompanies trips to Vietnam for Canadian medical professionals, treating the poorest of the poor in remote areas, concentrating on specialist eye care.

Nguyen Quyen (Interview HOF130 2020) appears to be among the most successful Vietnamese refugee interviewees. On arrival in Canada "I was shell shocked. The culture is completely different ... It's a struggle [getting] through everything. Back then we had no one to talk to. There's only forty to forty-five people around and who knows each other? Some of them live here for a year and they don't know each other ... We got off assistance as soon as possible, we want to work ... My oldest brother got work in a meat processing company, he worked to support both of us [the two younger brothers] to get an education." Nguyen is an engineer who has become the vice-president of a major Edmonton corporation. He has three adult children, all of them university-educated professionals. He and his family see themselves as fully Canadianized. He reached this position by working extremely hard "every day of the week, 365 days a year. I didn't have a youth life whatsoever." Nguyen insists that as an Asian immigrant, he had to work twice as hard in university and in his professional life as his Canadian-born fellow students and colleagues. He emphasizes the value of hard work and states that he has attempted to inculcate the importance of working hard and perseverance in his children. As well, one of the main goals of his life is contributing to Canadian society.

Nguyen Duc Mien (Interview HOF104 2019), Duong Kiem Minh, (Interview HOF107 2019), and Kathy Ma (Interview HOF170 2020) all represent a relatively typical life course in Canada for working-class Vietnamese refugees. They all started in difficult jobs, had to change jobs often to get better pay and better working conditions, and, along with their spouses, work extremely hard. Although all three of them were able to express themselves during their interviews, their English remains relatively weak. For them, a secure, good life in Canada and the possibility of upward mobility for their children is the essence of being Canadian. They have all managed to reach these goals and are grateful to Canada for having made this possible.

Finally, a few words about La Hoan Vo (Interview HOF157 2020). In Vietnam, La was released after spending nine years in a re-education camp. This wounded him profoundly both physically and, especially, mentally. His wife and children were already living in Canada, and he joined them in Montreal as a sponsored dependent, following many years of separation. He had many jobs in Montreal, but he could not restart a normal life with his family. Eventually, with deep regret, he left Montreal and joined his siblings who had resettled in Calgary. He now has a normal life, living with his Calgary family and participating in Vietnamese community activities. He says that he is happy in Canada.

Characteristics of the Canadian Vietnamese Community after Four Decades in Canada

Listening to their interviews, it is difficult to believe that in general, following the extreme traumas they had endured, most former Vietnamese refugees have made what they describe as successful and happy lives in Canada. They have a deep commitment to their families and their community. Many have sponsored family members left behind in Vietnam as soon as they were able, at a time when they themselves were still at the beginning of their adaptation to Canadian culture and society. While they insist that they had been lucky, in fact they have overcome enormous challenges. Their luck has largely been achieved through extremely hard work and perseverance.

They recognize and deeply value the compassion displayed toward them by many Canadians as private sponsors, government officials, and members of their new Canadian communities. They consider that without this compassion they would have found their early lives in Canada much harder. In those cases where the refugees had negative experiences on arrival to Canada, they were able overcome these through a willingness to work hard and a spirit of independence.

As soon as they could, they either joined community associations established by the earlier 1975 refugees or founded their own associations. These associations continue to exist and flourish as Buddhist temples, Vietnamese Catholic churches, and other faith-based organizations as well as secular community centres in cities across Canada. Vietnamese New Year celebrations have become important community events in which the larger Canadian community joins the Vietnamese community. With many Vietnamese restaurants across Canada, Vietnamese culinary culture has, over the decades, become a part of the Canadian mainstream.

The interviewees describe Canadians as kind and generous people, open to newcomers. They consider that this kindness is a part of Canada being a diverse multicultural society. In referring to Canada's role in the world, most interviewees have emphasized that it is important for Canada to maintain its traditions of respecting human rights and welcoming refugees.

Many of the Vietnamese Canadian interviewees have built successful professional and business careers in Canada. In talking about their success, some interviewees state that the Vietnamese refugee movement demonstrates the positive value of resettling refugees, and that Vietnamese refugees have given more back to Canada than they have taken in the form of support by Canadian taxpayers. Through a range of organizations many former refugees are actively involved in supporting refugee resettlement as well as community work inside Canada.

8

Boat People's Lives in Canada: Seven Stories

This chapter presents seven individual stories of Vietnamese boat people resettled in Canada. It showcases the important changes over time that Vietnamese refugees had experienced in Canada and follows their life stories in Canada. They started out as strangers to Canadian culture and most of them did not speak Canada's official languages. But over a period of several decades most describe themselves as fully Canadian. At the same time, most have also maintained their Vietnamese – and in some cases Chinese – culture and language. As these stories demonstrate, this long-term transformation has been different in each case, yet it has many common elements.

To ensure that the individual stories of refugees sponsored by private groups, government-assisted refugees, and family-sponsored refugees are fully covered, some interview stories from each group are presented in depth. In addition, one individual story is that of Buchan Tho Trong (Interview HOF018 2019), a child refugee adopted by a Canadian. Adoptions like his were officially grouped under the private group sponsorship category. However, his adoption was different from other private group sponsorships. People like his adoptive father agreed not only to sponsor a child refugee, but to act as the child's parent. Stories similar to this (see chapter 6) were part of the reaction of average Canadians to newly arrived Southeast Asian refugees and demonstrate the willingness of many Canadians to make personal commitments in favour of the refugees.

Privately Sponsored Refugees

Buchan Tho Trong

The quotes in this story are from an interview (Interview HOF018 2019).

After a long flight from the Philippines, passing through Vancouver, Buchan arrived in Toronto on 24 June 1982. He was eleven years old, going on twelve. He was met at the airport by his adoptive father. His cousin from Vietnam, already in Canada, was also there. During a one-hour drive to Richmond Hill in a crowded station wagon, he met Bryan Buchan, the man he would call his dad, for the first time.

In Toronto, on the way from the airport, "everything was green, it was an amazing feeling. [My dad Bryan] was tall, 1.8 metres; for Vietnamese standards he was a tall man. He was towering over me, and he looked gentle. I had to say everything through my cousin because I didn't speak much English back then; he was, he looked like, a gentle man … We got to his home; I thought it was so big." The house was a standard Canadian three-bedroom house. "I was the twelfth person to live in that house. I thought it was huge compared to what I lived in Vietnam … but it was tiny, about a thousand-square-feet home, and we had twelve people in it." His dad was an elementary school teacher who was still single at that time. In addition to him and his Canadian dad, there were ten Vietnamese refugees living in the house, including a family with two children, four more adults, and two more children. The three children with no adult family members, including the newly arrived Buchan, were all adopted by his Canadian dad.

Buchan's birth father, the man he would henceforth call father, was already living in Canada. Like Buchan, his Vietnamese father was also sponsored through his Canadian dad's church. "Father lived just a block away from my dad, I would come to see him every week." Throughout Buchan's childhood and adolescence, he lived with his Canadian dad but saw his Vietnamese father often. "Canada in the summer, it was great, a lot of green, nothing that I had seen in Vietnam, a lot of trees, grass … first impression of Canada, amazing."

The church to which his dad belonged sponsored several Vietnamese refugees and their families. Among them was the cousin who had abandoned Buchan on the boat during their escape from Vietnam and had left Buchan's older brother back in Vietnam. The older brother had been conscripted and fought in Cambodia. Later he escaped from the army and went into hiding. Still later, he developed serious mental problems and could no longer work. To this day, he is being supported by family members who remained in Vietnam. Being abandoned by his cousin may have destroyed his life.

Eventually, Buchan as a teenager in Toronto talked to the cousin who had abandoned him and his older brother. "I came to his house many times and I asked them what happened. They said … after that day they actually didn't know what happened to me … I don't think they were paying attention to me the whole week I was on the boat." Not only did his cousin abandon the two young boys entrusted to him; he then lied about Buchan's fate to his mother. He said to her that they thought that he had fallen into the sea from the escape boat and when they discovered his absence, "they prayed for him." Buchan thinks that his cousin was motivated by greed. "My mom asked them to take care of me, but they didn't pay any attention."

Buchan describes his integration as easy and rapid. His dad registered him for English classes in the summer and at the start of the school year he went into grade 7. He was in his dad's class, and his dad helped him with subjects where he had difficulties with English. For the first two years he referred to his dictionary often. "After about two years I integrated into Canadian life very well." In high school, he was like other Canadian kids. He had been given a second chance.

In 1984, the Vietnamese refugees living in Bryan Buchan's house started to establish their own homes, starting with his older cousin and his cousin's family. Then, one by one, all the children became adults, finished college, and went to live on their own. Buchan lived with his dad for ten years, until he graduated from college in 1992.

Bryan Buchan has remained in close contact with all his Vietnamese children over the years: they are part of his family. Most of them live in Toronto, Barrie, and Ottawa. They visit and talk on the phone often, and

Bryan Buchan is interested in his Vietnamese grandchildren. Much of the young Buchan's remaining Vietnamese family has made it to Canada. His father has passed away, but his mother lives in Toronto with a son.

Looking back on his life, he says, "Knowing what I know now, I don't think I would encourage the escape [from Vietnam]." It was too risky; many people perished along the way. But his family could not stay in Vietnam. They are Catholics and the communists had suppressed their freedom to worship. "We risked our lives, we risked everything. But I guess that's the price you pay for freedom. Over here you're free to do anything, to live your life. I think a lot of people are still persecuted over there."

Buchan thinks that Canada has done very good humanitarian work and has been a beacon of hope for refugees. Canadians are generous with their time and resources. "My dad treated us much better than my own parents. He treats me like his own son. He has no distinction between adopted and his own children. He made a commitment when he was only thirty-five, even though he was only a teacher. He made that lifelong decision to care for all of us. I can't imagine myself doing that."

Buchan is an IT professional, has a comfortable life, and believes that in Canada you can do anything your heart desires if you work hard. He has two teenage boys, eighteen and fifteen. His boys are not very interested in his experiences, so he does not talk much about them. He thinks that most Vietnamese refugees prefer not to talk too much about their experiences. And yet, in the course of the whole interview, he often recalls his life with considerable emotion.

Even though Buchan has occasionally experienced subtle unspoken prejudice, Canada has been good to him, and he would not choose to live anywhere but in Canada. He thinks that Canada should maintain its humanitarian programs since this country may provide the only hope for vulnerable refugees.

The large number of Vietnamese refugees adopted and otherwise supported by "Dad Bryan Buchan" became successful Canadians. To this day, they remain a close clan and often visit him, now in his late seventies and married to a Vietnamese woman. For this group of former refugees, Bryan Buchan remains their beloved dad, and a very special individual.

Dang Van Nghiem

The quotes in this story are from an interview (Interview HOF084 2019).

After spending five months in a crude jungle camp on a tiny Indonesian island in the Anambas Archipelago and three months in the Galang refugee camp, Dang Van Nghiem, his heavily pregnant wife, and their young child arrived in Montreal on 1 December 1979. They were sponsored by the Hamilton Mennonite Church. On arrival in Canada, "myself and my wife was frightened because it was the middle of winter … the weather was very cold … the cloud covered snow … I thought the trees are dead, the trees have no leaf, I was frightened, and I thought we were betrayed … and we would be sent to the concentration camp … to work as slave labourers." Dang's life experiences in Vietnam – terrible beyond the sufferings of many of his compatriots – prepared him for such thoughts.

Following reception formalities at the Longue-Pointe military base in Montreal, they flew to Hamilton, Ontario. "We did not know we were sponsored by the church … we did not know anything about the city. On 3 December 1979, we were greeted by the Hamilton Mennonite Church at the airport … They are very friendly, they treated us with respect … we felt so good about that, at that time our fear released … Then they give us a drive to 151 Queen Street apartment." A furnished two-bedroom apartment was waiting for them in an apartment house where other Vietnamese refugees had already settled in. The furniture was new, there were new clothes, and there were supplies in the apartment. The family now realized that they had nothing to fear, that they were well taken care of. Initially, the couple did not want to use any of the new things in their apartment. They thought that they would save them to send them to their relatives in Vietnam. Two church members were assigned to look after all the family needs. "The church members came to visit us and also they invited to go to attend church on Sunday and some time we went to their house for dinner." Their sponsors immediately did the paperwork to get their social insurance numbers, enrol them in the Ontario Health Insurance Plan, and find English instruction for them. "We are well taken care of."

Compared to other Vietnamese refugees, Dang realizes that he and his family were fortunate. "Unlike other Vietnamese families who are sponsored, maybe three, six months after they got a job and have to go to work. My family, fortunately, we were sponsored maybe nine years, [including] rental and also food," until Dang finished his education at Queen's University.

Why did the sponsors cover the Dang family's expenses so long? In March 1980, Mrs Dang gave birth to their second child, a boy. Meanwhile, the family received news from Vietnam that both Mr and Mrs Dang's families were living in terrible starvation conditions. As soon as possible, Dang started "working three low part-time jobs." At the end of 1980, he managed to find a better paying full-time job as shipper-dispatcher in a shoe company, where he stayed for two years. Learning about the living conditions of their parents' families in Vietnam, the "Hamilton Mennonite Church helped with my rent and food for my family. I used my income, most of my income, to send home to support my wife's family and my family" in Vietnam. As well, "I told them I wanted to go back to school, so they wanted me to have the money for my education."

Based on his family's terrible experiences with the Viet Cong before 1975, Dang became a committed anticommunist and intended to return to Vietnam to fight the communists. "In 1982, I heard about the National Front for the Liberation of Vietnam … I really like to be health care worker [for the guerrilla army] … because living in the jungle would be very dangerous." He was hoping to do this by obtaining a nursing degree that would qualify him as a battlefield medic.

"Because when we left Vietnam I could not bring any documents to prove my education background, so I have to go back to grade 13 … and I want to be sure to get an offer of acceptance at the university, so I went back to grade 13 in 1983." With the continued financial support of the Hamilton Mennonite Church, Dang finished grade 13 and enrolled in the four-year nursing degree program at Queen's University in Kingston in 1984. The church continued to support the Dang family until he graduated from university in 1988.

Meanwhile, his wife, who had given birth to a son in 1982, obtained a one-year practical nursing diploma and started to work as a registered practical nurse in 1983. She sent her earnings to Vietnam to help her family. The family's move to Kingston, as well as their apartment rent in Kingston, continued to be subsidized by the Hamilton Mennonite Church. Other university costs were covered through Mrs Dang's earnings as a practical nurse, bursaries, and Ontario Student Assistance Program loans.

In 1987, during his third year of university, Dang received news that the anticommunist guerillas in the jungles were wiped out by the Vietnamese Army. "I was shocked. I became hopeless. I did not know what to do because that's the only way we could liberate our country from the Communist government." There was no longer "hope to go back to Vietnam."

As soon as Dang graduated as a registered nurse in 1988, "I got three part-time jobs at Saint Mary's of the Lake Hospital where my wife was working, and also I got part-time job at Kingston General Hospital, and then one kind of part-time job at the Canadian Forces Base hospital." At two of these hospitals, his wife was also employed. "In 1991, I got full-time job at Correctional Services Canada at the Regional Treatment Centre." At the same time, he kept his part-time job at St Mary's Hospital in Kingston and whenever called upon to do so, he worked overtime. In effect, he worked a double workload as a nurse for twenty years. Since 2011, he has reduced his workload to his position at Correctional Services Canada where he still works.

The Dang family's relations with the Hamilton Mennonite Church continue to be close. "I went back home to Hamilton to attend church Mass on Sunday, to visit the members, and on any special occasions we went back home to visit ... I could not say thank you enough to the church members, the Hamilton Church manager, because without their support and encouragement I would not be able to finish my education."

Dang also thanks his wife and children, who provided indispensable moral and physical support during his university studies. Having to follow university-level courses with his still weak English was extremely hard. "Especially the first and second years were the most difficult years for me, especially when I took biology, biochemistry, and anatomy in English ... I have to remember long names in English. It's very difficult and I was stressed out." Because of the stress, he suffered from many physical symptoms, pain and numbness in his limbs and sleeplessness. "My Canadian classmates, they always help me. They took notes [that] I was unable to take ... I borrow their notes at the end of the lecture. I make copies and study from their notes ... You know, without their help I would not be able to make it."

Dang believes that Canadian refugee policies saved not only Vietnamese refugees but also many other refugees and "helped to make Canada into a great nation." When his children still lived with Dang and his wife, they often shared stories of the war, their lives in Vietnam, and their escape. They consider that "Canada is heaven on Earth" with generous people that provided a good life and opportunities for Vietnamese refugees.

Huynh Vinh

The quotes in this story are from an interview (Interview HOF114 2019).

Huynh Vinh is a well-spoken, very well-educated, articulate man in his early fifties. He is Hakka Chinese from Binh Hoa, South Vietnam, part of an ethnic group with its own language and culture. As he explained, the Hakka are a mobile group, at home in China and in a diaspora throughout Southeast Asia. His family had been in Vietnam for generations, but the Hakka are accustomed to displacements. When things do not work out in one place, they move. Before 1975, his father was a quartermaster corporal in the South Vietnamese army and his mother was a seamstress. After doing hard labour for one and a half years in a prison camp, his father knew that they had no place in the new Vietnam: they had to leave.

His family, consisting of his parents, himself, a brother, and two sisters, as well as two uncles, were boat people, leaving Vietnam in April 1979. Sponsored by a private group, they arrived in Montreal in early November 1979. "On landing, I looked out and thought, why are those people looking like they're smoking but they don't have cigarettes ... I found soon enough it's a bit cool." He was nine years old, about to turn ten. He experienced Canada for the first time at the Longue-Pointe military base in Montreal, where he had a delousing shower and was fitted out with winter clothes. "The food was rather strange. We're not accustomed to it; looking for rice, there's no rice. We came across these things that are bubbly squishy, green and red. They were Jell-O … Okay, it's going to take some getting used to … My parents meet with officials; actually an interpreter basically informed my parents that we have a sponsor family or a sponsor group in this place called Brandon, Manitoba." After four days in Montreal, the family flew to Winnipeg where they spent a night at the Balmoral Hotel. "I remember looking out the window at the Balmoral Hotel and just wondering what my place is in this new country." Next day they were put on a Greyhound bus going west. Looking out the bus window at the snowy prairie landscape, "my great-uncle said, 'You know, this looks like Siberia.'"

In Brandon they were greeted by their private sponsors. "A *Sun* reporter was there, captured pictures of us. My wife, after all these years, went back and found the article" in the Brandon newspaper. The owner of the local Chinese restaurant invited the newly arrived family to a meal with familiar flavours. They must have been among the first boat people to arrive in Brandon and were welcomed with open arms.

A member of their sponsoring group, a teacher, took them to their destination near Brandon, where a furnished three-bedroom house was waiting for them. "I still remember the kindness, how they were so patient with us and drove us [there] … Now we have a new home." The whole extended family, including the two uncles, "lived in a three-bedroom home." A young man came to their house to teach Huynh's uncles English, and the local Anglican pastor's wife taught his mother. His father could already communicate in English and became the family's principal contact with the sponsors. Huynh and his brother started to attend elementary school two days after arrival.

The extended family stayed together until "my two uncles wanted to strike out on their own … They left within four or five months." Eventually, one ended up in Vancouver and the other in Calgary. In May 1980, one of the sponsors found a job for Huynh's father with the Russell highway department. His father moved first, and during the next six weeks set up accommodations for the family in Russell, Manitoba. The four children finished the school year, and the family joined the father in Russell in June.

"He worked there for three and a half years in the highway department. And then, as well, on the weekend he started working in a Chinese restaurant. So, he worked seven days a week for a solid number of years." They lived in subsidized housing and Huynh's father was also responsible for maintenance at their housing complex. He had three jobs. In summer, it was doable, but during the cold prairie winters it became very difficult. Two Chinese doctors, a married couple, got to know his father and suggested that with his work ethic, he should think of opening a business, perhaps a restaurant.

For the next year Huynh's parents travelled all over the area, looking for a suitable restaurant to purchase. Eventually they found one in the tiny village of Rossburn, Manitoba, a pizza-chicken place. "We didn't have enough capital yet, so through the kindness of the two Chinese doctors, they said, 'We'll co-sign the loan for you.' We bought the Rossburn restaurant. That's how we dived into being Canadian."

The small restaurant they bought still exists; it can be viewed through Google Earth on Rossburn's main street. "The restaurant actually had a house attached right in the back, so everything was in one. All you had to do was open the back door of the kitchen and you were in our dining room and kitchen ... We were there a solid ten years, from 1983 to 1993." They had never run a restaurant, and it took a lot of very hard work to make it a success. The restaurant was open seven days a week, only closing for Christmas, Boxing Day, and New Year's Day. They expanded the menu, adding Asian, Ukrainian, and Polish specialties to the original chicken and pizza offerings. On Sundays there was a Chinese smorgasbord. Then they added catering local weddings to the in-house service. Everybody in the family worked; the children worked after school. When the parents had to be absent, the two boys ran the restaurant, which gradually became the community centre of Rossburn.

That restaurant was the family's school of Canadian integration. "We picked up both the vernacular language and also the academic language ... We had to drive pretty far to find another Asian person." They would meet other Vietnamese or Chinese only when they occasionally went to a larger town, or very rarely to the city. The children went to school and played with local Canadian kids. Their parents insisted that they had to become full members of Canadian society. The family sold their successful rural restaurant in 1993; "the pace of work was simply unsustainable."

Meanwhile, after finishing grade 10, Huynh moved to Winnipeg to finish high school. He continued his education at the University of Manitoba and obtained his degree in 1993. "I didn't have the whole ten-year experience in Rossburn. I had six full years and then for four years I would come back and help in the summer."

After selling the Rossburn restaurant in 1993, the family moved to Calgary, where Huynh's paternal grandfather had settled. Initially, Huynh moved with them, but teaching jobs were difficult to find in Alberta, so he moved back to Winnipeg. Ever since then, "it's been twenty-seven years, working in the inner city. I jokingly tell people, look inside my heart, there's four [Winnipeg inner city schools] for the four chambers." Since the start of his teaching career Huynh has served ten years as a teacher and four years as a vice-principal. At the time of his Hearts of Freedom project interview, he had been a school principal for fourteen years, the last two in the same school where he started his career, with many immigrant and Indigenous students.

In 2002, Huynh married his "Mennonite wife, the love of my life." He has two young daughters. He started his teaching career in a heavily Asian Canadian neighbourhood where many Vietnamese refugees settled. But there were also many Indigenous, Filipino, Kurdish, and other immigrant students in his school. Rapidly, he realized that "everybody is my people" and that his job was to provide "a safe, secure, healthy, viable learning environment" for all students. He went out of his way to actively reach out to the parents of his immigrant students. If they could not come to him, he went to them. Ten years into his teaching career he earned a master's degree in education, and after a lot of thought accepted the difficult challenge of becoming a vice-principal.

Over the years he has been active in immigrant reception and has worked with a range of immigrant settlement agencies. He has often spoken to various immigrant groups about his experiences and their relevance to new arrivals in Canada. He helped organize and gave a presentation at the University of Manitoba's "Stranger in a New Homeland" conference. He has "lost count of the many times he has spoken" to immigrants, but it is "a lot of work, it has to come from the heart."

In closing, Huynh insisted on the concepts of building relationships through openness and trust, daring to display one's vulnerability. As he states, relationships are not only with other human beings but formed through a sense of rootedness to earth and water, which for him means being fully at home in Winnipeg in the Assiniboine River valley. He is deeply grounded in Canada, but his Vietnamese Chinese Hakka family is scattered all over the world, from Melbourne to Calgary to California and Europe. He still has one cousin left in Vietnam who maintains the old graves. One day, he hopes to visit Vietnam again as well as all his family around the world.

Nhung Tran-Davies

The quotes in this story are from an interview (Interview HOF141 2020).

Nhung Tran-Davies arrived in Canada in 1979 as a five-year-old child, with her widowed minority Chinese mother. She was the youngest of six siblings in a half-Chinese family. Her Vietnamese father, a soldier in the South Vietnamese Army, perished in the war before the fall of Saigon. Her recollections of life in Vietnam, the refugee camp, and arrival in Canada are those of a very young child.

She remembers that in the refugee camp, "my mom prayed every day for someone to want us … She would even go up to the statue of Mother Mary and pray." Then, "we heard that Canada wanted us, but we didn't know who wanted us [in Canada]." When they arrived in Edmonton, reality hit: the family's mother was a seamstress with no education. Her mother was fearful and nervous until the interpreter at the airport told her that she was safe, that she had nothing to fear.

"When we first stepped through the gates of the Edmonton International Airport, our lives were forever changed because in that moment we were welcomed by this crowd of really warm individuals. The moment stuck in my mind … because as a little girl, there was another girl who came up to me and had given me a doll. From that moment and from a young girl's perspective my heart rejoiced." This was the first time they realized that they had sponsors, people in Canada who wanted them. Father Gauthier and the church group had specifically asked for a difficult to resettle family that nobody else wanted. A mother alone with six children fit the bill. To this day, the notion of being wanted is very important to her. "That moment stuck with me for my whole life and that doll that was given to me, I had held on to and cherished for the past forty years." Relations with the sponsoring church, and especially with four families from the church that had special responsibility for them, have remained very close to this day. Tran-Davies still considers these families her own family.

For the whole Tran family, the initial integration was not easy. The church families helped a great deal: they "introduced us to the different cultural aspects of Canada. They took us shopping and, through the early years they took us to the schools that we went to … so that we'd get used to it and would drive us to school … and for myself to have a sitter." They worked hard for a long time to accustom the family to everything that was strange and different in Canada. "They had a huge impact on our lives in the early years."

"Our relationship with our sponsors did not stop there … [Over time], Mom made sure that every Christmas our whole family [visited] our sponsors who mostly lived in the Spruce Grove area, so we would drive from Edmonton to Spruce Grove … That continued contact through the years allowed our families to grow together … We remained integral parts of each other's lives, I consider them our family."

Tran-Davies's mother felt deeply beholden to the sponsors. To demonstrate her gratitude and show her independence, she got as many low-paying, manual jobs as she could handle as soon as she could. She worked at three jobs at the same time. Later, she managed to get jobs in her own specialty and worked as a seamstress. Learning English and fitting into the school environment was a challenge for the older children. But Tran-Davies was still very young and adapted to Canada as soon as she entered grade 1.

There were some minor cultural issues within the family. Their mother considered that the children should show their gratitude to Canada and the sponsors by working and studying all the time. But her children were becoming Canadian and occasionally wanted to have some fun. They remained very good children, studied and worked hard, and they eventually all got good jobs, but this was not always enough for their mother.

Being very young, Tran-Davies integrated rapidly and easily. But her mother and her older siblings had some difficulties based on language acquisition and cultural differences. At the beginning they saved every penny they could and quickly bought their own townhouse. A government program helped subsidize their purchase and their sponsors acted as guarantors for the mortgage.

Tran-Davies was the only one of the six children to go to university and eventually medical school. She chose medicine partly because she felt that this was the profession she would be best at, but mostly because it was a helping profession. She feels, "All that I have, all that I have become, is because of the generosity of our sponsors." She wants to repay this generosity by helping people, especially sick kids.

Based on her life experience and the gratitude she felt to her sponsors, Tran-Davies is deeply motivated to be active in charity work, helping refugees and poverty-stricken people in developing countries. In 2019, she and some friends founded a registered charity called "Children of Vietnam" which helps children in poverty by providing them with basic needs and an education. As well, she has founded two private sponsorship groups to sponsor Syrian refugee families to come to Canada.

> In 2016, about forty years [after] I left [Vietnam], one of the [Syrian refugee] families is a mother with five kids. She's single with five kids, and I just identified with her. And so when they came through the [Edmonton Airport] gates, I had a doll waiting for the little one who was about my age [when I arrived in Canada]. So, it was my turn to be standing at the gate, giving this doll to this beautiful little Syrian girl. I just felt at that moment that I was passing, in some way, a torch; passing all the dreams of Canadians, all the kindness and compassion of Canadians to this little girl. Forty years from now, that little girl will probably be contributing to making Canada a more beautiful place.

Tran-Davies does not routinely tell her children about her life experiences as a refugee. But in specific situations she often does remind them of what she and their grandmother had to go through. She feels that in their relatively easy life circumstances, they need to remember to show gratitude to Canada and kindness to all. She says that it was the kindness of their sponsors that brought them to Canada, and kindness is the most important quality that they can show to others.

Government-Assisted Refugees

Du Chang

The quotes in this story are from an interview (Interview HOF140 2020).

Du Chang was born in 1972 near Haiphong, North Vietnam. One of five siblings, she is the youngest daughter of a Chinese minority father and a Vietnamese mother. Her father, the scion of a commercial family, was a Chinese herbalist and a poet. Her mother, a businesswoman, sold the herbal medicines her father made at the local market. In 1963, the North Vietnamese government jailed her father for seven years for writing anticommunist poems. He was released in 1970, allowed to continue his herbalist business, but branded a traitor. Her mother's uncles, prominent in Hanoi's political circles, could provide the family a degree of protection. Still, her parents planned to leave Vietnam at the earliest possibility.

In March 1979, during the expulsion of the Chinese from Vietnam, the Du family, considered to be Chinese because of the father, was allowed to leave North Vietnam for a price on a refugee boat and sailed to Hong Kong, where they spent two years in three different refugee camps. Chosen by Canada as government-assisted refugees, they were flown to Montreal in March 1981 and spent a few days at Longue-Pointe military base in Montreal, "where we were fitted out with winter gear because we came in March … and we were sent to Red Deer … We had no say in [where we would settle] … We knew absolutely nothing about Red Deer."

In Red Deer, the family was put up in the old Buffalo Hotel for three weeks. Asian food was not available, "so my dad made our own tofu for a while. Very tough process. We made our own bean sprouts. Once we found a friend who actually drove, we were able to go to Calgary for grocery shopping." The family experienced culture shock. "The hardest thing is the lack of Asian culture. We didn't have any familiar foods or really many Vietnamese people."

Nobody in the Du family spoke English. At the local Manpower office, "we were given a French-speaking individual because my dad spoke French … Somehow we were surprised by Red Deer because they didn't have any housing waiting for us, so we stayed at the hotel for three weeks … In about three weeks we ended up living in a duplex which we liked very much." Within a few weeks Manpower Canada placed every family member, including the seven-year-old Du Chang, in ESL classes. "We all spent one year in ESL and then next year we went into the school [system]." The parents got their first jobs through Manpower. The father's first job was operating a dry-cleaning machine while the mother worked as a cleaner for the rest of her working life. Eventually, for the sake of the children's education, the family "ended up in Edmonton. We're all gonna go to university anyway, so you might as well move to a university town." In Edmonton, Du Chang's father resumed his occupation as a Chinese herbalist, serving the local Asian community. Her mother stopped working outside their home and became a homemaker.

The educational attainments of this family are exceptional. The oldest brother earned a PhD in computer science, another brother became an engineer, the third brother became an electrician, Du Chang finished law school, and her sister is a banker. Du Chang now works for the Edmonton office of the federal Department of Justice.

Since she was very young when she arrived in Canada, her superficial integration, including language and culture acquisition, was very rapid. Yet at the same time, she says, "My parents felt that Vietnam was their home … The way we were raised, I didn't feel I was part of the full Canadian mosaic, having all the full freedoms, full rights, probably until my thirties, until I became a lawyer for about five, six years." Later, she recognized what she describes as "cultural schizophrenia." "I am very Western; I don't think I could ever marry a Vietnamese … but I also have very Vietnamese cultural beliefs." In other words, "I am in this Western country, doing Western things, but then I have this cultural limitation." Only when she had her own children and could see the world through their Canadian eyes was she able to recognize that "this is my country, this is where I belong, this is where my roots are."

The obstacles she faced in her early years in Canada were mainly a function of her refugee family's poverty, caused by low earnings when compared to Canadian standards. They were a family of seven people living in a three-bedroom house on $600 a month. Their parents managed to provide them with the necessities of life, but they never had any extras. When other kids went skiing, they could not. When Du Chang got a free ticket to the circus, she "could get into the circus, but I had no spending money." Because they had so little money, her parents were very careful with it, making sure that the family had enough for necessities. She grew up with the sense that she "had to hold on to everything, had to hoard everything." As a result of her childhood experiences, she made a conscious decision "that I had to succeed in this country."

The Du children worked very hard at school, worked especially hard on their English skills. Quickly, they began to communicate with each other in English. Gradually, Du Chang began to lose some of her Vietnamese language skills. She smiles as she recalls how her mother – "My poor mother" – could not understand what her children were talking about with each other. "Sometimes we would get into heated debates, and she would say, 'I don't even know what you are saying, what are you yelling at?'"

Du Chang considers the support Canada provided to the Vietnamese refugees exceptional. Canadians are open and can appreciate other people's perspective. In this sense it is relatively easy for a newcomer to assimilate in Canada. Having said this, she says that as children she and her sister did experience incidents of racism. But they did not even know that it was racism: they just entered the society of Canadian children with "audacity" and were accepted. When she got her first job as a lawyer, she was both the first Asian and the first woman at her law firm. She just did her job, and when it was seen that she was capable, she was quickly accepted. Again, her audacity and the openness of Canadians did their job.

She is "embarrassingly open about my background and where I come from; I have quite a bit of pride in it." Her Canadian children are the visible demonstration of "how far we have come"; they have no real idea of prejudice. They consider Du Chang to be just a normal Western mother. What they can learn from the refugee experience is where their mother came from, and that it was a long road, overcoming serious difficulties.

Nguyen Thi Kim Loan

The quotes in this story are translated from a Vietnamese interview (Interview HOF132 2020).

Nguyen is from Saigon, the second youngest of eight children. Nine years old in 1975, she lost her sick mother one month after the fall of Saigon because of health service deficiencies under the new authorities. Her police officer father was sent to re-education camp. The eight children had to manage on their own. The eldest ones, in their early twenties, took care of the younger ones, and they also received help from relatives. Even the youngest children tried to contribute. Two of her adult siblings managed to escape in 1980, but she was too young to go with them. As she grew older, she made several attempts to escape, all of which failed. She made it to Thailand in 1989 following an unusual escape route through Cambodia and the Gulf of Thailand.

Before arriving in Canada, she spent four years in in the enormous Phanat Nikhom refugee camp in Thailand. On arrival at the camp, she recalls: "We met people who had come before us who asked, 'Oh! Didn't you know that the camp was closed, honey?'… They said that the camp had been closed since March 14, 1989. So, we were detained in a locked up, confined camp, with no English lessons, no meetings with foreigner groups." The UN's Comprehensive Plan of Action (CPA), aiming to gradually put an end to the refugee movement, was already in place. Her siblings who had resettled in the United States attempted to sponsor her to go there, without success.

After four years Canada accepted her as a government-assisted refugee. She does not know why Canada accepted her. After the CPA came into force, "the rate of passing was very low, about 10 per cent in all the refugee camps in Southeast Asia, not just Thailand … I was lucky to pass the selection process … I was predestined for Canada." She had been a writer for years before her camp experiences, but afterwards, her writing became a central element of her life.

Nguyen arrived in Canada and was directed to Ottawa as a government-assisted refugee. She knew nothing about Ottawa at the time, except that it was Canada's capital city. "They subsidized me for two years, so I was able to go to ESL classes. I was here by myself, but there was no hardship at all in living or money. They found me an apartment and supported me … I went to an adult high school for recertification in Ottawa … it was the High School of Commerce." She also received help from the Ottawa Vietnamese Catholic Church. She is deeply grateful for all the help she received. Having said this, she was alone in Canada and wanted to join her family who had settled in Texas. But their sponsorship application for her was again rejected by American authorities.

Following two years of language training, she married another Vietnamese refugee who was a pharmacist, already well established in Canada. She had two children in quick succession. Her goal in Ottawa was to go back to college and qualify as a teacher, which was her occupation in Vietnam before her escape. But linguistic difficulties made this impossible at the time and once she was married, she had to take care of her new family.

"So, I had two kids, and when my son was two years old, he was diagnosed with autism. So, at the time, my family decided to move here [Edmonton], because the program for autistic kids was better here." Nguyen wanted to retrain as a pharmacy technician, but "at that time there were no program for pharmacy technicians here, just in Red Deer." She registered for the course and at the same time also registered in a Level Two daycare course. She obtained qualifications in both occupations. Afterwards she quickly realized that she did not have time to work outside the home; she needed to take care of her autistic son. Her husband was working as a pharmacist seven days a week. She was the only one to take care of the children. A "few years later, once my children were better and going to school, then I was able to take a job, but just a part-time one."

The major obstacle to her early integration was not knowing the language. She would have liked to requalify as a teacher, but this was impossible, since she could not speak English well enough. Writing was her passion and she continued to write many stories in Vietnamese, so she had no access to an English-language reading public. The language obstacle also affected other aspects of her life.

The second obstacle was the customs, the habits, in Canada. "Whatever we got from Vietnam, from Asia, was different from here." But this was only in the first few years. "Now I have embraced all the new things in Canada." She feels that her husband who arrived in Canada at a young age and her daughter who was born in Canada have taught her a great deal about Canadian life. "No regrets about Vietnam any more … I am very happy to live in this country." She likes the openness of Canada, the ability to explore things, the liberal, capitalist lifestyle.

Next, she describes some of the camp experiences contained in her two published books. It was a dark time. Many of her stories focus on the desperation of the camp, where refugees were in a limbo, not being accepted for resettlement, but unwilling to be repatriated. In her stories she describes suicides, riots, hunger strikes, food shortages, corruption, and mistreatment by the Thai authorities. She insists that responsibility for all this went back to the Communist authorities of Vietnam. The refugees were all victims of communism. "I thank God [for my life here] … My husband is the associate owner of a pharmacy, my daughter is close to graduating as a nurse from the University of Alberta, my autistic son has made good progress. My life, also my mental health, everything is comfortable … Every year we travel, we visit my family in the USA."

The main reason Nguyen writes her books is to pass her experiences down to her daughter, to make the next generation understand what their parents went through. At the same time, she doesn't want constantly to badger her daughter about her experiences. But she has good evidence that her daughter understands that the refugees' experience should be preserved.

She insists that Canada's efforts for the Vietnamese refugees have been "a most precious thing. I am indebted. Thank you, Canada."

A Family-Sponsored Refugee

Tran Duc Chi

The quotes in this story are from an interview (Interview HOF009 2019).

Tran Duc Chi is a well-spoken gentleman in his mid-fifties. The interview was in English, which he speaks very well. He also speaks French, which he learned during his early Canadian years in Quebec. He is the youngest child of a very large family, one of eleven siblings. His father was a South Vietnamese civil servant in modest circumstances. At the time of the fall of Saigon, he was thirteen years old. Within two years, experiencing indoctrination and lack of freedom at school, lack of trust among people, and the general unfairness of the new regime, he wanted to escape at all costs. His mother was already deceased, and it took a serious effort to persuade his elderly father to allow him to leave. He left Vietnam by boat with an older sister in late 1977. He was sixteen years old.

They spent six months in Pulau Tengah refugee camp and they were sponsored to come to Canada by a sister in Montreal, who had been a student in Canada since 1973. In Montreal, "I was very happy to be surrounded by my family, they all loved me, but for some reason I was fiercely independent … I don't want to be a burden to my sister and my brother." When offered the opportunity by the Quebec government, "I left my sponsor, my sister, right away [and moved to] Gatineau, [Quebec], with my other sister who escaped [from Vietnam] with me." He attended the Gatineau Centre d'orientation et de formation des immigrants (COFI), the Quebec government's main institution to facilitate the integration of newcomers to Quebec.

Tran's first impression of Canada, which stayed with him for the rest of his life, was of an open country that welcomed refugees and immigrants from all parts of the world. At the Gatineau COFI he met refugees from Eastern European communist countries and people who had escaped from right-wing dictatorships. Within "a couple of days I realized that we were the same. Communist, not communist, capitalist, not capitalist, don't mean a thing. We were actually the same. We just wanted to live a happy life, a normal life, with some kind of dignity and Canada accepted us … I am forever indebted to COFI." It was here, in French Canada, that he was introduced to positive aspects of Canadian culture, especially treating newcomers with dignity. He studied at COFI for eight months and was ready to find a job at age seventeen.

While studying at COFI, Tran went to the federal Manpower Canada office every two weeks to receive a $78 cheque for his daily expenses. He will never forget the Manpower officer who dealt with him. "The way he handed me the cheque was as if he thanked me, as if he wanted me to share with him the experience I went through, as if I was somebody very valuable." Exchanges with this official occasioned in him a deep respect for Canadian officialdom and were instrumental in causing him to join the Canadian civil service.

His first job was with a gardening company and then he was a dishwasher. At the same time, he studied on his own from books provided by Quebec's Education des Adultes/Adult Education program. The next year, he entered CEGEP (public college) and continued to study during the day, while working at night.

Tran faced some obstacles during his acculturation process to Canada. As he says, "The biggest obstacle common to all refugees and immigrants is language, language, language." Acquiring Canada's two official languages took a lot of effort. Another "big obstacle was the culture, was the misunderstanding of culture. There are many small things, but I tell you an example. When you go to apply for a job, it was in my upbringing that I have to be modest ... When they ask me, 'do you know how to do this,' [I reply,] 'no sir, I don't know how to do that, but I will try very hard' ... In Canada you [either show] a lot of confidence or you know nothing." He did not know how to apply for a job; his modesty implied that he lacked confidence. It took time and acculturation before he could show confidence in a job interview and display his abilities in the Canadian manner. He still spoke English and French in a laboured manner, so he learned computer languages – COBOL and FORTRAN at that time – and worked as a programmer for the government. He got his undergraduate degree at the same time.

How long did it take him to become fully Canadian? From the beginning, "Canada was nice, it was fantastic. I started to fall in love with Canada and that feeling made me feel guilty." He felt that he was betraying Vietnam, his original love. "It was during a CEGEP math class – and I am very good in mathematics" – that he thought of infinity, and considered that infinity divided by two still remains infinity. That's when he realized that he could love both Vietnam and Canada equally. "I felt that this was my adopted country that I loved wholeheartedly. And that was OK. I didn't have to abandon my previous love [for Vietnam]."

He believes that Canada is strong because of diversity. When Canada accepts refugees, Canadian media talk as if Canada is doing the refugees a favour. Yet it is a two-way street. Canada is doing the refugees a favour by saving their lives. But the refugees are doing Canada a favour "to further strengthen our nation. I personally gave my youth to Canada. I could have gone to private industry, made more money as an IT person. But I stayed. I actually believe that I gave a lot to this country."

He also states that he enthusiastically shares the lessons of his life with his children. He believes that immigrants are an investment, not an expense. Immigrants need to be valued when they arrive. But also, they need to be developed, their love for Canada needs to be maintained. His children are Vietnamese Canadians. "They respect their Vietnamese heritage but love this country. And that's beautiful."

Conclusion to Part Three

Contributing to Canadian Society

The North Vietnamese communist cadres ruling South Vietnam after 1975 frequently spoke of freeing the Vietnamese people from colonialism and exploitation. But their talk, repeated as dogma in schools, universities, and workplaces, and especially in re-education camps, was contradicted by the realities of people's daily lives. There was little food; paper money had little value; it was dangerous to talk openly.

The North Vietnamese victory in the war, which was supposed to unite Vietnam, instead directed revenge against the South Vietnamese urban and middle classes, especially the Chinese minority. The average urban person, not only supporters of the former regime, had to face an existence where nothing was certain, where the government and the police had to be feared, where officials, policemen, and the military were corrupt. The Hearts of Freedom interviewees decided that facing the dangers of a sea journey, the possibility of death on the high seas, and the challenges of new lives in Canada was preferable to miserable, terrified lives in Vietnam.

On arrival in Canada, most boat people faced difficulties of acculturation, language acquisition, low-level jobs, and climate. Yet they consider Canadians to be a kind people and think that this kindness is a part of Canada being a diverse multicultural society. In referring to Canada's role in the world, most interviewees have emphasized that it is important for Canada to maintain its traditions of respecting human rights and welcoming refugees.

Many of the Vietnamese Canadian interviewees have built successful professional and business careers in Canada. In talking about their success, some interviewees state that the Vietnamese refugee movement demonstrates the positive value of resettling refugees, that Vietnamese refugees have given more back to Canada than they have taken in the form of support by Canadian taxpayers. Through a range of organizations, former refugees are actively involved in supporting refugee resettlement as well as community work inside Canada.

The boat people and their offspring have become active participants in Canadian cultural activities. Several writers of Vietnamese refugee background have become prize-winning authors in Canada in English and in French. It is remarkable that of the eighty-two Vietnamese interviewees, five are published writers, including prize-winning author Dr Le Van Chau (Interview HOF044 2019); and one, Nguyen Van Nghia (Interview HOF083 2019), is even a publisher of Vietnamese books. As Nguyen Thi Kim Loan (Interview HOF132 2020) states, she writes to let future generations know what the refugees have gone through. Of course, to enable young Canadians of Vietnamese background to understand their parents' stories, they need to maintain knowledge of the Vietnamese language. The interviewees realize that this is a challenge.

On 3 April 1975, crew members from the USS *Durham* took on board Vietnamese who were attempting to sail across the South China Sea in a small boat. Source: United States National Archives and Records Administration (NARA), National Archives at College Park, Still Pictures, NAID: 558518.

In December 1978, this small boat with 168 Vietnamese refugees crammed on board was crossing to Malaysia. The boat sank a few metres from shore. Most of the refugees were rescued and made it to the shore safely. Source: ©UNHCR/Kaspar Gaugler.

It is unknown how many people perished while trying to escape from Vietnam in small boats. Here, people on shore assist exhausted and distressed children and adults who have narrowly escaped drowning as their boat reached land. Source: ©UNHCR/Kaspar Gaugler.

In a refugee camp, a Canadian immigration officer interviews a family with the assistance of a translator. Source: Neufeld/Molloy Archives, photo by Robert J. Shalka.

At a refugee camp in Southeast Asia, an immigration officer interviews a family with the help of a translator. Source: Murray Mosher, Photo Features Ltd.

In some camps, refugees were themselves responsible for building their own shelter. Source: Neufeld/Molloy Archives.

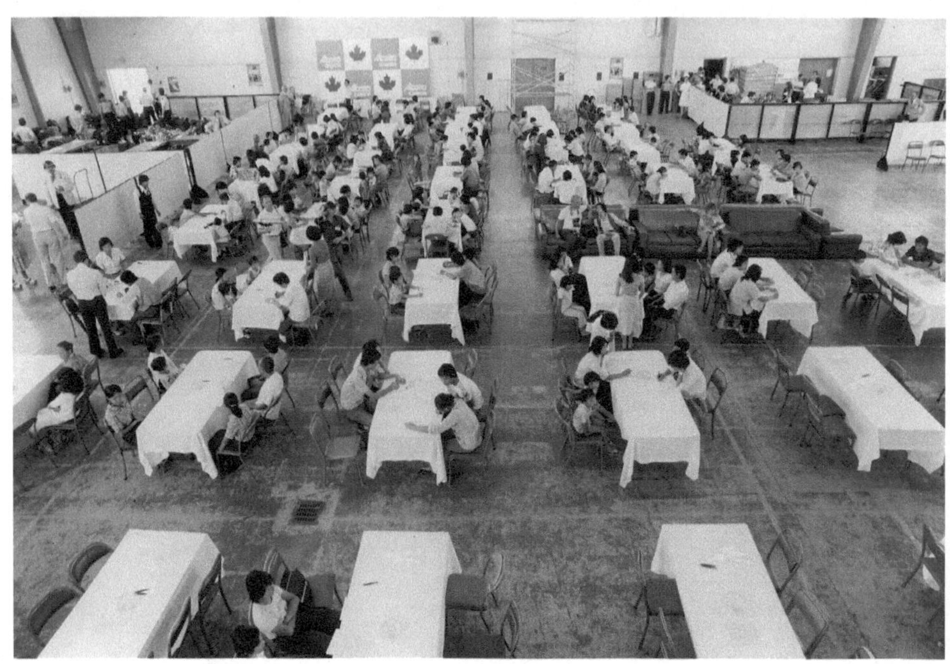

At the reception centre at Greisbach Barracks in Edmonton, dozens of newly arrived refugee families meet with Canadian officials who will issue them their permanent resident documents. The officials will also counsel them about their destination and whether they will be assisted by private sponsors or government officials. Source: Murray Mosher, Photo Features Ltd.

Having arrived in Canada, a family of nine waits at the reception centre at Greisbach Barracks to meet with Canadian immigration officials. Source: Murray Mosher, Photo Features Ltd.

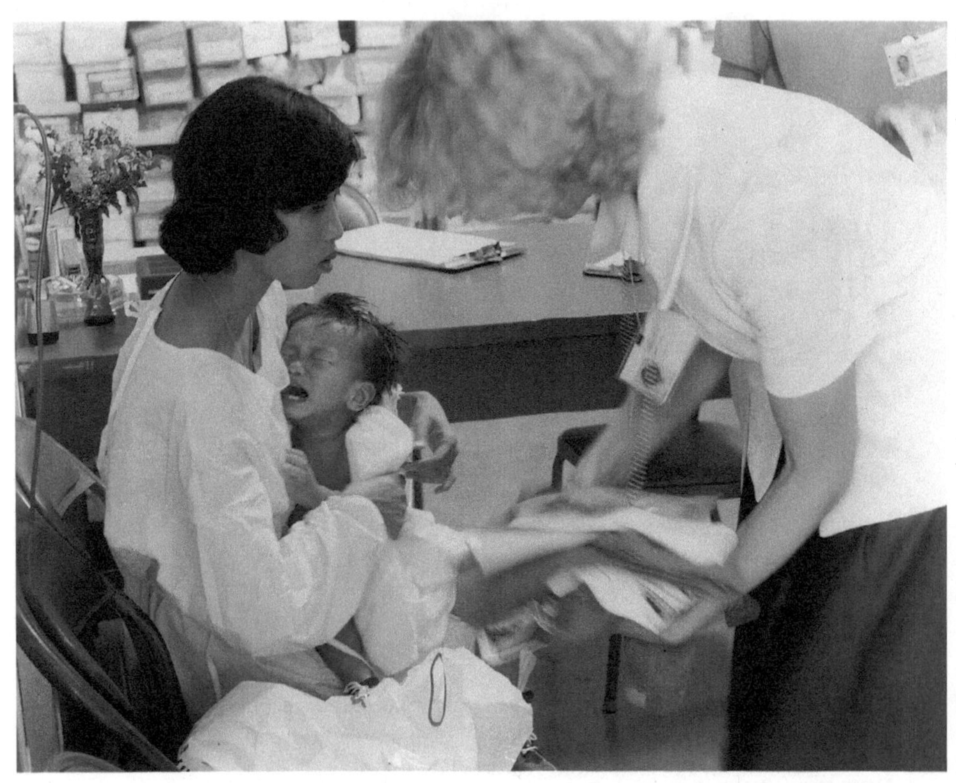

A refugee mother holds her child at the health clinic at the reception centre at Greisbach Barracks. Source: Murray Mosher, Photo Features Ltd.

Newly arrived youth and children pass the time. Source: Murray Mosher, Photo Features Ltd.

Two boys smile after arriving at the Griesbach Barracks reception centre in Edmonton. Source: Murray Mosher, Photo Features Ltd.

Dr Hieu C. Truong, PhD, P. Eng., is a prominent member of the Canadian Vietnamese community, now retired from the Royal Canadian Mint. The Mint's Hieu C. Truong Centre of Excellence for Research and Development was named for him. He was appointed to the Order of Canada in June 2017 for his outstanding service to Canada. Source: Photo collection of Le Phan.

Hmong women perform a line dance at the fortieth anniversary of their arrival in Canada. Source: Michael Molloy.

PART FOUR

Cambodian Refugees

9

Surviving War and Genocide, Escaping from Cambodia

This chapter describes the experiences of Cambodians who lived through bombing, war, fear, genocide, and terror, witnessing brutal executions and the radical reorganization and transformation of their country. Eventually they miraculously managed to escape. These are the experiences and the voices of those who endured and survived unthinkable conditions and challenges and can now tell the world what happened to them and their families.

The chapter highlights the experiences of thirty Cambodians, eight of whom are women. Of the interviews, sixteen were conducted in English, seven in French, and seven in Khmer. This chapter is organized under the themes of life under the Khmer Rouge, the escape journey, and refugee camp experiences. It closes with some concluding thoughts.

Vietnam War, Khmer Rouge, and Confusion

The ongoing wars and American bombing in Cambodia contributed to confusion when the Communist Party of Kampuchea (also known as the Khmer Rouge) came into power. Minar Chhor (Interview HOF077 2019) was in high school in 1975. "My father was a doctor, and my mother was a history and geography teacher. So, we lived well." He remembers two distinct periods: the war between the Khmer Rouge and the Lon Nol regime between 1970 and 1975, and the victory and rule of the Khmer Rouge under Pol Pot between 1975 and 1979. During the former, the population in Phnom Penh, the capital, did not suffer because the war was going on in rural areas. "They saw us as the people who are protected, the imperialists who are above everything. And once they won the war, that's when they really started to persecute us, to try and eliminate us, because they hated us so much … They wanted to build a society that is purely fair and egalitarian … we were seen as the population to be purged."

In the context of the civil war and United States bombing, many were confused regarding the Khmer Rouge victory and, hoping for the best, unknowingly welcomed them. When she heard that the Phnom Penh government had fallen, Un You Eng (Interview HOF129 2019) was initially happy about the Khmer Rouge emphasis on equality because there were great divisions between the rich and the poor, and she and other students had demonstrated demanding equality. On 17 April 1975, in a demonstration of support, "I went to cheer them on, excited and welcoming. After I returned from the demonstration, about three hours in, the military came and told us they had to clean up Phnom Penh. You have to evacuate out of the city for a few days."

Sovann Un (Interview HOF078 2019) was a teacher in a small village but made extra money to support his brother and cousin by selling rice at the Thai border. On 17 April 1975, he was at the border and could have escaped. But he believed in social equality and was under the impression that the communist Pol Pot regime had good intentions and would help the poor.

Similarly, Mao Ly (Interview HOF012 2019) recalls that in 1970–72, there was much confusion because of the war, first with Vietnam and then with the Khmer Rouge. When the Khmer Rouge seized Battambang he was sixteen years old. "We held up white shirts and waved with joy to welcome the new regime." Charlie Lim (Interview HOF024 2019), who was fifteen years of age when the Khmer Rouge began taking over the country and the capital Phnom Penh, remembers that "as a kid you ran around the tanks, armoured vehicles. You were so happy and at that time you don't know anything." He thought that the country would no longer be at war and that they would be free to go anywhere. When the Khmer Rouge, at gunpoint, immediately ordered the city of Phnom Penh to be emptied under the pretext that the US would be bombing, his father said, "Big trouble coming." Life in Cambodia was about to be drastically reorganized, resulting in severe hardship, starvation, illness, terror, and death.

Forced Evacuation

The entire population was ordered to leave the cities and travel into the countryside, taking only what they could carry. Hospitals were emptied and the ill and infirm were forced to join the long lines of people. The roads were jammed and there was no direction or village that they were to go to. Some were told to return to the villages where they were born. But many could not do so and settled in villages along the way. Soon food supplies and water were gone. Sovann Un (Interview HOF078 2019) recalls that the Khmer Rouge, brandishing guns, pushed everyone from the villages further from the Thai border because they feared people would escape. He headed to his wife's native village and stayed there until 1979.

The evacuation from the cities created life-threatening hardship as men, women, and children were forced to walk long hours in the heat without sufficient food, water, or medicine. During the evacuation, Saphan Noun (Interview HOF 125 2019) recounts what happened. "They came on 17 April and evacuated us all by the 23 April. On the night of 23 April, I had my first child. No midwife help and the umbilical cord was still attached for three to four hours. No one thought that I would survive." Her first child was just starting to walk and was starving without the availability of rice.

Several families got separated and many did not survive. Bodies soon scattered the roadways. Charlie Lim (Interview HOF024 2019) and his family – ten brothers and sisters, his parents, and his grandfather – fled to Vietnam, taking only a few belongings. His grandfather, who could not walk, soon became ill and died. Then his oldest sister died, then his brother and third sister, all due to starvation. Mao Ly (Interview HOF012 2019) remembers that it was the hot season, and when they slept on the roads their plastic mats would stick to the heated pavement. "Because of thirst some people drank water on the side of the road. Sometimes you would see floating corpses when trying to get a drink … Some people drank the water and got diarrhea immediately … If you drank the water in the morning, you had diarrhea in the evening, then the next day, you'd die." As each day passed there were more bodies on the roadside. When water supplies ran out, the only choice was to drink water from the side of the road.

Chamroeun Lay (Interview HOF011 2019) remembers that "if you have a car, the car has no gasoline, so it becomes like a carriage. You put your belongings in it and push." It took three to four days to get twenty kilometres. People evacuated and travelled without food or medicine, not knowing where they would go. Families were often separated – children sent to "youth mobile teams." Chamroeun was sent to a remote area to build a new rice field with his bare hands. Food was scarce and survival meant eating anything – "a snake, frog, or crab, or stolen potatoes." There was no medicine available and many attempted to make homemade medicine from roots. People quickly died from overwork, starvation, and illness, such as malaria.

It was a particularly difficult time for children, and families struggled to stay together on the crowded roads. Channa Kong (Interview HOF123 2019), who was twelve years old, had a high fever during the evacuation. Her father gave her some medication that offered some relief. With the extreme heat she eventually fainted and in the crowd was separated from her family. "We were separated until 1979, more than three years." In 1975, Yorp Sok (Interview HOF128 2019) had four children and was pregnant during the exodus to the countryside, not knowing where they were going. "It was my mother, my father, my younger siblings, and my younger siblings-in-law. We were three families." She lost her father in the crowd and did not see him again.

Overcome by grief, Neang Thong (Interview HOF032 2019) recalls that she "is the lucky one." She was ten years old and lost many of her family members – grandfather, uncle, two brothers, and two sisters. During the evacuation from the city, she became very ill and could not walk because of swollen legs. The family placed her in a cart, but the roads were not good, so they made her two sticks from bamboo so that she could walk. They tried to cross over a canal, making a raft out of bamboo. Her father helped pull her up a bank, and the family gave her food from their limited supply. Her brother became ill, and her sister who was out in the field became ill. Her father tried to rescue her sister, but leeches clung to him. and within a week he passed away.

Peng Ngy Lim (Interview HOF036 2019) and her husband were teachers in Phnom Penh, but when the city was evacuated, they decided to go to their natal village. After having to abandon their car, they walked seventy kilometres with young children ages three and five. After they had been in their home village for five months, the Khmer Rouge asked her husband to help with re-education/reform in the city. Instead, they took him away and executed him. She and her family were forced to walk thirty kilometres to the train station. On the train, their few belongings were confiscated, and at their destination they were separated by occupation (e.g., labourers, farmers, merchants, and so forth) and sent to different villages. Her mother, who was ill and forced to do farm work, died within two months. Her young son died a few months later of undernourishment. Her father followed and died from malnutrition.

Life under the Khmer Rouge

After the initial exodus from cities, everyone was forced to live on communal farms, forced labour camps, or small villages. The premise was to create a model classless, agrarian communist state, and to destroy the family structure so that loyalty shifted to Angkar – "the organization" – referring to the Khmer Rouge regime that controlled the people.

Family members could no longer live together, and there was collectivization of work and living arrangements. Children started working at a young age. Minar Chhor (Interview HOF077 2019) was placed in a group for young boys ten to fifteen years of age and given the task of building dams. His brother was placed in a group of children seven to ten years of age and took care of the cows. His mother, a teacher, was placed in a group of peasant women and had to cultivate rice, and his father, a doctor, was placed in a group who had to cut wood.

Those from the cities and from the professional class were considered "new people" and villagers "old people." Minar's father was a doctor and his mother a teacher, placing the family among those who were seen as expendable, the "population to be purged." He remembers "very hard work, hunger, and fear all of the time" in not knowing when he and his family would be killed. Similarly, Bokhara Bun (Interview HOF005 2019) also came from a privileged background, and the family was soon placed on a killing list, so they tried to hide his father in the village. Tragically, his father, betrayed by a former driver, died by suicide, slowly ingesting poisoned fruit, in 1975. However, the family hid the suicide, knowing that the Khmer Rouge considered suicide proof of hiding crimes and would execute the entire family. Bunkorn Yun (Interview HOF035 2019) lived a studious life with monks and by 1975 had earned his undergraduate degree in business and economics. He heard that the goal of Angkar was to get rid of a whole generation contaminated by capitalist influences and start a new society and generation that would adopt its new philosophy. That was when he saw that he had no future there and decided to escape.

Channa Kong's (Interview HOF123 2019) hair was long, but the Angkar ordered that it be cut short. As children, if they cried, they would be taken for re-education, and they "trained us not to behave like before." She was later reunited with her family and found out that all five siblings and her mother were alive, but Pol Pot had killed her father, who had been in the military.

As a young child Sophal Vonn (Interview HOF031 2019) experienced harsh conditions and brutality. Originally from Vietnam, she came to Cambodia at age four, and was twelve years old when the Khmer Rouge took over. She was taken from her parents to stay with a youth group for those thirteen years of age and up. She recalls that there "were around five hundred people living together at one time." There was collective eating and sleeping. She worked in the rice fields starting at three or four in the morning and had to dig trenches, ten metres a day. "For seven days I had nothing to eat." To survive she found a small papaya and ate it but then was tortured by getting no food or water for three days. "A month later they tied me up for one night and two days and tortured me by using red ants." The punishment was because of her Vietnamese background and coming from a good family. Fearing that she would be killed, Sophal attempted to escape but was caught and severely beaten. She was eventually saved by the Vietnamese invasion and released.

"One of the hardest things during that time was not wanting to live," states Bun Na Un (Interview HOF067 2019), "but I did not know what to do … One highly academic student bit his tongue until he died." He also comments how they were afraid of child soldiers who "didn't know who their parents or siblings were. To catch us, they would inform on us, tie us up, and kill us." He comments on how difficult "it was for three years, eight months, and twenty days." Kong Bun (Interview HOF124 2019) comments on how Angkar called everyone "friends," young or old, not using "aunt" or "uncle." The premise was that everyone was equal, and there was an attempt to transfer loyalty from the family to Angkar.

Knowing that the Khmer Rouge would torture and eliminate professionals and military people, Sovann Un (Interview HOF078 2019) worked as a farmer. Honouring the rules of Angkar was a strategy for survival. Everyone lived in fear.

There were some who attempted to escape the ruthlessness of the Khmer Rouge regime by immediately retreating to the mountains or jungle. Prom Sorn (Interview HOF025 2019) came from Battambang Province and was part of a large farming family of three girls and nine boys. He was twenty years old when the Khmer Rouge came into power, and he remembers that they constantly tested him and suspected that he had been in the army. Fearing the regime, in 1978 he and his wife and newborn child "ran away into the mountains until the Vietnamese took over." They survived by eating leaves and occasionally sneaking into villages to steal "some potatoes, tomatoes, everything that they grow" from the Khmer Rouge gardens.

Marriage

In Cambodian culture, marriages are traditionally a union between two families, as well as two people. However, during the Khmer Rouge era, in an attempt to shift family allegiances to Angkar, marriages were controlled, and families had no role. Most marriages were arranged in the interests of the regime with little emotional attachment or the celebratory aspects of traditional weddings. Forced marriage was used to advance the unique socio-political and ideological goals of the Khmer Rouge:

"First, forced marriage was used as a mechanism to both secure absolute loyalty to the regime and further the Khmer Rouge's goal of an agrarian revolutionary order. Second, forced marriage was used to systematically dismantle families of origin, while constructing a 'new family, representing the regime itself, once again ensuring compliance and obedience' and hopefully producing the next generation of loyal members" (Denov et al. 2022, 1549).

Kong Toeun (Interview HOF165 2020) describes how he placed his name on a list to get married and named a potential partner, then waited for the woman to make her choice. Multiple couples were married at the same time, and when their names were called, they shook hands. Those who got married had the possibility of staying close to the village and not being sent to a work unit. Kong Bun (Interview HOF124 2019) explains that "for me to stay close to the village, I requested for a woman to be my wife. I was not seeking love or loved anyone, but in this case my father was sick and unable to walk." Being dedicated to an ailing father, he asked his supervisor, "Friend-supervisor, can request a friend-woman for me?" He made out a request to a woman, and she agreed. At the wedding there was traditional music. They wore black and stood in front of each other, along with two other couples, and they made vows that they would live together and continue the revolution together. Bun brought his new wife home to introduce her to his father, saying, "This is a friend-woman I am engaged to, Dad. Please accept her as your daughter-in-law." His father gave his approval; but the next day, the new bride was sent away to work. But Bun was able to stay and care for his ailing father, the marriage being a means to an end. Similarly, Bunkorn Yun (Interview HOF035 2019) also married a young woman in order not to be sent to the field camp and remain in the village. They were only married for a month before he caught malaria and had to quarantine.

Pressure was placed on young adults to get married. Neang Thong (Interview HOF032 2019), a young woman of nineteen, resisted getting married despite numerous attempts to force her to do so. Finally, at gunpoint, she agreed for the sake of her family. "I say 'yes,' and after that about six weeks we get married, not only one couple, eleven couples the same time."

Killing by Khmer Rouge

It was not long before executions by the Khmer Rouge became known and visible. Peng Ngy Lim (Interview HOF036 2019) becomes emotional as she describes "a traumatizing event, an unforgettable scene," where everyone in the village, children included, was called to a public meeting to witness the torture and killing of a young couple. Members of the Khmer Rouge made speeches and announced that it was forbidden to love each other without marriage. They then brought a young man out with his hands tied to a cross and then the young woman, who was pregnant, also had her hands tied to a cross. They proceeded to beat them with a shovel, and after four or five blows, the young man fell. The young woman was beaten with even more blows because she was pregnant. Both died. Every night people were killed for different reasons, and Peng lived in constant fear.

Such executions were not uncommon. Bun Na Un (Interview HOF067 2019) describes a similar killing where if any couples showing romantic interests were discovered, "they would place the man on one end of a pole and the female on the other end, then beat them on the back of the head" until they died. The entire village would be called to bear witness.

Kong Bun (Interview HOF124 2019), who hid his identity as a student and learned to plow the fields, recalls a time that he tied the cows while collecting hay and loading the cart. A man approached him and told him that a person was just killed on the site. "I then went there, and I saw a woman's bra hung over the coconut tree and a trail of blood underneath." The man told him a woman had been executed there and said that the wooden house on the other side of the tree held prisoners. The man recalled that one woman had a plastic bag placed over her head so she could not breathe, and she struggled and kicked. She wore a skirt without underwear and the skirt came off. The Khmer Rouge laughed and poked the tips of their guns at her genitals. This was Kong's first encounter with the homicidal aspects of the Khmer Rouge regime.

In 1977, Mao Ly (Interview HOF012 2019) and his family were taken to be executed because they were accused of being Vietnamese. They were placed in a truck with others and taken to Katch Ro Test, an area where executions took place. "We sat in the truck looking at one another wondering how we were going to die. For some, they died from having their organs taken out, or get beaten to death. We could only look at one another and sob in silence, helplessly." However, it was night by the time they got there, and they were placed in a detention centre and shackled together until morning. Two other trucks full of prisoners arrived in the morning and were executed, leaving Mao Ly and his family in the centre. "During our time there they let us eat a tablespoon of porridge each. If we needed to urinate, they gave us a bottle. They would get one of us to pour it out. If we needed to defecate, they would bring us an ammunition box to defecate in. Once you were done, no one cleaned it … If you were grossed out by the feces, they made you eat it." During internal strife among the Khmer Rouge, they were eventually let go.

Mao Ly speaks of another horrific experience with Khmer Rouge killing. After his close experience with execution, he was given the task of burying the bodies of those executed – five to six a night. The earth was dry during the hot season, making it difficult to dig the two metres required for a body. "There were times I was able to dig a metre or so. I had to chop off the legs to have them fit in the burials." If he refused to do it, he would also be killed. There were seven who were executed, and three people were there to bury them. Then, one of the men who buried the bodies was also executed, leaving two to bury. He witnessed the executions. "They would take out the beating heart and play with it. For women, they cut out their breasts. I saw it!" Once they finished the executions, he had to bury the bodies. "At first when they would execute someone, I would urinate on myself … I was only sixteen witnessing executions … There was one time I defecated on myself." The soil was so hard, and he was so weak, that often only a small amount of dirt covered the bodies, and the next day there would be a leg, the buttocks, or a hand appearing from the surface.

Witnessing brutality by the Khmer Rouge was particularly horrifying to youth. Nhem Pheap (Interview HOF131 2019), who was only ten years old in 1978, remembers people being arrested, tied up, and sent to be killed. One day during the rainy season he heard frogs and decided to catch some to eat. He noticed "a gross smell" and "stepped into a hole that had a lot of dead bodies." He had discovered a mass grave of people who had been executed.

The Khmer Rouge made no attempt at hiding their executions, shocking treatment of women, and ritual cannibalism. Samath Yi (Interview HOF127 2019) sewed black clothing worn by the Khmer Rouge military. He recalls that on one occasion they came with red scratches on their faces. "They wore necklaces, bracelets, jewellery, and such, not like we wore it but on their arms, legs, even on their dogs. They said, 'Last night we cooked humans to eat.'" These people were to be transferred to another village, but instead they were executed by the Khmer Rouge. "The night that they were killed, the soldiers played a stereo loudly. Before the women were killed, they were raped, whether elderly or children. And all their jewellery was taken."

At this time, Samath Yi discovered that he and his family were on a list to be killed. Surprisingly, a member of the Khmer Rouge told him to escape to a village across the river. He comments, "Some were good people." During the day they were all ordered to go to the rice field, and Samath Yi, his wife Un You Eng (Interview HOF129 2019), and her family planned their escape. They all gathered and made a raft out of palms for the mother-in-law, who could not swim, and crossed the river. The group of around ten immediately split up in the jungle to avoid detection by the Khmer Rouge and finally found each other six hours later.

They ended up in Salong Village, Kandal Province, where the village chief allowed them to stay. Life was less harsh in some villages and there were pockets of resistance against the Khmer Rouge. The next day the Khmer Rouge soldiers came and confirmed that people had been sent off to be killed, as Samath Yi shares: "The village chief had to speak to Yuthea [Khmer Rouge] responsible for prosecuting us. He stated, 'These people are innocent' and 'They don't look like they used to work for the government. Allow me to educate them. If these people disobey, then you can take them.'" Un You Eng remembers the generosity of the people in the village. She was asked to be a teacher and given fifteen kilograms of rice a month, earning her the nickname "Teacher Fifteen Kilograms." They were given some land and could grow potatoes, watermelons, and bananas to eat. They were able to live peacefully in the village until around 1979 when the regime changed again, and the Vietnamese invaded. They eventually made their way to Khao I Dang refugee camp.

Starvation and Illness

It was not long before meagre rations of porridge resulted in starvation and illness. Charlie Lim (Interview HOF024 2019), as a young boy, faced harsh conditions and it was not long before everyone got sick in his family and lost weight. Charlie becomes very emotional as he recalls that time in his life when food was so scarce. "In 1976 everyone got sick, lost weight. Grandfather got sick because he was old, not last long, six months he passed away, father died, oldest sister died, brother died, third sister died." There was no food, "everyone skinny, flies on your eyes, no energy. You look for any animal that you can catch and eat, bring to the family to share." They all died of starvation. Charlie recalls that they were skin and bones and had no energy. He searched for food for the family and one time was caught stealing bamboo, tied up, and sent to a densely populated concentration camp where he was forced into hard labour. He was sent to the rice fields to build a dyke where the soil was hard. He worked for two months and had to be carried back to the camp from weakness and exhaustion. It was not long after that he learned his mother had died, as well as his younger brother.

For Yorp Sok (Interview HOF128 2019), family members, including her mother and older sibling, died of starvation. In 1976, one child became seriously ill with worms. "He would cough out the worms. They came out of mouth and out of his rectum. I counted fifty worms." Although she brought him to hospital, nothing was done for him, and he soon died.

Others suffered with diarrhea. Yorp Sok comments, "We looked like corpses." She had also hurt herself in a fall and her legs were cramping and twisted. She asked others if they could breastfeed her child. "We did things to survive like burning charcoals, Gua Sha." Bun Na Un (Interview HOF067 2019) explains that the only medicine available was "rolled up branches for us to swallow. They would also inject coconut water."

There was never enough food, and the rations were insufficient. To survive, people were forced to forage for anything edible and steal from the Khmer Rouge gardens. Kong Bun (Interview HOF124 2019) ate banana tree worms and stole baby jackfruit and coconut fruit. "I stole anything to survive." He recalls all the strategies to survive with little food. "As time went by, my father went hungry, and I couldn't find anything for him. I kept searching and then found a rice granary, which is called a barn here." He found some dried cow skin, cut it into strips and grilled them, and boiled them all day for him to eat. His father said it was delicious: "It tastes like barbecue pork."

He also stole vegetables from a plot owned by the Khmer Rouge. He had a friend who had a cap which Khmer Rouge officials wore, and he had a spare one for him, and one day they went to steal bananas. There were spies everywhere so they were very cautious. When they arrived at the tree, they saw that other people had cut the bananas and were carrying them out but saw his cap and dropped the bananas and left. "We got the bananas without stealing since they did it for us." He and friends also had a clever way of stealing potatoes: "We were crawling to avoid the spies who would shoot if we were seen. So, we crawled until we reached the potatoes. We had to figure out a trick, so they had no idea the potatoes were stolen. The only way was to use a knife to dig around the stem. When you see the potatoes, just cut it off so that the stem stays intact. Instead of a hoe we used a knife to dig around the stem, removed the potatoes, and left the stem intact. The stem would continue to live but there would be no potatoes."

One time when he was asked to guard the dining area of the Khmer Rouge, Kong Bun drank some watergrass soup left in a pot. Just then an official came downstairs and asked him what he was doing. "Guarding, brother," he replied. Then he was asked, "Do you want to eat?" Without hesitation Kong replied "yes." He recalls, "The most valuable items I kept with me was a pot, a spoon, a scarf [kroma], and a backpack, which had my mom's photos and a few clothes in it." He remembers that he had his spoon "tucked at my waistline like a weapon." He was able to eat a small amount of rice, not porridge, for the first time.

Soon after, Kong's father, who had been ill, passed away. "He died in my arms, only the two of us, father and son. We didn't have a light, or a candle. I used a car tire that I had cut up in pieces to keep for emergency purposes only. I lit it up the next day after he died. I hid the fact that my father passed away so that I can get an extra meal for that one day." Kong was so weak from starvation that he had no strength, so he asked three women from the village to carry his father to a burial site. "I was so thin, having a large head on a cane … I lived alone now, and I didn't know when I would die."

Sorpong Peou remembers being ill a lot during that time. "I was so sick I could not even walk or get out of bed from exhaustion to hunger and then malaria." In his experience the Khmer Rouge had nurses come to the village and come and treat those who were ill. "So, when the nurses saw me lying in bed and lying on the floor, they took me to the hospital and let me stay for probably months." He comments that although the regime was murderous, he was well cared for by the nurses.

The Vietnamese invasion in December 1978 replaced the Khmer Rouge with a new communist regime and many took the opportunity to flee to the border in Thailand (Robinson 2000). By the summer of 1979, there was a refugee crisis at the border with the arrival of half a million Cambodians. Khao I Dang, established by UNHCR and the Thai government in November 1979, was the largest camp for refugees to be settled in a third country. Since it officially closed for new arrivals in January 1980, Cambodians arriving after that date were forced to bribe officials or smuggle themselves into the camp. Others were retained in border camps where humanitarian aid was provided by the United Nations Border Relief Operation (UNBRO). Thailand was also a sanctuary for the Khmer Rouge who operated a network of military camps.

For others, after the Vietnamese invasion there was a painful rebuilding period as many were in search of family members and found out who had been killed and who had survived. Neang Thong (Interview HOF032 2019) was able to find her mother, brother, sister, and her husband. Charlie Lim (Interview HOF024 2019) and his only surviving sister returned to their childhood home and began to make a life for themselves. He found a friend and they started working together on several jobs such as cooking in a noodle house until they decided to leave Cambodia.

The Escape Journey

All those interviewed escaped by walking through the jungle and mountains to the Thai border. On the treacherous journey, they had to negotiate landmines, bamboo spikes that had been sharpened to a razor point and buried under a thin cover of ground, and the bodies of those who died before them. While the Thai border camps provided food and shelter for the fleeing Cambodians, they also provided sanctuary for Khmer Rouge soldiers who had established a network of military camps. When Cambodians reached the Thai border, they were often met with gunfire by the Thai soldiers. Initially, the Thai government considered them "illegal migrants" and they were not considered eligible for third-country resettlement (Jackson 1987).

In 1975, Mean Bonn Taing (Interview HOF037 2019) was about to graduate with a degree in electrical engineering when all his dreams were shattered. Like many who were educated, he had to hide his identity and be a worker, not an intellectual. He was soon separated from his uncle and his brother and was moved to a remote area. He remembers: "I live but I don't have spirit anymore." He was able to see his mom, who died shortly after. He felt that he too would soon die and decided to plan an escape with a friend. They saved rice each day from the kitchen until they had half a kilogram. Mean Bonn had knowledge of geography and knew that the stars would be most visible from midnight to 6:00 a.m. On the fifth day they ran out of water and became dehydrated. Then they came upon bamboo everywhere and saw a creek. "Buddha didn't let us down … I caught a big frog, cut the head off, and cut it into four pieces and we ate it." They continued. He was becoming tired and weak. "I saw a lot of fireflies … had a military course on survival in the forest." When he saw several fireflies, he knew that there would be water somewhere. He found a pool, jumped in, filled water bottles, and placed a wet scarf around his neck. They continued avoiding landmines and climbed the highest mountain hoping that the Khmer Rouge would not be there. On reaching the summit and knowing that Thailand was close, they decided to sleep on a flat rock. Mean Bonn looked back at the landscape of Cambodia, thinking that this may be the last time he would see his country, and remembers thinking, "I cannot describe how beautiful it is."

In 1976, the Khmer Rouge decided to let young people go and search for their parents to celebrate the New Year. Bunkorn Yun (Interview HOF035 2019) used the pretext that he was looking for his parents to escape with his friend and headed for the Thai border. They were stopped along the way by the Khmer Rouge to work briefly in a field. Bunkorn used this time to further prepare for his escape. Using what he learned in a physics class, he built two compasses using a magnet that he stole from a Khmer Rouge bicycle. He also strengthened the soles of his feet by walking on needles and thorns since he had no shoes for the long journey. He figured that it would take three to five days to get to Thailand. Knowing that the Thai police and military were vicious, he decided to escape on 25 December 1977, hoping to arrive around 30–31 December, a time of New Year celebrations. He and a friend left in the evening with two compasses, a small container for water, a small axe, a lighter, a bit of salt, and a small amount of rice. After a few hours they came across a pond full of fish and caught a few. They walked at night and slept during the day arriving in Thailand on 2 January 1978. On arrival, they were caught by military police and imprisoned in a camp with terrible conditions. Like Mean Bonn, Bunkorn recalls the beauty of his escape journey and speaks of the lush flora and fauna, canopies of orchid flowers, and deer. He looked for the same area when he returned many years later but was not able to find the location.

Bun Na Un (Interview HOF067 2019) was in the army when the Khmer Rouge decided to permit young people to go and search for their parents. He immediately left the army and ran away from his hometown to Takeo Province. After seven to eight months, he was sent to Battambang Province, and from there he escaped to Thailand in mid-1976. He describes a harrowing journey. It took him and several elders three weeks, cutting through jungle. On arrival at the Thai border, they encountered Khmer Rouge soldiers. Bun Na grabbed an elder's arm and ran toward the soldiers and held the rifle up. Two people behind him were killed. Four of them were able to reach the summit, but one of the men was bleeding and died. Bun Na carried the elder, who was shot in the shoulder, until he saw a small hut close to the Thai border. They slept there for the night. Upon reaching Thailand, he was placed in prison for three weeks until he was released to a refugee camp.

Children and Childbirth

Children were particularly vulnerable during the escape through the jungle, and women who were pregnant often faced a traumatic childbirth. In 1979, on the way to the Thai border, Nhem Pheap (Interview HOF131 2020) and his family saw dead bodies and mass graves everywhere. His sister passed away in the jungle. His pregnant mother went into labour and gave birth to a baby boy. Then the area was bombarded by artillery. "My dad grabs my mom, I grab my brother by the hand, he was just born. We run, all bloody, we run." On the border, Communist Thai soldiers pointed guns at them, but then realized that they needed assistance and took them. "They gave me dry beef. They see that we are hungry. They give my mom some wine to help her." They eventually went to a refugee camp.

In 1979, during the Vietnamese invasion, Yorp Sok (Interview HOF128 2019) lost two children to illness. Yorp Sok was pregnant as they ran into the jungle. "I was in full term … my stomach was hurting, and we were in the middle of the jungle and mountains. At night we heard tigers crying." She was unable to go forward, and her husband went ahead looking for a midwife. However, she gave birth before he returned: "My baby was born on the ground." Luckily, a stranger came by to offer his help and tied the umbilical cord. Her husband returned and made a fire that lasted three days; then they moved on, not knowing where to go. They followed the Thai cornfields and they all found safety in a Thai refugee camp.

Sam An Eam (Interview HOF023 2019), the youngest of five brothers and one sister, was educated in a Buddhist school, and then a regular school. He recalls that from 1975 to 1979 life was very hard: "no food, no nothing." In 1979, when the Vietnamese invaded and began fighting against the Khmer Rouge, he had no choice but to leave. He, his nine-months-pregnant wife, and their five children travelled toward the Thai border along with his brother. They escaped with no food or medicine and travelled for twenty-two days and nights. One morning his wife looked tired, tried to walk, but started sobbing and said, "Baby coming." She delivered a baby girl, named Samnang, meaning "lucky." She was placed in a makeshift hammock. They came to the river, but his wife could not swim. They cut a tree, made a raft, and crossed the river. Their nine-year-old son, Yung, helped push the raft across the river. Then, after one day and one night, they reached the Thai border and went to live in the Khao I Dang camp. There, four of his children became ill and died. "Four children, one month, gone." He only had his oldest son and newly born daughter. The loss was more than he could endure, and he became delusional. When a truck of refugees arrived, he believed that his lost children were returning to him.

The Vietnamese Invasion

During the Vietnam invasion, many were fearful of the Vietnamese and ran toward the mountains of Thailand. However, Dim Meas (Interview HOF030 2019) urged his family to stay and later found out that most of those who fled did not survive. He also recalls that it was rice-growing season, and the fields were flourishing with rice available to all because the Khmer Rouge had fled. "Lucky you can fish. Nobody controls you, just whatever you want to do, that's okay."

Soth Chhlam (Interview HOF099 2019) witnessed the Khmer Rouge marching south toward a forest and thought that they had been pushed back by the Vietnamese army. He encountered some villagers who needed help carrying some essential goods like cooking pots and food. He went along with them and arrived at a village and found his family. Shortly after, the Khmer Rouge took him and his family as hostages and brought them to the forest to work carrying ammunition. His parents were eventually released, but he remained in the forest. He saw people who stepped on landmines dying, "gone in a blue light." He incurred a serious leg wound that left him unable to walk. "I cannot walk anymore and just sleep there and see if I die because I cannot do anything." But villagers took care of him and took him to the Khmer Rouge–controlled area. One morning he heard artillery. Others ran, but he could only use a crutch, two bamboo sticks. He walked and walked, finally coming to a Thai border camp where he was placed on a stretcher. He remembers that it was September 1978.

When the Vietnamese entered Cambodia, they pushed the Khmer Rouge back, and Kong Toeun (Interview HOF165 2020) decided it was time to escape to a Thai border camp with his wife and young baby. They received some food at the border camp and then travelled to Khao I Dang camp, where they had to sneak in because the camp was no longer accepting refugees.

Sarin Ouch (Interview HOF151 2020) remembers that when the Vietnamese army invaded, he feared both the Vietnamese army and the Khmer Rouge. "The Vietnamese would shoot at you because they don't know if you are Khmer Rouge or civilian." He decided to escape to Thailand and trekked through the jungle for two months followed by the Khmer Rouge. On the way, he and others foraged for food, and some died eating poisonous mushrooms. Before the Thai border there is a rapid river, and many people drowned. He crossed the hundred-metre-wide river by placing air in a plastic bag and using it to float. Others found pieces of wood. Sarin remembers how difficult it was to determine when they crossed into Thailand, and the tremendous relief when they saw the Thai vegetation, cars, and infrastructure. There were tents and they were given food – rice, chicken, and salt. He felt, "Oh, I am alive."

Prom Sorn (Interview HOF025 2019), who had retreated to the jungle when Pol Pot came into power, returned to his village and found that he had nothing. His land and home had been occupied. He headed to the Thai border, and the UNHCR brought him to Khao I Dang camp. In June 1979, after the Vietnamese invaded, Sovann Un (Interview HOF078 2019) decided to leave Cambodia with his family. They stayed at the Thai border for one month waiting for aid from the UN. They were pushed back out of concern that they were communist Khmers, and no UN aid had arrived. He recalls how the Thai had dumped busloads of people over the mountain, leaving them to descend a route full of landmines.

After the Vietnam invasion, Bokhara Bun (Interview HOF005 2019), who was ten years old, decided to escape with an uncle. He comments on how a child of that age during the war was already very mature with survival skills. They saw no future under Vietnamese occupation and were afraid that the Khmer Rouge would return. There was freedom of movement, and they managed to reach the Thai border using false papers. Trucks were allowed to bring merchandise across the border, so they crossed in 1982 by getting a few chickens and joining a group of merchants. It was monsoon season, and they paid a guide to cross the border during combat between the Vietnamese army and the Khmer Rouge. He describes a harrowing scene of how they dodged live fire running across the battlefield, holding a live chicken in each hand. On the other side, he found he had clenched his fists so hard that the chickens were dead. They bribed their way into Khao I Dang camp. He still has nightmares of these events, and he cannot tell his children of the details of his experiences because, he says, he does not have the courage to go through it again.

Many families had lost members to overwork, starvation, disease, or execution. After the end of the Khmer Rouge regime, Minar Chhor (Interview HOF077 2019) discovered how many had been massacred and realized how lucky his family was to be together and alive. "We were one of the luckiest families because it was only after meeting other families and friends that we realized that many of my parents' friends lost many family members ... If the father was a soldier, it was not only the soldier who was eliminated but the whole family, even the babies." The family decided to leave the country and after two to three months crossed the Thai border at Surin. They were immediately taken to a well-organized refugee camp and given food and clothing. Minar's father was a doctor and was able to connect with some friends in France. After two months in the camp, they were selected by France and left for a transit camp for another month. They left for France around mid-October 1979.

Life in the Refugee Camps

After escaping to Thailand, the refugees found themselves in one of the camps along the border. The camps varied in size and in the resources they provided. Khao I Dang camp, one of the largest, was constructed by the UNHCR on orders of the Thai government and opened in November 1979. By July 1980, the population of the camp was 136,000. The camp included a hospital, a temple, and a Christian church, and many huts, and became one of the most important holding centres. It was situated thirty kilometres north of Aranyaprathet and fifteen kilometres from the Thai-Cambodian border. By the mid-1980s, there were at least twenty camps near or on the Thai-Cambodian border with a population of about 300,000. There were several transit centres in Bangkok (Vickery

1990). Other camps included Sakeo I, set up in October 1979; eventually the population of 28,000 was moved to a new site at Sakeo II. Kamput closed in 1981.

Some refugees, like Bunkorn Yun (Interview HOF035 2019), spent several months imprisoned by the military on arrival. One night, his camp was attacked by communist Thai, and he was injured by a rocket and sent to an infirmary in a police camp further in the interior. He was allowed to do small jobs for the police and saved enough money for transportation to Bangkok. From there, the French embassy sent him to Surin refugee camp where he remained for almost one year before being accepted by Canada.

Kong Bun (Interview HOF124 2019) arrived at the Khao I Dang refugee camp in 1979 shortly after it had been opened. "There was only a UNHCR office and a hospital hall. Other than that, it was an empty field with bushes at the foot of the mountain." He and his two siblings and two cousins were given a tent and a tarp to tie to a tree branch, mosquito nets, a blanket, and water buckets. "We got a lot of rice to eat, and we were no longer eating porridge." Later they were provided bamboo to build a home. During his stay at Khao I Dang camp, he worked as a police district officer doing surveillance and then with the hospital assisting people with their medication and recording patient names and taking weight measurements. "I worked for a while until the camp got too crowded and they had to split the camp." "I volunteered to go to Kamput camp where all my family were going." He moved to Kamput camp until it closed. He reports that there were many robberies in the camps. He then returned to Khao I Dang until the end of 1987 when he was accepted to come to Canada.

Getting into a camp was not always easy. Samath Yi (Interview HOF127 2019) had to sneak across the Thai-Cambodian border into Khao I Dang camp, and the guide made them hide until he spoke with the guards. "If someone tried to sneak in, they would shoot. They would shoot to kill. It didn't matter who you were. For the children, we held their mouths shut. We couldn't have them cry … we didn't have the money so they wouldn't let us in." Finally they entered, had to pay 500 baht each for the family to stay, and were given a small dwelling to live in. His wife's family was unable to gain entry and were in a new refugee camp by the border.

Although his brother-in-law sponsored him and the family to come to Canada, his leg injury created a problem. "They said I couldn't go to Canada because of the heavy snow … It would be too slippery to walk." He was sent to Bangkok for rehabilitation and then back to another refugee camp for approximately a month before the family finally made it to Montreal, sponsored by family.

From 1980 to 1984, Saphan Noun (Interview HOF125 2019) lived in the Khao I Dang camp and did sewing to earn a living and also had a small grocery business. She found the experience was very chaotic and confusing as they applied to different countries. Although her husband was a doctor he was not believed. Suddenly they were sent to the Chunbory camp and at one point US immigration officers made false accusations that their second child was not their own – "the second child who was born during the regime and had shorter than normal hands and legs." They were accepted by France and Canada and chose Canada in 1984.

Chamroeun Lay (Interview HOF011 2019) describes Khao I Dang camp as "another big prison" surrounded by a three-metre barbed-wire fence. "If you go out you have to ask permission or you would be shot by a Thai soldier." He arrived in 1979, registered with UNHCR as a refugee, and was guaranteed a food ration of some rice and either fish or chicken. The worst was not having sufficient drinking water and the lack of toilet facilities. Chamroeun began working for a team from the Canadian embassy and was immediately accepted to come to Canada. He explains that most Cambodians applied to the US because they knew little about Canada. Stories about Canada being an extremely cold country in the wintertime circulated in the camp. "They say that Canada is a cold country – in the wintertime they do not work with time to relax – they work in the summertime."

Sorpong Peou was successful in joining his family in Khao I Dang and was recruited to be a primary school teacher. He learned English on his own and became the main radio operator with the UNHCR office connecting with other Cambodian radio operators. His life also was changed spiritually. "Khao I Dang was the place where I became a Christian … My life is full of twists and turns and not knowing where I am going … I don't know where I am going but God knows what he is doing … one door closes, another opens."

It was March 1982 when Charlie Lim (Interview HOF024 2019) arrived at Khao I Dang camp and he and a friend immediately registered as brothers since they both had the same last name. Since birth dates were not regularly kept, he had the strategy of choosing "the year of his birth to be younger and eligible for a chance to go to school when going to a third country." He was finally accepted by Canada and arrived on 6 March 1983.

There was an active black market in Khao I Dang, but it came with some danger. Prom Sorn (Interview HOF025 2019) explains: "If you want to make money … you go buy some stuff, when they catch you, they are going to take some, maybe shoot you. The people who have a brother, a mother, they send them money to buy something – they can buy anything. They have good food but for me, no." To supplement the UNHCR rations, Prom, who had little money, would buy noodles or rice from Thailand to sell inside the camp. However, he had to deal with the corruption of Thai soldiers who demanded a cut. He could not speak Thai and often faced the brutality of the soldiers. In 1984–85, after the Thai government closed access to the camps, people would come without identification. Prom remembers that during this time a lot of people died because of brutality by the Thai soldiers as they searched for "illegal" refugees.

Similarly, Bokhara Bun (Interview HOF005 2019) and his uncle bribed their way into the camp and stayed two years. He found miserable conditions. Water and rice were highly rationed, but they were able to get a bit of meat from UN organizations. He studied French and English and his uncle who spoke French worked as an interpreter with the UNHCR, and within eight months of their arrival at the camp, they went to a transit camp to get their medicals and prepare to come to Canada. It was here that he met a missionary priest who was giving orientation classes on life in Canada. The priest later became his adoptive father and helped him to settle in Canada.

Nhem Pheap (Interview HOF131 2020) and his family spent eleven years in Thai camps including SAS Keo I, SAS Keo II, and Khao I Dang camps. He was trained on multiculturalism and the customs of different places, and he was learning English. His hopes of coming to Canada were shattered when the family's application was rejected because his brother (who had been born in the jungle during their escape) was physically and mentally disabled. They ended up staying another two years. Fearing that he would be returned to Cambodia, Nhem Pheap applied to New Zealand and was approved. At the same time, Canadian immigration officers assisted with the documentation and finally the family was accepted. He gives thanks to "all those people kind in their heart."

Those in the refugee camps took advantage of the opportunity to learn English. Sophal Vonn (Interview HOF031 2019) worked in the orphanage while in Chonburi camp and took advantage of the opportunity to learn English. She was in the refugee camp from 1981 to 1983. In 1981, at age nineteen, she met and married her husband. Others also realized that knowing English would be of benefit. Similarly, Soth Chhlam (Interview HOF099 2019), who spent several years in the camps, found a library of English books and would read them every night. He worked in the camp hospital, and he remembers by name one doctor helping him with English. When picked by the Canadian government, not knowing much about Canada, he thinks, "Any country that take me out of hell here, I go, and thanks to them."

Dim Meas (Interview HOF030 2019) and his family were in transition for a long period, and he was one of the last to arrive in Canada after spending the years from 1982 to 1984 on the Thai-Cambodian border, 1984 to 1987 in Khao I Dang, and two years at Chonburi. He arrived in Montreal on 23 January 1989.

Prom Sorn (Interview HOF025 2019) and his family arrived in Montreal in January 1986 and were government sponsored. Many who arrived in the winter were not prepared for the cold. He recalls that he was given a winter jacket, pants, and boots. But it was so warm in the airplane that he placed them under the seat. When he got off the plane and realized how cold it was, he raced back to get his winter clothes and was stopped by security. The worst was behind them but the struggle to adapt to a new country was about to begin.

10

Cambodian Resettlement in Canada: Perseverance, Courage, and Hope

Departure and Arrival

People who lived through traumatic circumstances began to create new lives. There were mixed feelings of joy, sadness, and fear of the unknown when leaving the refugee camps in Thailand. For Dourn Sam (Interview HOF006 2019), when the plane took off, he screamed loudly in Khmer: "Yes, I have freedom … I am released, and I am flying." Feelings of relief were soon replaced by uncertainty in relocating to a foreign country with language, cultural, and geographic differences and initial isolation. Before he arrived, Kong Bun (Interview HOF124 2019) took a course for newcomers to Canada and heard it mentioned that it was daylight for six months and dark for six months and wondered how he would survive.

Positive Impact of Sponsorship

Overall, those who were privately sponsored quickly felt a connection and were often less isolated than those government sponsored. Bun Na Un (Interview HOF067 2019) and his wife, who came with a group of seven hundred, said that they were met at Montreal's Mirabel Airport by a Cambodian organization and brought to a military base for three days. Their private sponsor picked them up and they settled in a furnished apartment. "They gave us clothing, shirts and shoes." Bun Na felt that he did not know how to live in such a cold climate and asked to be returned to Cambodia, but after a month he felt more at home. He speaks highly of his sponsor, a member of the Italian association, who would drive them to school, and even stayed with his wife and child for a week to help them. "If there was something we did not know, they had a Cambodian tutor come to assist us. They told us that the home rented for us is to be treated like it was ours, and for us not to hesitate to use anything." Reflecting, Bun Na remarks that acquiring language skills was the most difficult. It took around six to seven months before he felt comfortable shopping.

Samath Yi (Interview HOF127 2019) reflects on how, coming from a hot climate, they didn't know how to warm themselves. "If the sun was shining brightly, we assumed it was hot, so we stepped out, but it was freezing … They informed us about how to protect ourselves from the weather, but we didn't know better." Getting to the next bus stop often meant slipping on the ice.

Settlement Challenges

When Dourn Sam (Interview HOF006 2019) arrived in Montreal in 1979 at age twenty-five as a single man, he was housed in an army base for the night. He remembers having difficulty with the shower, not knowing how to regulate hot and cold. He took the bus to Ottawa the next morning and lived with Father MacNamara for one year. He went to school for six months and then worked in a factory. After five years he went to work in hospital food services, retiring after thirty-three years. He reflects and recalls that it was a "bumpy road, the new life was not easy – sad to leave my country, my culture, but I had no choice." Being one of the first Cambodian refugees, he could not easily find ethnic food. He also encountered some racism in the workplace. In 1986, he married a Cambodian woman and now has two children. Neang Thong (Interview HOF032 2019) also arrived in Ottawa in 1979 sponsored by a Catholic church. Although she was separated from her mother, who was in France, she made a life in Canada with her husband, and they have two daughters and one son. She is thankful for the support of the Canadian government and her church sponsor. Although she attended language classes, learning

English was one of her biggest challenges. She has been back to Cambodia three times.

The challenges of living in a different culture and country soon became paramount. Chamroeun Lay (Interview HOF011 2019) arrived in Montreal on 17 November 1982, "looked through the window and it was all white." He was housed in a hotel with others. "When you walk in there you look like refugees … and I remember perfectly the indoor pool and people taking a plunge in there … so cold." He immediately encountered the challenges of new culture and customs, language, and the social system. When he got to his room, he wondered how to use the television, how to regulate hot and cold water in the bathroom, and how to use the sheets and blankets on the bed: "Should I sleep on the bed or peel those sheets off?" The next day they travelled to Ottawa and were put up in the Beacon Arms Hotel for several weeks. They immediately faced other challenges. They were given a key to their room but did not know how to find the room or use the elevator. He soon learned that 2040 meant room 40 on the twentieth floor. They were given pocket money for food but didn't know what to order. They saw "hot dog" on the menu and thought, "These people eat dog? … So many things to learn." They wanted to buy rice and went to Chinatown and met the next challenge of riding the bus and getting off at the right stop. He remembers learning by trial and error and at times thinking, "Why did I come to this country?" Initially, their only support was each other. At first, they were afraid to venture out. "We were suppressed too long by the regime … traumatized." And there was no temple where they could gather. For some, the experiences took a toll on their health. For Saphan Noun (Interview HOF125 2019), who had lost all members of her family, the memories were too great, and she had episodes of fainting. She was eventually told that "it was post-trauma" – she had post-traumatic stress disorder.

Similarly, Channa Kong (Interview HOF123 2019) experienced challenges when she arrived in Hamilton on 13 October 1987 and was housed in a hotel. She didn't know how to use the elevator so used the stairs. "There was a free breakfast, but we didn't know. Breakfast was Eggo pancakes … I fed my oldest the pancake, but she would beg for rice." There were no Asian grocers in Hamilton at that time and she did not know where to buy rice.

Those who were government sponsored often faced isolation, loneliness, and depression. Kong Bun (Interview HOF124 2019) was placed in a hotel in St Catharine's for three months because the government had difficulty finding him a home. "I was depressed while staying in the hotel. I looked outside through the windows, and I saw no leaves on the trees. It was January. I thought, if all the trees died, why not just cut them down? We didn't know that in spring the leaves would return." He had no contact with anyone other than a Cambodian man at Manpower who was a friend from the camp. He provided help to other Cambodians living in the hotel. Although Kong received money from Manpower for food, there were no cooking facilities in the hotel. He purchased food at the Chinese grocer and cooked the rice at his friend's home. He was sent for language classes but found it difficult to concentrate. For others, settlement often meant a change in eating habits.

Samath Yi (Interview HOF127 2019) remembers fear of embarrassment. "When I went to work, I didn't eat rice, I'd make sandwiches. Our food is distinctively different … [It] has an odour. So we would pack sandwiches." Yorp Sok (Interview HOF128 2019) found it difficult not knowing the language and recalls the slippery conditions because of the freezing rain. Going to school for the required six months was frustrating because she did not even know the alphabet.

Adapting to Canada

Sovann Un (Interview HOF078 2019) and his family arrived at Longue-Pointe military base in Montreal on 22 January 1980 and then relocated to a village near Quebec City. They were sponsored by United Way. The children started school and he and his wife took French courses at the language institute. By summer he began earning money to send to his brothers and sisters in Cambodia. There was a demand for machinists, and he started professional training courses at a CEGEP in Quebec City. He finished the course in 1982 and the family moved to Montreal for work opportunities. He found a job in an electroplating company and has worked there for thirty-two years. He is still in contact with his sponsorship group, and they visit him in Montreal. As a former teacher, he and his wife believe in education and have supported their children through university. Sovann, coming from a poor family of farmers in Cambodia, established "a small charity organization that has built eighteen schools in Cambodia and sponsored high school students to help them go to university."

Sorpong Peou came to Ottawa in 1982 and immediately explored the possibility of attending university even though he had not completed high school. After completing two courses at the adult high school, he was admitted to the University of Waterloo and travelled there by bus. It was the beginning of his academic career, and he is now an internationally noted professor of global peace and security. His daughter also went to the University of Waterloo: "one went in as a nobody, one in as a star." Sorpong reflects on his life and states, "I am Canadian with Cambodian background."

Charlie Lim (Interview HOF024 2019) was sponsored by a Seventh Day Adventist church group and arrived in Vancouver on 16 March 1983. When noodle houses opened, Charlie Lim used his noodle cooking skills while he was attending ESL classes. After one year in Vancouver, he moved to Toronto. In 1990 he relocated to Ottawa and soon after got married. He studied by correspondence and read a lot of newspapers. He remembers working hard for twenty years and now he operates a business with sixty to seventy employees. He is proud of his son and daughter who both have a university education. Soth Chhlam (Interview HOF099 2019) arrived in Winnipeg in late August 1989 and was instructed to buy warm boots and coats and warned about the weather to come. He immediately went to school, but in the middle of grade 12 heard that his family in Cambodia needed more assistance and he relocated to a mushroom farm in Hamilton to make more money. He later moved to Newmarket for a better paying job and was able to purchase a home. He was married in 1993. He is proud of his daughter and son, who have both finished university. "Canada is my land too. I feel that I am Canadian."

Bokhara Bun (Interview HOF005 2019) arrived in Windsor with his uncle in April 1984. Because of the orientation course he had high expectations of what Canada was like and was disappointed in what he found. Social services provided one bedroom at the Holiday Inn for about two months and registered him in ESL classes. Other than that, they were left on their own. "Asian food was difficult to find, especially rice besides Uncle Ben's." His uncle met someone, became engaged, and moved to the United States with his fiancée. However, the priest whom he met in Cambodia returned to Canada, picked him up in Windsor, and brought him to Winnipeg. That's where, at age twelve or thirteen, his life changed for the better. He had "a nice bed and a room at the rectory of the Archbishop of St Boniface." The priest enrolled him in a very welcoming French school. School replaced family for him – he was welcomed and felt like an adopted brother. He communicated by finding words in a French-Cambodian dictionary, studied hard, and passed eighth grade along with everyone else. His photographic memory helped him to continue through high school and to enter the College of St Boniface (of the University of Manitoba). Bokhara then joined the family of a close friend whose father was in the Armed Forces and was transferred to Hull, Quebec. He continued with his education and has been with the federal government since 1999 in information network systems.

Despite the initial challenges, Cambodian refugees quickly found employment and thrived. Yorp Sok (Interview HOF128 2019) had three jobs and "no time to sleep … I worked ninety hours a week. At the beginning it was factory work. I did spooling for sewing, winding the needle. I had another job which was cleaning a military base. The job started from 7 a.m. to 3 p.m. The cleaning job started from 4 p.m. to 12 a.m." She also took care of children to earn money. Her second child was born in 1988. Manpower gave her $500 to buy winter clothing. She went with a friend to buy the children's clothing. Her friend's children were all boys, and she did not know that there were clothes for girls and clothes for boys. Later looking at photographs her daughter would laugh and ask why she had to wear boy's clothing. Her first job was in a shoe company at $7 an hour. She made additional money for each pair of finished shoes and could make $100 a night. She became a citizen in 1992 because she wanted to vote. She had her driver's licence and brought her children to the library twice a week. She reflects and says that not knowing the language was one of the hardest settlement challenges.

Samath Yi (Interview HOF127 2019) arrived in Montreal in July 1981 and immediately began to work as a tailor. After five years, he was proud to buy a home for the family. He eventually opened his own successful tailor shop in a mall and worked there for fifteen years. It was many years before he felt totally integrated. "The moment I knew I was comfortable was when I was able to pick up the language and interact with other Canadians. It's the happiest moment when you can interact in their language. If we needed to take the bus, we knew where. If we needed to take the metro, we knew where. If we needed to go grocery shopping, we knew where. We were able to go back and forth, and that's when we knew that we were settled. It was from 1988 to 1990 that I began to get comfortable." Samath Yi sees Canada as a country one can thrive in and is thankful for it. He calls it the best country in the world, backed by his travels around the world. He also emphasizes how Canadians are accommodating to those with disabilities, especially himself. He mentions that in Canada, nearly all restrooms are free of charge, which says a lot about the generosity of Canadians.

Sophal Vonn (Interview HOF031 2019) arrived in April of 1983 and, like many government-assisted refugees, was placed in a hotel. She found the cold to be isolating. "I felt so lonely at that time." She found companionship in her fellow refugees, both Vietnamese and Cambodian. She was expecting her first child. "I could only go back to school [English classes] for three months. I could not take the bus because I had morning sickness all the time and keep on throwing up." After the birth of her daughter, she was told that her "English was good enough" and worked peeling and preparing vegetables. Then she thought: "I don't think that I am going to do this because it's a good chance for me to go back to school, so I put my daughter in daycare. I went back to high school." Sophal then went to college after the birth of her second child. She then earned a certificate from Algonquin College in their accounting program. She is now proud of the educational accomplishments of her children. She has been back to Cambodia three times. "Everything is changed. I don't think that I could recall where I lived." Her mother and aunt have passed away. "It is not so easy to go back."

Many interviewees said they were thankful for support from Canada. Bun Na Un (Interview HOF067 2019) states: "I want to thank Canada for allowing people to gain citizenship after three years of living. Thank you, Canada, for your contribution to freedom." Dim Meas (Interview HOF030 2019) quickly settled in Ottawa with his family. His sponsor gave him a bicycle and he creatively added a long stick so he could hang the many grocery bags while he transported them home. He has maintained contact with an extended family and every Sunday his four brothers and families get together.

Nhem Pheap (Interview HOF131 2019) was twenty-two years old when he and his family of six arrived in Edmonton in November 1990. They stayed in a hotel for one week and then they were moved into an apartment. He thanks those who came before him to assist with settlement challenges. He quickly began working as a carpenter building and restoring houses. He comments that life is good here, "but not enough to erase what I saw." He is thankful for all of the countries with people "who opened their hearts."

Charlie Lim (Interview HOF024 2019) ends his interview with a powerful statement of why the Canadian government should accept and welcome refugees: "I hope that anyone who sees this interview realizes that many people need help, that is my wish."

At Home in Canada, Remembering Cambodia

For Minar Chhor (Interview HOF077 2019), his settlement in Canada followed a circuitous route. After graduating from engineering in France and working there for three years, he had the opportunity to work in Montreal and decided to stay. He has never felt like an outsider and credits Canada's emphasis on multiculturalism. "There is the Canadian charter which respects a lot of beliefs on multiculturalism." When asked if there was anything that he would like to share with Canadian youth, Minar, overcome with emotion, states that "war is a great tragedy that must be avoided at all costs. But you can still remake your life … All this is very important because in life the most important thing is that someone is reaching out to you to get back on track." As a Southeast Asian refugee, he feels fortunate. "We have been welcomed and we have been able to integrate well … we have contributed to the richness of art and to the economy of the host country … Our children have also contributed a lot. They are proud Canadians, and I am proud of them too." As for speaking about the past tragedies to young people, Minar replies, "they understand it, but they don't feel it." He credits successful settlement to "perseverance, courage and not forgetting where you come from and always keeping hope."

The inspiring and poignant accounts of survival of those interviewed reflect their tremendous strength and resilience. They persevered and worked hard to overcome their past hardships and create a future for their children. For many the settlement period was difficult. Bokhara Bun (Interview HOF005 2019) suggests that those assisting with refugee settlement could have been much better prepared and more knowledgeable about Cambodians. And he feels that there is still a need for Cambodians to organize and be recognized as a culture and mentions that there is no real reminder of the Khmer Rouge genocide in Canada.

Settlement in Canada does not mean forgetting Cambodia. Many, such as Bunkorn Yun (Interview HOF035 2019), sent money back to the camps to help fellow Cambodians who had few resources for food. Most have travelled back to Cambodia and many still have family there. For Chamroeun Lay (Interview HOF011 2019) it was during a trip back when he realized that he was fully integrated and is now a Canadian. In Canada, Bokhara Bun created a group to help young Cambodians face obstacles and connect with the employment market through an online job bank system at the Department of Employment. After retirement, he looks forward to helping young Cambodians in Canada to appreciate their heritage.

Many of those interviewed are actively working to preserve their culture in Canada. Bunkorn Yun is secretary and former vice-president of the Cambodian Association, which opened a centre for cultural events, cultural dances, and shows to promote Cambodian culture to the public. They celebrate their New Year with all the traditions.

Although settled in Canada, like many others, Mean Bonn Taing (Interview HOF037 2019) reflects on his life in Cambodia and the Cambodian genocide. "One question remains in my head: Why did the Khmer Rouge do this to us? … Why kill your own people?"

11

Against the Odds: Three Cambodian Refugee Stories of Survival

What follows are the summarized accounts of three of the Cambodians who participated in the Hearts of Freedom project. Their experiences are unique, yet they have some common elements. Both Rivaux Lay and Paulie Phoeuk survived the forced return to Cambodia from Thailand by the Thai soldiers down Preah Vihear Mountain – a remarkable feat as profiled in the film *Ghost Mountain*.[1]

Rivaux Lay was an adult when he escaped; Paulie Pheouk was an adolescent when he escaped and was still a minor on arrival to Canada. Vichuta Ly was a teenager when she arrived in Canada.

Rivaux Lay

The quotes in this story are from an interview (Interview HOF003 2019).

Rivaux Lay was born in Phnom Penh into a middle-class family. His parents owned several rental apartments and several businesses. He used to have his own personal servant who would prepare everything for him. Life was good and peaceful before General Lon Nol overthrew King Norodom Sihanouk in 1970. Fighting broke out everywhere; many young people joined the military trying to defend what they thought was their

1 Filmmaker James Taing talks about the 1979 massacre of survivors of Pol Pot's Killing Fields along the Thailand-Cambodia border and about his documentary film *Ghost Mountain* in C-Span Q&A, 2020, "James Taing," accessed 29 July 2024, https://www.c-span.org/video/?476652–1/qa-james-taing.

freedom and democracy. During that time, there were battles closer to the capital, sometimes around five kilometres from his house. He could see bullets and rockets and United States warplanes dropping bombs. After the planes left, the Khmer Rouge sent rockets into the capital.

On 17 April 1975, when Cambodia fell to the Khmer Rouge, a convoy of soldiers came into the capital and ordered everyone to lay down their weapons and leave for a couple days because Americans would be bombing the city.

"No one knew where to go." The Khmer Rouge confiscated cars, trucks, and motorcycles from everyone, so they had to travel on foot. Rivaux's family joined others on the overcrowded roads, taking only what they could carry on their backs. "It was chaotic … everyone panicked and sometimes some people separated from each other. I was lucky because we have a small family, we stick together."

Two months later the Khmer Rouge ordered everyone to stop moving, leave the roads, find a place in the villages, and stay there. Anyone caught travelling would be arrested. Rivaux's family rushed to Kompong Cham to meet his grandmother there. "They put us in the jungle, and we had to make our own house from bamboo." The house they built was five square metres for six people. He and his brother were twelve and fourteen and had never built anything in their life, but they were forced to learn and adapt.

Then, six months later, they were sent to Komputang, and "that is where the hardship happened." They were treated like prisoners, had little freedom, and were stripped of all belongings, except a few clothes. "I never saw a member of my own family." Family members were separated into different work units to do hard labour, such as farming, building dams, and digging canals, so if anyone planned on escaping, they had to think about the consequences to their relatives. Only seniors and those with medical problems stayed in the villages.

"During that time, it taught me everything on how to survive. … We work very hard and sometimes we start from eight o'clock in the morning until twelve midnight and break for about a half an hour for the whole day." Overwork and starvation took their toll and to be able to survive Rivaux had to forage for food. "Any living thing we eat." Villagers knew how to find plants and wild potatoes in the jungle to add to what they had, but they would not show him, so Rivaux would sneak behind them and steal their knowledge.

Not long after he got there, he got malaria and was sent back to the village for treatment. There was no medicine except home remedies such as the roots of plants that were ineffective. He had a fever and almost died.

You could not trust anyone, including your closest friend, because "they would sell you for a bowl of rice … I lived in fear every day." Saying anything against the regime could result in your disappearance. He was asked frequently what he did in the past and any inconsistent answers could result in his death. Educated people, anyone who used to work for the previous government, and soldiers were targeted. "When they asked me to write something, I used my right hand (I am left-handed)."

At one point, he was forced to work from 4:00 a.m. to midnight. He was so skinny, "you can see all the bones in my body at that time." But that did not stop him from trying his best to earn his spot in the best group in that unit. He carried more than one hundred kilograms on his back every day. If anyone tried to escape and got caught, they would bring them back and make them dig their own grave, and they would be killed in front of everyone to warn others from doing the same. Some feared the possibility and hanged themselves.

One evening in late 1977 after Rivaux came home from work, his top commander called him in and asked if he was sick. He could not disagree with his superior, so he answered, "Yes." The commander said, "Pack up and go to the hospital now." He took his clothes bag, hopped on a food truck, and was off to the hospital. A few weeks later his second commander went to the hospital and asked the doctor to release him from the hospital, but the doctor refused. The second commander tried a couple of times more to take him out and the doctor continued to refuse to release him. Six or seven months later, the doctor finally released him from his care. He did not go back to his unit but was placed with the province's construction group. There, he met his best friend who whispered to him that he was so lucky that he was not at the unit a few months ago because twenty-nine people were sent to jail and executed, and his name was the thirtieth. He then knew the reason his top commander sent him to the hospital in a rush and the second commander tried very hard to take him back. He could not thank his commander and the doctor for saving his life because at that time, if someone was caught helping others, he or she would be in trouble.

He became a state worker with better food and regular work hours. There, he saw horse-drawn carts driving from the jail to a burial place, covered only with mats. Sometimes corpses fell out of the carts, but he pretended that he saw nothing. Rivaux was humiliated, tortured, witnessed many killings, and was targeted because of his Chinese heritage. He survived two execution attempts. "I was so lucky, every time someone wanted to kill me, someone else saved me."

When Vietnam invaded Cambodia in 1979, there was a powerful song: "Vietnamese are the enemy of Cambodia." Rivaux took up arms and went to the front line: "I forgot what they did to me the last four years. It is time for me to defend my country." However, he did not have a chance fighting against Soviet-made tanks and had to run away from three front lines. He finally gave up and went back to his family.

After his experience with the Khmer Rouge, he did not want to live under another communist regime, so in May 1979, he and the family escaped into Thailand and stayed at Nong Chan camp. One month after he got there, the Thai government sent all refugees from the camp back to Cambodia through Preah Vihear Mountain.

At Preah Vihear Mountain, Thai solders handed refugees over to the "Red Thai" (communist Thai) and "let them do the dirty work for them." They were forced down the steep escarpment at gunpoint. The mountain was littered with landmines, and they were not provided with food or water. Some Thai people knew the conditions that they would face and tried to hand out rice and water to the refugees along the way; he got ten kilograms of rice from them. Those who came earlier stepped on mines and died instantly. They had to follow each other's footsteps and dared not pass because they feared landmines. "We could walk only five metres a day." He was forced to sleep with corpses along the way. It took them close to three weeks to get down that mountain. They finally met Vietnamese soldiers who gave them some bread powder and helped clear the mines to make a path, allowing them to walk faster down the mountain. What the Thai government did to the refugees was inhumane. The CIA estimates that 10,000 people died on that mountain (Kamm 1979).

It took Rivaux one month before he reached Mongkol Borey, Battambang. Shortly after, his mother led the family to Thailand again, and this time they stayed in Khao I Dang refugee camp. His mother hired a human smuggler to bring Rivaux and his brother to Aranyaprathet camp in early 1980. He started learning English there and worked with the Catholic Church providing nutrition to children and pregnant women. He also worked as an interpreter to help refugees with their needs and as a supervisor with the US Department of Immigration. In mid-1981, they closed Aranyaprathet camp, and he was sent to Surin, where he helped provide health care services to refugees. He married a brief time later his first girlfriend, Thavay Senghirann. When the Surin camp closed in 1982, he moved to Phanat Nikhom Chonburi camp where he worked for a US agency that prepared people for settlement in the US.

Finally, in 1983 he was accepted by Canadian Immigration through government sponsorship, and he arrived in Ottawa on 6 May 1983 with his wife and baby. They stayed in a hotel for one month before moving to an apartment. It was a difficult and lonely time because they had no friends. His wife cried every day and wanted to go back to Cambodia. There were not many Cambodians in Ottawa at the time and there were no services for new immigrants. Getting around was exceedingly difficult, and he would walk a long distance carrying a forty-five-kilogram bag of rice and groceries from the only local Chinese store because he did not know how to take a bus. Life improved after more Cambodian families moved into the apartment building. Throughout his settlement, he received six months of ESL classes from Algonquin College, but his wife was not able to take any ESL classes because her English was so weak.

He struggled even though he knew some English, so he felt that he had to step up and help others. He became an ESL teacher in 1988 and a community outreach worker with Somerset West Community and Health Centre in 1989. He provided cultural interpretation and counselling to Cambodian, Laotian, and Thai populations and worked as a multicultural liaison officer in the Ottawa District School Board and with the Ottawa Immigration Services Organization in 1990.

Rivaux has been involved with several organizations including the Cambodian Association. He is dedicated to preserving Cambodian culture and was the art director and founder of Selepak Culture Association, a Cambodian traditional dance troupe in Ottawa. In the interview, Rivaux reflected on his experiences of survival: "If you asked me to tell my story ten or fifteen years ago, you may see me crying through the whole tape" because the pain was so fresh in his memory. He hates war because nothing good comes out of it. Many people lost everything including their lives and the impact did not stop after the war ended. It continues for many years or generations after. He lost everything, his childhood, his property, his country, and everything that he loved, because of war.

He was separated from his parents since he was fourteen, was tortured, starved, and almost killed by the Khmer Rouge. He endured many struggles as a refugee, almost died on the Preah Vihear Mountain, and went through struggles in refugee camps before coming to Canada. Rivaux feels lucky to be alive.

Paulie Phoeuk

The quotes in this story are from an interview (Interview HOF038 2019).

Paulie Phoeuk was born in 1963 in a small village into a large family of six sisters, one brother, and a niece and nephew who also lived with them. They had a big house with a large property. He went to school with the monks in the pagoda. However, he was only twelve years old when his education was interrupted by the civil war, when Lon Nol soldiers were fighting the Khmer Rouge. Paulie was unable to continue his education and comments, "My generation was born at the wrong time in the wrong country."

In 1969, the Khmer Rouge had killed his brother for his property. When the Khmer Rouge, claiming victory, captured the capital in 1975 and took over his village, the family escaped to Battambang Province. The schools were closed; children were immediately separated from their parents and parents from each other. They were all sent to collective farms. His father was a tailor and worked for the Khmer Rouge and his mother was a cook. From 1976 to 1979 he did not see them, and as a child, he needed to survive on his own. "If I don't steal, I die."

Paulie was ordered to dig canals and work in the rice field. He remembers having nothing to eat and getting very thin. As he saw friends dying, "every day I think, When is my turn to die?" He had to steal food to survive, and one time was caught and beaten. Another time he was shackled with twenty other people but, being so small at ten years old, he was able to slip out of the shackles to go to the bathroom and was confronted by the Khmer Rouge.

In 1979 when the Vietnamese overthrew the Khmer Rouge, he escaped to Thailand with the family and reached a UNHCR camp which provided rice, fish, and chicken. He had to make his own shelter to sleep. There were no proper toilets. "Thai soldiers don't treat us well. Look down on us." After ten days they were told that "thirty buses were coming to pick us up – we would be going to a third country. We were happy." But instead, after a twenty-four-hour trip from Nong Chan to Preah Vihear, they were "dumped like garbage" down the steep mountain while Thai soldiers shot at them.

He remembers the difficulty of going down the steep escarpment and seeing the bodies of people who had gone before and had set off landmines. He saw a lot of people "floating on the water, died because of the minefields." He had to "push away blood to get clean water to drink, step on dead bodies and sleep with dead people." Finally, the family saw Vietnamese soldiers who picked them up and guided them by cutting leaves for paths where there were no land mines. They walked for "four days in the mountains following the Vietnamese." It took another month to get to Battambang. After three months back in Battambang, his mother feared escaping again, so Paulie escaped to Thailand accompanied by one relative, but otherwise as a minor on his own. The main reason was to find food to eat.

He managed to get across the Thai border again and entered Khao I Dang refugee camp. He was then placed in an orphanage centre, where he lived in a tent. The food was good and every morning he received an injection for malaria. In November 1980, he was chosen to go to the US sponsored by a family in Iowa. But already at age seventeen he was past the age of fostering. As an unaccompanied minor, he had little control over where he went. The refugee orphanage camp treated him very well. It was "heaven," "paradise" after what he had experienced. He remembers having a blanket placed over him at night and was so grateful for the caring kindness. "I'd like to say thank you." He quickly learned English, worked for the UN, and then went to Chonburi camp in preparation for going to a third country. There he worked for a Canadian immigration officer who asked him if he wanted to go to Canada and supported him in arranging the paperwork. He was shown a film about Canada and chose Toronto because he saw several Asian people in the city. He had no way of informing his family of his departure.

Paulie's settlement challenges began on the flight to Canada, and he recalls an embarrassing event on the airplane. Although he had read a book on how to use the washroom during the flight, he had a perplexing situation. When he opened the door, he saw a reflection of himself in the mirror and said "OK, sorry" and stood outside thinking that he had disturbed someone. After a long wait, he repeated entering one more time and realized that the reflection was his own. Also, he was hesitant to flush the toilet or touch anything on the plane, fearing that "whole plane could be destroyed by you."

Paulie arrived at Montreal's Mirabel Airport on 24 April 1983 and was given a jacket and boots. Looking out the window at the bare trees, he thought, "This country has a lot of dead wood to cook food." He travelled to Toronto and was placed with five Vietnamese youth in one room in the Shelbourne Hotel. They were all minors, and they took turns sleeping. "Cleaner never had a chance to clean the room." When going out together they would all hold hands to cross the street. He tried to find rice besides "Uncle Sam" (Uncle Ben's) and set out to Chinatown using the subway, counting the stops.

There were not many Cambodian families and there was so much to learn about life in Canada. For example, it was hard to know how to eat in a restaurant – he would eat all the bread not knowing more food was coming and would have little room for the main course. Shortly after, Paulie met a Cambodian woman who helped him learn how to use a stove and go to the supermarkets. The Manpower department sent him to learn English for six months. Soon he met other Cambodian families, went to their homes to eat, found his own place to live, and started feeling comfortable in Canada.

Manpower arranged his first job as a caretaker. "I thought that I would take care of somebody." He soon found out that he was to clean three floors in a building and was paid $4.40 an hour. He also had a job in a restaurant setting tables and chopping vegetables.

Paulie's fondest work memories are as a school bus driver from 2006 to 2019, and he is proud of his contribution to the lives of children. Along with remembering the stops for all forty-eight students, he would playfully engage the children with funny stories of his past, saying, "You are lucky to have a bus driver imported from Cambodia." Paulie also emphasized to the children the importance of going to school and listening to their parents. He felt acceptance from children and says, "They tell you the truth." Children still remember him and reach out when they see him in shopping malls.

Paulie went back to Cambodia in 1990 and brought his family. He is proud of his children, who are university educated and fortunate to have received the education that he was denied in Cambodia. He is grateful to have arrived in Canada. "Canada is my home. Canada gave me a new life." "I'd love to say thank you. I tell my children that without Canada I might be dead." At age fifty-six he has lived in Canada for thirty-six years and feels that it is his home. "Most people in Canada do not look like me but they accept me as I am." He comments on how during the Pol Pot regime the Khmer Rouge looked like him but treated him very badly. "I almost died by them."

Vichuta Ly

The quotes in this story are translated from an interview conducted in French (Interview HOF079 2019).

Vichuta Ly was born in 1965 in Phnom Penh, the youngest of ten children. "At the beginning of the war we are a whole family with cousins, brothers-in-law, sisters-in-law, we are thirty-five, and at the end we are only five survivors … Between 1972 and 1975 my father was the minister of justice during the Republican regime. My mother was simply a housewife … Before the war, we were fine. On the weekends we went with our family to the province to visit other families. We had a good time … It was wonderful because it was peaceful. It's a fascinating country, the culture as well as the landscape and development."

"My father was a patriot. In 1975, when the evacuations took place, the US embassy asked my father to leave. He said that if he left, it was like he was against his own country … He was asked three times, but my father refused all three times." She recalls a memory in which her father had gathered her and her siblings in his arms so that they could feel safe falling asleep while they heard rockets outside. She says she managed to fall asleep but when she woke up, everyone was crying because her father had been taken away. The last time she saw him was 17 April 1975.

When the Khmer Rouge soldiers evacuated everyone living in urban areas to the countryside under the pretense that the US would bomb the cities, Vichuta and her family left their home with little food and clothing. Walking all night "we start to see people dying … Everyone was tired … we sleep about ten to twenty minutes and even an hour and they wake us up. We have to keep walking." Her mother realized that the new regime would impose an oppressive program that would be extremely dangerous for her family. She hoped to escape with all her family members to Thailand, but the large family included many young children which made it difficult to reach the border as a group.

By early 1976, only five members of her family were together. The others either disappeared or died due to forced labour, starvation, or execution. In 1977 during the monsoon season, Vichuta's brother-in-law was arrested for a second time and eventually killed by the Khmer Rouge. During that time, the soldiers also arrested Vichuta and her sister. They were denounced for being members of the country's bourgeoisie and an intellectual family. Vichuta remembers her mother's words: "Our lives depend on you." She urged her daughter to tell the Khmer Rouge that "the family was poor, their father was a retired man, they owned a small store with one motorcycle and two bicycles."

When Vichuta was only twelve years old, she was taken away to a re-education camp where she was questioned about her family and tortured by authorities. Her mother had told her to lie about the family as it was the only way they could survive. "When they took me to the work centre, they woke me up every twenty or thirty minutes or every hour to ask the same questions: 'What does your father do? What does your brother-in-law do? Who are you?' Always the same questions and they whip me from time to time."

During their detention, Vichuta and her sister were separated and tortured as criminals against Angkar. She continued to resist and repeated her mother's words to the authorities. "They ask me to write in the Khmer, and this is what saves my life, because I don't know how to write in Khmer because I studied at a French school, and I am the only one in my family who didn't know how to write in Khmer." The authorities released her after holding her for ten days in a re-education centre. She was reunited with her mother, sister, and nephew.

The Khmer Rouge had forced Vichuta and her family to move from village to village. "They transported us in American military trucks and sent us to a train station. They put us on a train cargo and close the door … People are sick, they have diarrhea, it smells awful. You can't see anything … Some people died in the car."

Along the way, her family members were separated. She remembers horrific scenes she came across and how they had little to eat on the journeys. Many members of her family, including her sister, who was eighteen years old and had dreams of one day becoming a doctor, died. After her sister's death, they were forced to bury her in the forest and continue. "My brother-in-law wrote her name and date, probably just the year, and put it in a bottle to be buried with the body, hoping that if the country changes, we can go back and get it."

Every month she and her family had to bury other relatives who had died along the way. "At the end of 1977, the Khmer Rouge were killing each other." There was conflict between the Khmer Rouge from different regions and Vichuta discovered that her family was on a list of those to be killed.

In early 1979 her mother, who had hidden a radio, heard on *The Voice of America* that there was a change in the country. The Vietnamese army defeated the Khmer Rouge and Vichuta found one of her brothers in their father's hometown. Together, they decided to leave Cambodia and reached a refugee camp in Thailand.

On 30 May 1980, Vichuta and her remaining family travelled to Canada and settled in Hudson Heights, Quebec. During their first months in Canada, she explains how she and her family were frightened by the sounds of thunderstorms as it reminded them of war. She says it took time to adjust and reminded themselves that they were safe in Canada. She says it was not difficult for her to adjust to her new life in Canada because she was still a young teenager. She says that the most difficult part was living between two cultures (Cambodian and Canadian). Despite this challenge, Vichuta entered university and graduated with a law degree.

However, Vichuta never forgot those back in Cambodia and returned to her homeland for the first time in 2002. She established a nonprofit, nonpolitical organization, Legal Support for Children and Women (LSCW), that provides free legal aid to women and children who are the victims of human trafficking (sex and forced labour), domestic violence, and rape in Cambodia (End Slavery Now 2024). She believes strongly in humanitarian aid for people in need and was highly impressed by the work of Doctors Without Borders when she was in refugee camps. Because she is a lawyer, not a doctor, she wanted to apply a similar model for legal services. The organization works with lawyers from around the world. Because of her passion for education, Vichuta also uses the organization to offer young Cambodian women who are pursuing law careers the chance to work and develop their skills. More information about the programs Vichuta developed through her Legal Support for Women and Children initiative is available online.[2]

Rivaux Lay, Paulie Phoeuk, and Vichuta Ly all endured the hardships of the Khmer Rouge regime. Paulie was a minor, and Rivaux and Vichuta represented the "class to be eliminated." As a woman, Vichuta was particularly vulnerable. All displayed tremendous strength, courage, and resilience. That they survived with their sanity intact is amazing, and their ability to rebuild their lives, pursue meaningful employment, and raise families is a tribute to the human spirit.

2 See End Slavery Now, 2024, "Legal Support for Children and Women," accessed 29 July 2024, https://www.endslaverynow.org/legal-support-for-children-and-women-lscw.

Conclusion to Part Four

Mean Bonn Taing's (Interview HOF037 2019) question remains in our thoughts: "Why did the Khmer Rouge do this to us? … Why kill your own people?" The Khmer Rouge came to power in the context of the Vietnam war, relentless bombing of the countryside, a devastating civil war, loss of lands, destruction of homes, deaths of family members, and tremendous socio-economic upheaval. These conditions impacted the peasant population to a greater extent than those in the cities, and many peasants joined the Khmer Rouge "to find meaning in a chaotic and violent world" (Hinton 2005, 282). They were then indoctrinated with extremist ideology, an adaptation of Marxist-Leninist and Maoist ideas. The result further fuelled peasant anger and class rage, construing city people as the enemy. Alexander Hinton has referred to these conditions as "genocidal priming," resulting in one of the most brutal regimes in recorded history (Hinton 2005, 282).

The Khmer Rouge, despite their violence and brutality and their policies aimed to undermine the family, were unsuccessful in destroying family bonds and transferring family loyalty to Angkar (Mam 2006). The practice of separating family members by age and sex into work brigades in various locations and the collectivization of living arrangements were often met with acts of resistance. Kong Bun's (Interview HOF124 2019) situation demonstrates how, when formal traditions were opposed, allegiance to the family continued to remain primary. Traditionally, marriages, along with being a union between two people, are also a union between two families. Although the Khmer Rouge controlled the selection of marriage partners and the ceremony, there are examples of including family, such as when Kong brought his new wife home and asked for his father's blessing. Also, getting married allowed him to remain in the village and care for his father, fulfilling his role to care for him in his old age. Although the Khmer Rouge banned funeral ceremonies, Kong mourned his father by lighting a small flame in his honour. Kong also describes listening to music knowing that all art forms in connection to the past were suppressed and punishable by death if discovered. A villager had tapes of an old musician, and they would take turns on a bicycle to run power to secretly listen to the tapes.

Similarly, Neang Thong (Interview HOF032 2019) was a young child working at a sugarcane farm and would break the rules to see her mother and bring her some sugarcane. On another occasion, she was placed in a different work site from her husband, learned that he was ill, and made a request to see him. Although the Khmer Rouge declined her request, she persisted and was allowed to go at night.

There were also pockets of resistance among village chiefs who intervened to spare people from execution, as was the case for Samath Yi (Interview HOF127 2019) and Un You Eng (Interview HOF129 2019) in Salong village. Others, such as the physician who sent Rivaux Lay (Interview HOF003 2019) to the hospital to save him from execution, acted against the genocidal practices. Sorpong Peou recounts the time that he was starving, weak, and ill from malaria. The Khmer Rouge nurses took him to the hospital where he stayed for a month and was brought back to health. Similarly, although Khmer Rouge soldiers were sent to arrest Saphan Noun (Interview HOF125 2019) and her husband, the village leader protected them, the commander who made the order realized that he knew the family, and the accusations were called off.

The interviewees demonstrated remarkable strength and resilience during their life under the Khmer Rouge, during their escape and adjustment in the refugee camps, and during their resettlement in Canada. Many took advantage of opportunities in the refugee camps for language instruction and employment. They read the books that were available and worked alongside those in the camp services assisting at hospitals and refugee agencies. On arrival in Canada, perseverance, courage, and hope carried them as they settled, established a new life, and made significant contributions in their communities.

PART FIVE

Laotian Refugees

12

Laos: The Secret War, Escape, and Refugee Camps

Following the communist Pathet Lao takeover of Laos in December 1975, life changed dramatically as the country became the Lao People's Democratic Republic. This chapter describes and analyzes twenty-eight Laotian interviews comprising thirty-one participants, including two couples and a pair of siblings.

All the Laotian interviewees arrived in Canada between 1978 and 1980. At the time of their arrival, they were between the ages of seven and thirty-nine. The thirty-one interviewees included seven children, six young adults, and eighteen young families. Within the group there were thirteen women and eighteen men. Twenty-eight participants identified themselves as Lao (Lowland Lao) while three identified as Hmong (Highland Lao), an ethic minority group in Laos. The participants' occupations in Laos (or in the case of those who arrived as children, the occupations of their breadwinner parents) included: people working as a military private/pilot in the Royal Lao Army or CIA (2); Royal Lao Government official/civil servant/police/pilot (7); medical doctor/pharmacist/paramedic (4); veterinarian (1); teacher/principal (6); technical occupation worker (1); small business owner (3); worker/labourer (2); farmer (2); college/university student (2); and unknown (1). Six interviewees had family members who worked in the Royal Lao military and ten interviewees had family members who worked in the Royal Lao Government. Over 51 per cent of the refugees interviewed (sixteen out of thirty-one) had families in the Royal Lao military or government. Upon arrival in Canada, seven of the thirty-one people were minors and did not speak English or French. Of the twenty-four remaining people, four were fluent in English, four were fluent in French, and four were fluent in both languages. Twelve of the adults had limited or no proficiency in either English or French. As children, single adults, and young families, they took up residences across Canada from British Columbia to Quebec.

Laotian interviewees describe their lives during the civil war in Laos and, following the communist takeover, their escapes and experiences of refugee camps in Thailand. The analysis discusses common themes, with both shared and unique tragedies and experiences. These interviews illustrate the importance of storytelling that connects people with common experiences. In chapters 12, 13, and 14, the interviewees' own words are used to tell their stories, and where possible, they are quoted directly. This places emphasis on the interviewees' words and powerful emotions. Direct quotes naturally reflect the fact that the interviewees are speaking in a second language. Full names will appear initially, after which first names are used for identification, in accordance with Laotian custom.

Life in Laos During the Civil War

The Civil War in Laos between the Royal Lao Government and the communist Pathet Lao lasted from 1962 to 1975. It affected all parts of the country, with 48 to 58 per cent of the Royal Lao Government's expenditures going to the military (Stuart-Fox 2010, 346). However, unless one lived close to one of the war zones, Laotians continued with their routine lives.

Children went to school, played with their friends, and helped their families at home. Ly Vang (Interview HOF092 2019) lived in a rural area. She helped care for the horses and water buffalo on her family's farm. She had a favorite white horse and speaks of the freedom and peace she felt while riding it.

Young adults remember playing sports, hanging out with friends, and attending college. Oudom Pravat (Interview HOF028 2019) describes how he dropped out of school, spent time with girls, and played music in nightclubs, while Doumphet Phanthavong (Interview HOF119 2019) lived in a dormitory and "focused on school and study." Khamla Inthadeth (Interview HOF033 2019) speaks about attending a police academy for three years until 1975 when he was forced to quit. Interviewees who were adults in Laos before 1975 all speak about their work. They include an industrial worker, a veterinarian working for the Royal Lao Government, a transportation office worker, a teacher, a farmer, and a cabinet maker.

For those with family members in the Royal Lao Military and associated services, life was somewhat different. Oudong and Thepouthith Vongsouneth (Interview HOF057 2019) recollect moving often, as their father was an air traffic controller for the military. Stephanie Phetsamay Stobbe (Interview HOF113 2019) recalls walking to school with her older sister to attend kindergarten, but she also remembers moving from house to house so the family could avoid spies and enemy soldiers. An early childhood memory is of airplanes and bombing and being rushed into a small hole beneath her house for protection; she asked her parents and sister, "Why are we in a hole in the dark?" Lou Xiong (Interview HOF089 2019) was born close to the Ho Chi Minh trail along the Laos-Vietnam border. His childhood revolved around the war as his father was a soldier working with the CIA, which required the family to live and move around in the war zones.

Hardship and Fear Under the Pathet Lao

Life changed drastically after 2 December 1975 when the communist Pathet Lao took over the government and established the Lao People's Democratic Republic. Massive social and economic changes enforced by terror, especially the brutal re-education camps, or *semina*, produced hardship and fear. The intense stress of those years hurt many Laotians. Many interviewees still feel the impact of those painful years to this day. Oudom (Interview HOF028 2019) describes how everything came to a halt under the new regime – they closed businesses, including nightclubs, and there were no jobs. He survived by doing things he had never done before, including going to the mountains to cut wood to sell as firewood. He was an aspiring artist but found it very difficult to finish high school and go to art school.

Khamong Phommarinh (Interview HOF080 2019) states, "Every day we lived there, there was no freedom at all. We had to listen and do what they asked. We couldn't refuse or talk too much about the politics or critique the politicians or government." Doumphet (Interview HOF119 2019) describes how freedom was limited: "I can't say what I [want]. I cannot say that so and because at that time it is very, very tough the government, and they know who you are." Xay Bounnapha (Interview HOF059 2019) states that in 1975, as a former public servant, he had to "keep a low profile" for fear of being "round up and arbitrarily arrested." Inpone Luangaphay (Interview HOF160 2020) describes how "they changed the system from a free country to a communist system. They put oppression on the people, hardship. Lots of people get hardship, running out of food. And ... people [were] not happy about the system, so that's why they escape." Noulath Sayaphet (Interview HOF056 2019) states, "I think that when the regime has been changed ... You didn't have rights actually, and freedoms, and you live in fear. Fear means that [when] you sleep at night, they can come and take you away anytime ... every day is fear."

The oppressive and controlling nature of the new government caused significant mistrust in Lao society. People no longer felt safe talking and discussing things with their friends, neighbours, and even their families. Noulath and his wife Vatsana Sayaphet (Interview HOF056 2019) describe how they were afraid to talk to each other. Noulath says, "Even sister, brother, mother ... nothing [said] to people. Just keep to themselves because they are afraid to say something bad ... you don't trust nobody at that time." Paspaporn Vong (Interview HOF115 2019) recalls, "At that time, there is no trust. You fear anybody, not just the authorities. Even your friends, the neighbours. They try to create that kind of atmosphere that's easy for them to control."

Economic Changes and Hardships

The end of substantial economic aid from the United States caused the collapse of the somewhat artificial economy that had sustained the Royal Lao Government. The Pathet Lao government then controlled and socialized the economy. Industry, commerce, and finance were taken over by the government and agriculture was collectivized. Collectivization was implemented in nine of thirteen provinces. The peasants were deeply upset at having their farms become communal property, even going so far as to destroy their crops to show their anger (Stuart-Fox 1997).

The Pathet Lao government abolished the previous currency and replaced it with the new "kip," a devalued "liberation currency" which led to rampant inflation (Stuart-Fox 1997, 172). Many recall the horror of having all their savings and investments disappear with the introduction of the new Lao kip. Khamong (Interview HOF080 2019) explains, "If you had a lot of money, when you exchanged it for the new kip – let's say the amount passed 20,000, they didn't give you everything. You had to keep it in the bank. You could only withdraw accordingly, but only if you had a good reason to do so. And if you had foreign currency, like the dollar and all, all of it had to be given to the bank and controlled by the government. To carry any money, you had to have a good reason. Many people committed suicide over this because they [lost] millions. Imagine 100 kip for 1 kip [Communist currency]." Chanthai Taillefer (Interview HOF118 2019) remembers money changing with the new currency, more gun control, and more soldiers walking the street: "Change happen so fast in our country and make everybody scared." The Pathet Lao government attempted to control the prices of basic commodities, and to stop hoarding and black-market dealings by restricting the movement of people and goods.

Many civil servants lost their jobs. Xay (Interview HOF059 2019) managed to retain a lower-level civil service position. He recalls that many people were reassigned to jobs not related to their training, and that the more he worked, the less freedom he had. Civil servants were often paid in vouchers that could be exchanged for food and other items in state stores. As the government pay was insufficient to support their families, civil servants often had to work two or three jobs to support themselves (Stuart-Fox 2008, 89).

Sisters Oudong and Thepouthith (Interview HOF057 2019) came from an upper-middle-class family under the previous government. However, the new government took their money, and they were given coupons for rice, sugar, and meat. The food shortage was crippling. Their parents said, "This is not good, this is not a living. You don't survive. You stay, you die. You go, you might have a future. You only take a risk. So, people that escaped, they take a risk for better." Keota and Khamong (Interview HOF080 2019) were a teacher and a school principal, but they still decided to leave Laos. Keota says, "There was poverty – poverty in the sense that we weren't being paid regularly. We had nothing. It was difficult everywhere. To get one kilogram of meat and rice, we had to line up all morning. It was too hard for us, and we had three kids. We decided to leave for our children's future." Inpone (Interview HOF160 2020) states in his interview: "They change the system from freedom country to a communist system. They put oppression on the people, the hardship. Lots of people get hardship, running out of food. And ... people not happy about the system, so that's why they escape."

The Re-Education Camps

As soon as the Pathet Lao took power, it created re-education camps (semina) to control the population, especially the more highly educated people. Presented as places to teach people the new communist way of life, in reality, the re-education camps were brutal concentration camps in which thousands of people died from malnutrition, disease, and attempted escape. Estimates place the number of imprisoned Laotians at 40,000 to 50,000. Many people were forced to remain in the re-education camps for five years and more (Stuart-Fox 1997).

Phanomnhong Aryavong (Interview HOF014 2019) and Khamong and Keota (Interview HOF080 2019) recall those who worked for the former government had to learn "the politics of the new regime ... learn socialist theory and all. But to be honest, it wasn't like that at all – they brought people to concentration camps. And many died in these camps." Khamong discusses which people were taken, and the importance and priority of certain individuals being removed from society. She says, "They started with people in the military, police, and then government workers. After that, teachers and people who worked in education. They started with people who worked in administration and then school principals. We were teachers, so our turn would have come. We decided to leave because we heard from these people that had gone that it was not to learn about theory like at school, these were actually concentration camps."

Thongsouk Vongphackdy (Interview HOF098 2019) worked at a teacher's college in 1974–75 and experienced drastic changes in 1977 when "the situation was unstable because people get arrested from their home without knowing anything, without warning. So, we don't know what's going to happen to our life and to our family. And actually, it happened right after that, but because I was a teacher, so they don't look into that yet."

Milana Ward's (Interview HOF134 2020) father had been a pharmacist at the Royal Lao military hospital. The family saw how "people were starting to be shipped to re-education camps, especially the people that were educated." Friends warned the family that their father's name was on the list of those about to be imprisoned, prompting the family to leave swiftly. Xay (Interview HOF059 2019) describes "a friend accused of US spy without proof, arrested before my eyes, crying family, haven't seen him since then, sent to re-education camp."

Viengsamay Phanvongkham's (Interview HOF161 2020) grandfather had worked for the French army in the first Indochina War and was murdered by a Vietnamese communist. Years later, that Western legacy was still enough reason for Viengsamay's father to fear being sent to semina. His father had warned his family not to believe the tactics that the communists would use to destroy their family. One day, a man came by with a human ear supposedly belonging to Viengsamay's father, but Viengsamay's mother would not believe him. They came back with a human heart, and again told her that he was dead and she should move on. Again, she did not believe them. Viengsamay's father did eventually escape from the re-education camp with both ears and his heart. Of course, they had to get the ear and heart from someone for the macabre ruse. Many people were less fortunate than Viengsamay's father.

Stephanie (Interview HOF113 2019) remembers her family constantly worrying about being sent to a semina. Eventually the family left the country "so that the children would have a better life and be in a more peaceful country." Although the Laotians loved their country, they were gravely concerned for their future and the future of their children. Siblings Oudong and Thepouthith (Interview HOF057 2019) share how their parents were worried about their jobs, the children's education, their well-being, and how money was tight. Their mother was a teacher and was on the list to be sent to a re-education camp. They recall, "It's hard for my dad to take care of six kids … They decide that we can't stay there because for our own future."

Young people with no future were making difficult decisions to flee the country on their own. Sengsouvanh Sengdeuanepheng (Interview HOF135 2020) had just graduated and began teaching at a junior high school. She also feared semina and, she says, "I don't know what I am supposed to do … If I escape, I have to leave something behind like my parents and younger brothers, right? And all of a sudden, I say no matter what I have to escape to get a better life."

Escape

It is estimated that 10 per cent of the entire population of Laos and 30 per cent of the Hmong population left Laos. The Hmong feared retaliation since many had fought with the CIA forces. About 90 per cent of the educated middle class and virtually the entire Vietnamese and Chinese business community fled (Stuart-Fox 2010, 279). Due to its close proximity and similar language and culture, the great majority of refugees escaped to Thailand, with most crossing the Mekong River, the natural border that separates the two countries, although small groups also escaped through the short land border in the jungle.

Many families swam or took a canoe across the Mekong River. Parts of the Mekong River are wide and dangerous, with whirlpools and jutting boulders. Soldiers with machine guns often patrolled both sides of the river to prevent Laotians from entering Thailand. Noulath (Interview HOF056 2019) shares that it was a "very scary moment because we have to be quiet, and it's so dark, and so … nobody around. And we didn't really know can we make it or not. And now depend on the guy who take us at that time. If he didn't choose the right time, and we might get shot anytime if we move. As long as we get out from the house, then your life is danger. As long as they see you, then they shoot before they ask." As a child at the time, Stephanie (Interview HOF113 2019) remembers her parents being "very careful of trying to get across the Mekong River without being seen by the soldiers … The Lao soldiers were told to shoot anyone trying to leave, and the Thai soldiers were told to shoot anyone trying to land because they didn't want any refugees there. And then, our boat hit a whirlpool, and that spun us around and around and around. And our boat kept filling up water … The two older kids took buckets, and we were scooping water out of the boat, and our parents were trying to steer the boat through the whirlpool so that we would get to safety across in Thailand." Sengsouvanh (Interview HOF135 2020) describes how she and two friends took a leaky canoe and paddled across the river at night, not knowing how to swim or paddle, with the sounds of gunshots all around them. She feared, "If soldiers see you, they shoot you no matter what. No matter what they don't want you to escape from the country to the other country. That's very dangerous journey to escape, yeah and with the darkness and by the … gunshots around us over the Mekong River."

Some people did not have a boat or canoe to cross the Mekong River. Paspaporn (Interview HOF115 2019) and Manisorn Vong (Interview HOF116 2019) hired someone to pick them up in a boat that never showed up. Manisorn recalls how her husband and another man "cut the banana tree … to make a boat [raft]" and being seven months pregnant, she was able to sit on the raft with a two-year-old girl while the others swam hanging onto the raft. Doumphet (Interview HOF119 2019) describes how he and his friends swam across the river holding onto a one-gallon gas tank. He says, "We nearly halfway … We can't go to the destination that we going to get there because due to the current very strong and push us over and over and past the marine … station for the border." Eventually a boat with guns and spotlights picked them up and took them to the Thai police.

Soldiers and strong currents were not the only concern. Khouanta Phommarath (Interview HOF117 2019) courageously escaped Laos with her four young children in a small boat. She recalls, "As [we] were nearing the Thai border, there was a big boat that came and that really scared [us] because it caused a lot of waves, so [we] threw over whatever items they had in the boat, and [we] quickly made it across." Chanthai (Interview HOF118 2019), along with two female cousins, left Laos with the assistance of three young men by running through the bush and wet rice fields before getting into a boat. She remembers, "The helicopter up there, shine the spotlight all over around us. And we went – I don't know how to swim and one of my cousins don't know how to swim, but the other one know how to swim ... and they ... cover us with the boat but we ducked ourselves into the boat [canoe]. I mean into the water then the boat cover us."

The smuggling industry was flourishing, sometimes charging exorbitant amounts of money to sneak Laotians into Thailand. Oudong and Thepouthith (Interview HOF057 2019) say that their parents paid US$50,000 for the eight of them to be smuggled out of Laos, as her mother refused to separate the family. "Because when they put you on the boat, you hear all kinds of horror stories, right? And you see people dying in the Mekong River. People got shot, people got ... their boat, their canoe tip over." When they arrived on the Thai shores of the Mekong River, Thai soldiers came to the bank of the river and ordered them to get out of the canoe. She says one of the soldiers "point the gun right at us, and my dad went down on his knees. And he point the gun right at my dad's forehead, and he said he's gonna kill all of us." Apparently, the soldiers thought he was Vietnamese (which for some reason made killing acceptable). Realizing he was Lao, they let the family go.

Xay (Interview HOF059 2019) also paid smugglers to get his family of six to Thailand. He recalls how the boat's "load capacity was just enough to hold my kids and the belongings and two women ... If one more passenger was in, the boat would be sinking." The boat in fact would not hold him, and he ended up swimming along in the river:

> My eyeball distance between jumping into the water and the shore is approximately 150 metres. When you are swimming with clothes on, the water resistance is heavy. I was completely exhausted at about 24 metres from the shore. I am at the very dangerous event. What I was using was that I tried to punch my body down deeper until I reach the bottom of the river. Luckily my feet push myself upward to the surface and catch the breath. And I kept repeating that a few times until I reached the shore. I was completely exhausted. I faint, I laid on the ground.

Milana (Interview HOF134 2019) recalls her father escaped a week earlier and that her grandfather or father paid some gunmen who dressed up as fishermen to get the rest of the family. She describes her mother "putting us in the boat, it was just a small fishing boat and covering us up with what she said was banana leaves but I remember it as being blankets just so that we weren't visible and they crossed and I remember my experience was just peeking behind the covers and seeing the water and wanting to touch it and sticking out my hand and my mom pushing my hand back."

Those who fled through the jungles before crossing to Thailand had different challenges to overcome, including endless trekking through the dense forests and avoiding soldier patrols. They tended to be people who lived in the mountains in Laos, particularly ethnic minority groups such as the Khammu (the largest ethnic minority group living in northern and central Laos) and Hmong. Lou Xiong's (Interview HOF089 2019) family, who were Hmong, trekked for twenty days and nights without food, carrying guns and a few clothes in their backpacks. He recalls eating whatever they could find in the forest for survival – bamboo shoots, banana leaves, and banana shoots. Lou describes their traumatic escape: "And soon as we get close to the border of Thailand, there's the Mekong River that runs across. That's the border. And we are not lucky, and we got ambushed, so they captured my parents and other people … back to Laos. Somewhere in Laos. And I was fortunate, I and four others … we can [be called] kids at that time because we only fourteen, thirteen years old. So, we escaped from there. We swimming across the Mekong River to Thailand. And then from there, they put us into a refugee camp."

Ly (Interview HOF092 2019) recalls as a young Hmong girl escaping with her family through the jungles and how her feet were sore and bleeding after walking for two weeks though the mountains with no rest. Ly also recollects her own experience:

> And I remember at one point climbing the mountain. It was a lot of pain, but my dad would do his very best just to carry me a little bit, but because I have four others who's younger than me that he had to carry one on the back and sometimes one on the front. And my mom had to carry two. And so, my brother and sister carry food and other things for survival, so I know that there was no one listen to my complaints. Though I cry, but I don't get picked up. I still had to walk and walk.

She remembers looking for food along the way – mushrooms, fruits, berries, leaves, and insects. Along the road, they saw some people who had died and were left behind. Ly recalls, "You could smell the foul, and the skeletons of the people were quite scary. But my dad say, 'Walk very quiet and slow, and don't step on them because they are people like us, but they die because they have no choice. So, then find your step carefully.'"

Viengsamay's (Interview HOF161 2020) family drove in the jungle and met up with other families who walked through the night to their escape route with hired men. He remembers "walking, walking, and then, all of the sudden, there's a bunch of … guys came to us with machine guns. And we – my mom, everybody drop on the floor, on the ground, and say, 'Oh, this is it. We're done.' Right? But … then, the two gentlemen that taking us now were talking to them, and we had realized that they are in a group together. They're the ones in the jungle waiting with machine guns and everything, right? Now, it's getting scary." He recalls walking chest deep in water and in rice fields carrying little children and remembered how "the ants – because your shoes … the ants would bite your feet, and you thought, you know, 'What is this?! Is it like a snake?' Or whatever. You can't see, but you can see a little bit in the moonlight, right? And we walk, walk, walk until we get to the Mekong River."

These stories demonstrate how desperate many Laotians were to escape the Pathet Lao government and build a better future somewhere else. Clandestine and dangerous escape routes across the Mekong River and through the thick jungles, on their own or with paid smugglers, were common. Their courage and determination finally led them to refugee camps in Thailand.

Life in Thai Refugee Camps

Thailand became the country of first asylum for most Laotian refugees. At its peak in 1978, Thailand hosted 100,000 refugees. However, the Thai government was unwilling to let the refugees stay and expected the international community to resettle them in third countries (Molloy et al. 2017, 280–1). After the refugees were identified by Thai officials, they would begin the process of entering official refugee camps. Often, they were held in jails or other detention centres until their refugee status could be determined and paperwork could be filled out. This lasted weeks, sometimes months. Only after entering official camps could the refugees be interviewed and processed for third-country resettlement. There were many refugee camps in northern Thailand, mostly housing Lao people. From the twenty-eight interviews we conducted, eighteen individuals went to Nongkai refugee camp in northeastern Thailand directly across from Vientiane, Laos, on the banks of the Mekong River. The remainder went to various other refugee camps including Ubon, Ubol, Ban Vinai, Sob Tuang, Ban Thong, Pua, and Ban Nam Yao.

After many months or even years of filling out applications and being interviewed by immigration officials, those refugees approved for resettlement in Canada and other third countries were sent to another transit centre (camp) in Bangkok. They remained there for weeks or months for further processing and medical examinations before boarding flights to their new homes in Canada.

The refugee camps in Thailand were characterized by overcrowding, inadequate sanitation, poor nutrition, and a general lack of services. Experiences were varied depending on the different camps. The big ones, including Nong Khai and Ban Vinai, were like small, overcrowded cities. Most refugees in the large camps spent some time in detention centres before entering the main camps. The smaller ones like Soptuang or Ban Thong were in the middle of the forest, where people had to forage for supplies to build a hut and even find food.

People in the smaller camps typically avoided lengthy stays in detention centres. In Nong Khai and Ubol camps, the Lowland Lao were mostly from the middle-class population of civil servants, teachers, and small-business owners, and many had studied abroad (Molloy et al. 2017, 280–1). Ban Vinai and Soptuang camps were mostly made up of Hmong and other ethnic minority groups. Some problems affected all camps, whether big or small. Sexual assault was a constant concern for females, and probably some males as well, and bribes were accepted and expected as a way of accessing services or moving to the head of the line.

Khouanta Phommarath (Interview HOF117 2019) says when she and her children arrived in Thailand, they were taken to a detention centre and placed in a small room with two hundred people for three days and then sent to a larger jail near Nong Khai refugee camp where there were one thousand people. She was required to pay 5,000 baht (US$246) but did not have the money, so the judge said, "If you don't have 5,000 baht, you have to go to jail." Khouanta and her children sat around in jail for one month with nothing to do. Xay (Interview HOF059 2019) recalls his family being taken to a Thai detention centre located near Nong Khai refugee camp:

> We were among the eight hundred people in that particular cell … The centre was not adequate to hold such … numbers of people … The centre was completely blocked by high steel metal fences. There was one house, a long bamboo hut, the toilet was overloaded and no water to clean up so people would ease themselves and urinate wherever they can. Hygiene was almost zero. Even feces odor filled up the centre. No matter where you go. We stayed in the centre for ten days. Food was distributed twice daily, lunch, supper time. We did not take a shower.

Sengsouvanh (Interview HOF135 2020) also describes her experience at the detention centre. "Everything stinky and then dirty and when there we want to go for bathroom, take a shower, the soldier come to open the door for us. They don't put man and lady together because man in one room and lady in other room, but we can see each other … No privacy at all." Sengsouvanh found it difficult to live in Nong Khai refugee camp and feared for her safety, especially as a young woman. She recalls, "When you in Nong Khai camp you don't have to make yourself look good … You have to be humble, you have to [do] whatever [not to stand out] … The people killing, stealing, the shooting sometime at nighttime." Noulath (Interview HOF056 2019) describes Nong Khai refugee camp as having approximately 37,000 people with fifty buildings that housed 700 to 800 people each. He says, "Each building, they have leader to deal with the Thai government, make sure everybody has food, has clothes, has shelter. In Laos, we call it *soun*. *Soun*, it means zero. Like it's a zero in there. So, we start from the beginning. It's the same thing. It's not safe there, too. So, a lot of people every day, people get killed.

People get taken away. Even we escaped to Thailand, but yet we still fear because Thailand authority … We are no land. We are no country. We are no rights, and they do whatever they want to do."

Manisorn (Interview HOF116 2019) sadly describes being sent to a temporary camp where there was "no toilet, no water, food not very good … By that time, I was pregnant and … so sick. The baby cannot move because to have to stay in line for so many hours and then the baby is gone, and he died." She was sent to a camp hospital and her husband Paspaporn (Interview HOF115 2019) recalls that "they don't have modern equipment, just a nurse … so we lost the first baby." Noulath (Interview HOF056 2019) describes when his son was born in the refugee camp: it was "pretty hard because in the camp we don't have anything. Even the hospital, it's very limited supply. And somehow, we have to spend money to buy the medication, to buy all the equipment a baby needs, to raise the child there. And even somehow that we have buy medication, go to the pharmacy." As he was a veterinarian in Laos, he decided to deliver the baby himself. Oudom (Interview HOF028 2019) spent two years and five months in Nong Khai refugee camp. He describes, "It's no life there. You spend today without nothing … Every camp allowed you to go to the town, but you had to buy a pass. I didn't have money. I have a group of friends and we were good in music, and we were hired by Thai people once in a while to play in town. That's how I survived." Viengsamay (Interview HOF161 2020) describes Nong Khai refugee camp as "pretty dirty … You live like an animal, basically, but it is what it is, right? That's what happens in wartime. Because it's overcrowded … There's not enough room for all those refugees."

Ban Vinai and Ubol camps seemed to be somewhat better than Nong Khai. Khamong and Keota (Interview HOF080 2019) were some of the luckier ones to arrive in Ubol refugee camp and stayed in a small cabin. Keota describes, "We ate there, slept there, we were lucky. We were lucky because we spoke French, English, and Lao, and we understood Thai too. We found work almost right away." Lou (Interview HOF089 2019) spent one year in Ban Vinai camp in 1977 with his uncle in a long house, similar to an apartment unit. He describes the camp as "not too bad because a lot of people in there, and I think, we have food delivery every week that is from United Nations or somebody … You can go to outside the camp and go do little work for Thai people, get a little money here and there to buy stuff that you need." While at the camp, he went to school to learn Thai and paid to study English until he had no money. A Canadian immigration officer came to the camp and he decided to go with his cousin's family to Canada. Three months after their interview, they came to Canada.

Other smaller camps had no housing or basic services. Ly (Interview HOF092 2019) describes the refugee camp Pua (Ban Nam Yao), where they had to build a small hut for their family and the UN provided food twice or three times a week. Her father brought along her favorite white horse, but there was nothing to feed him for two months. The horse was taken to a creek to feed on some grass and got strangled by vines. Her father had to put the horse down and their friends came and "they took every part of my horse. And I heard my dad say even the skin because it was in the refugee camp, and there's not much food, so people took all his bones, all his skin, all his meats." One of her mother's friends took the meat, dried it, and gave it to her mother to barbecue. Ly ate it as she thought it was deer meat until her aunt told her, "You had just ate [eaten] your horse. That was your horse." Ly was sick and traumatized by the whole experience, and for fifteen years she felt guilty. She also says at the camp they "were free to go here and there and wherever that we may go. But it was not really safe for, especially for all the ladies." In fact, she had two friends who were sexually assaulted on their way home from work.

Stephanie (Interview HOF113 2019) remembers the Ban Thong refugee camp, where her "parents had to build the hut for our family just because in that camp there were no buildings or tents or anything like that for the refugees. And so, everyone had to build their own homes or huts … with thatched roof, and no walls." There "was not enough food to eat. Food was rationed. I think they got some rice and some dried fish, and that was about it." Water had to be carried in buckets from a nearby creek for cooking and drinking as there was no running water at the camp. There was security around the whole camp which was "fenced off with barbed wire" to prevent people from entering and leaving.

By 1991, 55,000 remained in refugee camps in Thailand, including 10,000 Lao Loum (Lowland) and 45,000 people from hill tribes. Many Hmong refugees refused to return to Laos, and those who did not resettle in the United States remained in Thailand – approximately 7,000 as of late 2006 (Stuart-Fox 2010, 279).

The interviewees told stories of the varied Lao experience during the war years, from those who noticed very little to those who were deeply affected by the violence. Ironically, it was not just the war that caused the exodus of people, but the policies instituted by the new Communist government that became the basis of a common national suffering. Difficulties in providing basic needs, fears for safety and being sent to re-education camps, and total oppression under the new regime were enough to drive 10 per cent of the Lao population to leave their home country. In short, many people fled because the risk of death from fleeing was less unnerving than the risk of death from staying.

There were many routes of escape for the Lao, whether it be over the Mekong River or through the jungles. All the routes involved planning, deception, and risk and ended up in the squalor of a refugee camp. The intensity and immediacy of the fear of living in and fleeing Laos was over once they were admitted to the camps.

Unfortunately, hunger, poor sanitation, and safety concerns were a part of that environment too. Waiting to be accepted into a new country began the next part of their journey.

13

Resettlement of Laotian Refugees in Canada: Struggles and Successes

Between 1975 and 1978, approximately 244 Laotians, mainly middle-class government, military, and business employees, arrived in Canada. As the flow of refugees grew exponentially, the UNHCR pressured Canada and other countries to resettle more refugees. By the end of 1980, a total of 10,093 Laotians had resettled in Canada, with 1,753 sponsored by the Mennonite Central Committee Canada under the new Private Sponsorship of Refugees program. Between 1981 and 1997, an additional 7,272 Laotians arrived, with approximately half coming through the family reunification program (see appendix 2).

When the Laotian interviewees arrived in Canada, they were between the ages of seven and thirty-nine. They settled in different places across the country. Their stories describe extraordinary experiences in a new country, and their courage and resilience in starting new lives in Canada.

Arrival and Initial Experiences in Canada

The refugees flew on charters with Air Canada, Ward Air, and Canadian Pacific and on commercial flights. According to the interviewees, some flights carried between three hundred and five hundred people from various refugee camps. From the twenty-eight interviews, most Laotians' first point of entry in Canada was at the Canadian Forces Base (CFB) Longue-Pointe (Montreal) or the CFB Griesbach (Edmonton). At these bases, the refugees were given permanent resident status, counselling, medical examinations, and winter clothing if they arrived during the cold months. The refugees stayed on the bases from a few days to a month. Refugees who arrived with or without a sponsor would be sent to various destinations as either government assisted or privately sponsored. In early 1979, before the CFB reception centres were established, a few of the refugees arrived through Toronto and Vancouver. These few exceptions would wait on the plane for take-off to their final destination city. Twenty-one interviewees had private sponsorship and the remaining seven interviewees were government assisted.

There was not much for the refugees to do at the CFB bases besides catch up on sleep and get over jetlag. Many of the soldiers stationed there entertained the refugees with games, built snowmen, and engaged in other activities (Molloy et al. 2017). The interviews provided some insights into the refugees' first experiences in Canada at the military bases. Oudong and Theopouthith (Interview HOF057 2019) remember the embarrassment of having to strip and shower at the Montreal base. They were told, "'Okay, you need to strip.' And then, they give you this robe. You know those paper towel robe? You cannot hold on too tight. They'll rip. And then … you line up, and they just spray you. They spray you first," making them feel like animals. They understood that it was to get rid of lice and any bacteria, but nonetheless it was a humiliating experience. Viengsamay (Interview HOF161 2020) remembers the food at the Edmonton base. He says, "Although it's good food, but it's the taste, acquired taste … I remember seeing all those soldiers. In the morning, they would have cereal and milk. We couldn't do it." At Longue-Pointe military base, Paspaporn (Interview HOF0115 2019) remembers eating "a lot of apples because we don't have apples back home."

Khouanta's (Interview HOF117 2019) family arrived in Montreal in March 1980 and stayed at the military base. She thought it was wonderful when they were given a bagful of clothes and were called when it was time to eat. After four days, they flew to Winnipeg, where two families who were part of the sponsorship group picked them up at the airport to go to St Pierre. She says, "They rented them a big house and the fridge was full of food and that … surprised them." Khouanta's family owed Can$3,000 for airfare to come to Canada from Thailand, and the sponsors paid for the rest of the costs.

Like Khouanta, Oudom (Interview HOF028 2019) was privately sponsored. His family arrived in 1979 and remained in Longue-Pointe for a few days completing paperwork. There were about one thousand people at the army base, waiting to go to their final destinations. Oudom's family was flown to Winnipeg and picked up by their sponsors, who took them for tea and then to their rented home. It was a one-bedroom house converted into two bedrooms. He describes how, "in the morning, we wake up, go to kitchen, open the fridge, and it was full of food. Couldn't believe it. It's our house, small, they rented, with big backyard. We grew a garden back there. My wife planted some Asian herbs, vegetables. Stayed in St Boniface – French Canadians live. They were good people. Very generous people." Manisorn (Interview HOF116 2019) states that when they arrived in Leamington, Ontario, "Our sponsor had already had a house for us … They took us to shopping to buy groceries and they looking for a job for us."

However, not all the arrival experiences were positive. Stephanie's (Interview HOF113 2019) family landed in Montreal in December 1979 and were given winter boots and coats. They remained there for two weeks until Canadian immigration officials found them a private sponsor. When they arrived in Winnipeg, they were picked up by two people who were part of the group of five families sponsoring them. They were driven to a small, rural community in the snow and placed in a "two-room house with no running water, no heat except for a wood-burning stove, no washroom. So, there was an outhouse nearby, and this was located in the church's graveyard. So, coming from a Buddhist culture, that … was an extreme shock for our family … The kids were scared because now we're living with the ghosts in the cemetery, and the outhouse was right by the tombstones." No one from the refugee liaison office or any settlement agency came by to check on how the family was doing in their new home. Such harsh beginnings were not common but there were a few families who had similar difficult experiences.

The experiences of government-assisted refugees were somewhat different from those of the privately sponsored refugees. They were often taken to a hotel until more appropriate accommodations could be found for them. They were usually met at the airport and their first real contacts were with their assigned government employment officers. Sengsouvanh (Interview HOF135 2020) arrived in 1980 and spent three days in Longue-Pointe where she was given a choice to go to Montreal or Edmonton. She thought at the time, "In Edmonton, I can speak two languages, and my brother and I make decision, maybe we go to Edmonton because the oil city, right? And maybe the best economy. That's why we make decision." She was excited to be in a new city in a big country. Her first impression was, "Oh, we stay here and the good life … And then I say okay, that's why the first impression when we come to big city, come to see different thing, and see the snowing. At that time, it was snowing so much, right? In November, oh my goodness! I never ever seen the snow in my whole life." Upon arriving in Edmonton, they stayed in a hotel until an immigration counsellor came to take them to Manpower to fill out forms, find an apartment, and look for a job.

Khamong and Keota (Interview HOF080 2019) recall, "Some families stay in the camp for eight years, seven years waiting for sponsors. We were sponsored by the government because we didn't need a group of people to take care of us in Canada." Their family was processed in Longue-Pointe when "normally those documents, which are yellow, are processed in the camp, but we brought them here and had them processed." Once they were processed, they stayed in a hotel for one week until the government found a place for them. Because they did not have sponsors to help them, they had many challenges, including grocery shopping, taking public transit, and dressing for the winter. Keota remembers many phone calls from school telling her, "Ma'am, you know your kids can't be barefoot during the winter, they're going to lose their feet because they'll freeze, and we'll have to amputate."

Overall, the refugees who were privately sponsored received more assistance and guidance from their sponsors than those who were government sponsored. Milana (Interview HOF134 2020) recalls how they lived with their church sponsors for a few months before moving into their own apartment. The sponsors helped them navigate grocery and furniture shopping and setting up the apartment. Viengsamay (Interview HOF161 2020) describes the beauty of Canadian people who opened their hearts to them. He shares how they would "take us to the doctor … take us to school … take us to learn English, look for a job for us." There was also more opportunity to learn English as a second language and take other courses, whereas the government-assisted refugees often went to work soon upon arrival. Doumphet (Interview HOF119 2019) was government sponsored and describes being picked up at the airport by one man and taken to a one-bedroom apartment shared with a Cambodian man. He regrets not being able to get an education in Canada and felt that if he had a private sponsor, he might have been able to obtain a degree.

Adapting to a New Life

There were many struggles in learning to live in Canada. Refugees had been warned about the cold weather, but it was still a shock. A few refugees came with strong English or French language skills, but for the most part communication was slow and arduous. Almost all the refugees were given employment very soon after arriving. They are all grateful for the opportunities, but many had hoped for jobs more suited to their education and abilities. Adapting to a new life in a new country with different customs and languages is difficult in any circumstances. Refugees invariably arrive with trauma and pain from their previous experiences. Nevertheless, they faced their early challenges with much dignity and humour.

Those few Laotian refugees who spoke English and/or French upon arrival in Canada came with a little less anxiety because they felt they could at least communicate basic needs. Several of the refugees who spoke French found Canadian French to be very different from what they had been educated in. Khamong and Keota (Interview HOF080 2019) learned English and French in school in Laos so when they arrived at their destination, Longueil, Quebec, they were able to communicate. Keota says, "The only thing that was certain was that we could communicate in French and English before coming here. At least a bit so that we wouldn't starve to death because we could ask." Although Khamong and Keota were schoolteachers and a principal in Laos, they were willing to work anywhere in Longueil. Khamong states, "We were ready for any job. We took on any job because the only thing we had in mind was to provide for the family, especially the children, and of course also the family we had left behind." Khamong began to work at a watch company in shipping and his wife Keota worked for a women's clothing manufacturer. Ly (Interview HOF092 2019) and Phanomnhong (Interview HOF014 2019), who had learned Parisian French in Laos, both found Quebec French difficult.

The results of a study of Laotian refugees who arrived in Canada in the late 1970s and early 1980s showed that only 60 per cent of the sponsors were able to use the services of translators (often relatives or former refugees) upon arrival, and that sponsors and refugees relied on nonverbal communication, including gestures and drawings, to talk to one another (Stobbe 2006). Even with those difficulties, priority was often given to finding jobs. Stephanie's (Interview HOF113 2019) mother used a Thai-English dictionary to communicate with their sponsors, and there were no ESL classes in their town. They recall using a lot of hand gestures to try to communicate, but mostly with mixed results. Their sponsors preferred that the parents focus on work rather than study English. Within a few days of arriving in Manitoba, Stephanie's mother was sent to work in a sewing factory and her father was sent to work as a farm hand. Phanomnhong (Interview HOF014 2019) recalls one of his sponsors saying, "You don't need to go to study ESL. Why? Because you have enough right now." He regrets not having had more educational opportunities.

Some refugees were able to take English or French classes at the beginning of their lives in Canada in different cities. Oudom (Interview HOF028 2019) and his wife studied English for three months at Red River College in Winnipeg. After three years in Winnipeg they moved to Ottawa, and then to Toronto, where he worked at a car parts plant as a floor sweeper and worked his way up to a machine worker. Eventually he moved back to Ottawa and took a course in electronics at Algonquin College and went to work at high-tech companies (Mitel, New Bridge) where his wife also worked.

Sengsouvanh (Interview HOF135 2020) was able to take some French courses and ESL classes at night at a local high school in Edmonton. The daytime classes were free, but the evening classes cost money. Most people worked during the day so were forced to pay for the evening classes. Xay (Interview HOF059 2019) states, "All of us had a language barrier. My wife and I had to attend language training courses called ESL for three months sponsored by the Canada Employment Centre" in Ottawa. Thongsouk (Interview HOF098 2019) recalls his wife taking ESL classes but was not taught how to read or write. He wrote on a piece of paper for her to carry around, "My name is … and my address, my phone number, my husband's name, telephone number."

The Laotians who came to Canada feel that learning to communicate and finding work to support their families was very significant for their integration in Canada. They came prepared, as research suggests 61 per cent of Laotians in Thailand refugee camps had five years or more of formal education and 43 per cent were civil servants (Thomson 1980, 126). However, as the refugees discuss, getting access to ESL classes and having their previous work experience and skills recognized was a challenge. Other research on Laotian refugees in British Columbia and Manitoba indicates that 90 per cent of those interviewed would have liked to have had more matching of their skills to various occupations, and support for retraining and fast-tracking of foreign credentials. Mentors from their own refugee communities were almost nonexistent (Stobbe 2006). Milana (Interview HOF134 2020) describes how her parents were unable to find work in their original field and did cleaning and newspaper delivery jobs to support the family at the beginning. Eventually her father got a job with Northwest Drug Company, but not as a pharmacist, and her mother became an aide in a nursing home in Edmonton.

After losing everything, it was important for the refugees to feel a sense of control in their lives. They were willing to accept any kind of work that would give them independence and create a feeling of self-sufficiency. Chanthai (Interview HOF118 2019) remembers going to work in a sewing factory within two weeks of arrival in Steinbach, Manitoba. She recalls, "We are exciting to get a job, I want to work, I want to make money. If I have money, I will send money to my family and now we know how Canada look like and we want our family to come here too." Doumphet (Interview HOF119 2019) describes how he began working at a radiator shop for $3.50 per hour after arriving in Winnipeg, and today both he and his wife still work at Palliser Furniture.

The Establishment of Cultural Associations

"Laos is a land of festivals. Every village, every temple, and every ethnic minority not only holds its own special festivals but also joins the wider Lao community in celebrating the national ones as well" (Stuart-Fox 2008, 1). Religious and cultural celebrations have long been a staple of Laotian culture, and the Lao refugees were quick to organize them into their new lives in Canada. Ethnic associations provided mutual support and places where Laotians could maintain their language and traditions. Research has shown that these organizations did invaluable work in helping Laotians adapt to life in Canada (Dorais 2000; Van Esterik 2003; Winland 1992, 2006). The Laotian refugees discuss the importance of these organizations in their integration process and in their cultural connections.

The majority of Laotians were Theravada Buddhists, while the Hmong were often Christians. As Paul Robert Magosci notes, Buddhist temples are natural "venues for the establishment of support networks" (Stobbe 2016, 120). A Hmong Association was established soon after the Hmong arrived in Canada and several Hmong Mennonite churches were organized as the Hmong and Mennonites had shared values, a history of persecution, and an emphasis on community solidarity and mutual aid (Winland 2006).

Thongsouk (Interview HOF098 2019) arrived in Canada in 1978 and started the first Lao Association in his flat in Toronto, which became the Lao Association of Ontario. He recalls, "The government, at that time, they have programs, a sponsorship program under the government, under private groups, and churches, so on. And at that time, the government need us to help translate." He would pick up refugees from the airport and take them to the immigration office, help them find a place to live, and help with general orientation. Under the Canadian Laos Vietnam Program sponsored by the government, the Laotian and Vietnamese Associations were housed in the same office building. He shares: "That's when the big amount, the huge amounts of refugees came. In my … flat, I remember, we had almost about sixty people in that small room. We were cramped. To greet them because everyone was so happy. We came to Canada without knowing each other. Now the government bring us together. We celebrated that night to welcome them."

Lou (Interview HOF089 2019) describes the Hmong Association: "This is my community and my people, and we're still working together to help our children and grandchildren to understand our culture, religious, and making sure they keep our culture and their language too." Ly (Interview HOF092 2019) discusses how she joined the Hmong Christian church and association in Waterloo to celebrate New Year's events. Today, however, Ly, like other interviewees, fears that her language will disappear. When she speaks Hmong to her grandchildren, they answer in English. She laments that, most likely, "the third generation will not speak Hmong." She also worries that the Hmong tradition of the children caring for their elderly parents will weaken.

Life in Canada

All the Laotians interviewed for the HOF project are grateful for the opportunity to come to Canada, and to realize their desires for freedom and the opportunities to make a good life for themselves and their families. Most of the Laotians who came to Canada were part of families with young children. Several young men and women met their prospective spouses while in the refugee camps. Some got married there before coming to Canada, while others managed to reconnect once they arrived at their final destinations. Still others became adults in Canada and found their partners here. Laotian communities in earlier years frequently lacked the leadership of people who understand Canadian bureaucracy and the official languages (Chan 1988; Indra 1987), but today there are many leaders who have those qualifications.

The life of a single man or woman coming to Canada on their own is quite different from that of a family. Many single Laotians were in their teens or early twenties when they courageously made their way to Canada for a better life. Lou (Interview HOF089 2019), at age fifteen, came to Canada in 1979 as part of his cousin's family and lived in Watrous, Saskatchewan, for three years. He describes his first years as living in a "cold country and you're lonely. No parents, no support. I lived a hard life, really hard life." When his cousins moved to Kitchener-Waterloo because there was a Hmong community there, he remained in Watrous with his sponsor to try to complete high school before moving to Markham, Ontario, where his cousins now lived. He was able to write an exam to go straight to Centennial College. He attended college during the day and worked for a cleaning company at night to pay for his tuition. He graduated with a business management degree. During that time, he met his Hmong girlfriend, got married, and moved to Kitchener where his wife's family lived. He began working at Zellers department store as a management trainee. Lou was involved in the Hmong church as secretary and treasurer and helped the Hmong Association of Canada with newcomers, including translating and preparing taxes for newcomers and the elderly. Lou did not see his father for over thirty years, as he was closely watched in Laos. In 2011, his father was finally able to move to the United States to be with Lou's sister, but his father "couldn't recognize me" and then wept when he realized Lou was his son.

Doumphet (Interview HOF119 2019) was twenty-three years old when he came to Winnipeg as a government-assisted single refugee in 1979. The rest of his family was resettled in France, but Doumphet followed his girlfriend's family to Canada. While he was at the Edmonton military base, he was able to contact his girlfriend in Vancouver. He recalls not taking any English courses as "nobody guide me, nobody tell me the direction … I always work." His boss at Nikan Radiator helped him to organize a wedding, along with others from McIvor Mennonite Brethren Church who were connected to his wife's sponsors. He says, "[When] we marry I remember we had six family to my wedding [who were] Laotian people and all the rest is Mennonite." Doumphet founded the Lao Association with six other families and continues to celebrate That Luang and New Year's events. After Nikan Radiator, he went to work at Kitchen Craft, while his wife worked at Planned Parenthood. She now works at Palliser Furniture in Research and Development. They have two children and five grandchildren and are in contact with his family in France and Germany. Doumphet shares, "I feel now like Canada is my hometown. I feel like but I don't forget where I came from, from Laos, who I am, but that's for me. Because I came here, and I spent time to live here more than I live in Laos."

After forty years, the refugees have lived in Canada longer than any other place and consider Canada home.

Family Legacy

From these interviews, it is evident how proud the first generation of Laotian refugees are of their children and grandchildren, with their achievements in education, employment, and life in Canada. This was the hope and dream of the refugees when they made the difficult decision to flee Laos and start a new life in Canada. The interviews show the encouragement and support parents have given their children in pursuing their careers and taking advantage of the opportunities they have as Canadians. There is also gratitude to Canada. Doumphet (Interview HOF119 2019) says, "My daughter and my son have a good education and you know they always finish the University of Manitoba and Winnipeg and that's why I thank you very much … Canada."

Many parents talk about the sacrifices they made in their own lives so that their children could have a better future. Today, Lou (Interview HOF089 2019) has five children and four grandchildren, and the hardships are in the past. Regarding his children, he shares that "two finished college, and three finished university. And the oldest is working for the federal government … One is civil engineering, one is mechanic, one is nurse." In coming to Canada, Lou says, "We worked hard. We want a better life for your children. And us, we are the oldest generation. We come to Canada without a penny, without knowing English, but we can still survive. Like right now, most people own a house, have a couple cars outside the garage … You should be better than your grandpa and grandma. So, we encourage our kids to be better people … better citizens for the country."

Conclusions

After forty years, these interviews reveal how the Laotians have been able to successfully adapt and integrate in Canada. They have worked their way up in various employment positions and many have obtained post-secondary education degrees. In return, they are giving back to their communities by assisting new refugees with settlement and contributing to the Canadian workforce and society.

The interviewees acknowledge the people who helped them along their journey. Their successful integration means that they, in return, can also contribute to helping others and create a caring community. Keota (Interview HOF080 2019) remembers meeting people from different countries in Canada and felt, "These people knew where I was coming from. This meant seeking freedom, equality, working to build a life and future for the family. Everyone does their part, that's how I see it. Ah! Those people are just like me, why should I be scared? We are strong and brave, and if we become sick, the government is there to help us, so that was encouraging." Sengsouvanh (Interview HOF135 2020) describes the people in Edmonton who helped her integration as "very friendly, very helpful to helping each other, do not like snob, that's why I am very impressed with Canadian people, very awesome. If you need help, they always be there for you." Keota recalls the first years of being in Canada: "We were well received, well surrounded. Well surrounded in the sense that volunteers from the neighbourhood would often check on us and ask if there was anything they could do to help us … I think to the generosity of Quebecois friends, and Canadians."

A statement by Viengsamay (Interview HOF161 2020) summarizes the feelings of many Laotian Canadians when he says that he "experienced … the kind heart of Canadians, what it means to be Canadian. And I share that, in my heart. And now, I'm Canadian, and I, hopefully, will reciprocate that someday."

14

Constantly Adapting: Stories of Three Laotian Refugees

This chapter provides an in-depth view of the Laotian refugee experience by following the lives of three individual refugees over four decades from Southeast Asia to Canada. These stories add historical breadth to the understanding of the refugee experience, starting from persecution and deep suffering in their homelands, to new lives in a strange land, eventually making Canada their home.

Sengphet Chanthavong

The quotes in this story are from an interview. The interviewee has declined to have the interview published and is referred to by a pseudonym.

Sengphet Chanthavong was born in a rural village outside Pak Lay, a city in the northwest of Laos along the Mekong River near the Thailand border. He went to school until grade 6 in the village and then had to walk through the jungle along the Mekong River to Pak Lay for further schooling. As he remembers, "It's sixty kilometres walking at that time. No road, nothing, just go by the jungle along the river." After completing his studies in Pak Lay, he did teacher training in Luang Prabang, a city in north-central Laos, and became a primary school teacher in 1969. Then he moved to Vientiane, the capital of Laos, for further education. After graduating from a three-year program in 1973, Sengphet was qualified to teach in a junior high school. He followed this by another four years of studies at Dongdok National University to become a high school teacher. In 1976, at age twenty-seven, he received a bachelor's degree in natural sciences and was promoted to principal of a junior high school with 1,200 students, two vice-principals, and twenty-five teachers from 1976 to 1978.

Sengphet recalls drastic changes under the new Communist government while working as a high school principal. It was a "difficult time for us. We got used to the old system that had freedom, we had everything. But the new system was very hard to live in. It's against our ideology that we already learned from modern countries, the Western countries. The communist system that governed Laos in 1975 – that's horrible. You cannot survive. If you say anything against the government, they come to knock at your door and bring you out [to *semina*, or re-education camps]."

Sengphet describes how the new regime affected his school. "When they [the new government] came in, [they] only give us … a political, communist ideology – teaching that almost every day. Even myself, I am a principal. Before opening the school year, each year, I have to gather all the teachers, the students in a big, big hall – containing four hundred students and teachers, right? To teach them communist politics … Everything bad was thrown to the old government, the old regime, and the Western world. Everything … best is from China, Russia. That's the best. Powerful."

Teachers' salaries were sporadic:

> We sometimes get paid three months … We had to wait three months to get paid for the first time. Same as right now too … That's why the education over there is no quality. The teachers went to teach at the school only a couple of hours, then they go out to sell the items to work extra to earn money to feed the family. Otherwise, they won't survive. Me, too, like at that time after school, I had to go teach Laos languages to foreign diplomats like American diplomats, French diplomats, we teach the diplomats. Japanese diplomats. We teach Lao language to them.

Even though Sengphet was a high school principal and his wife was a nurse, it was difficult to find enough money to purchase the essentials to live.

Sengphet describes how when the Communist government arrested someone, they ended up in re-education camps. "The seminars. But actually, it's like a prison. It's like a nice word to say to the people – 're-education camp.' But actually, it's a prison." He heard about the re-education camps from various people. "A lot of people were tortured and died … Even, you heard about king of Laos? The king and the queen. They were in the same position. [Interviewer: They were in a re-education camp?] Yeah. Locked up there and they died there. And until now, nobody knows where they're buried. No … no trace at all. And there were a lot of high-ranking people that died there."

In 1978, Sengphet made the difficult decision to escape Laos with his wife and a childhood friend. He and his friend paid 1,200 baht (US$60) each to the people who would help them cross the Mekong River into Thailand. After giving them the money, they waited at the house for one of the men to get a boat. After three hours, the man showed up and said they could not take the boat across as there were too many soldiers patrolling the river. Sengphet realized the men only wanted their money and were not going to help, so they left the area and lost their money.

Sengphet decided to make another escape attempt after talking to his wife's uncle, who was an army captain and had previously been sent to re-education camps to work in the woods. They contacted an old man whom the uncle knew who lived four or five kilometres away, close to the Mekong River. With his brother-in-law, Sengphet dressed as a farmer and went to work on this man's farm for two weeks to ensure the police recognized them as farmers. After two weeks the police became less suspicious. The old farmer offered to sell them a boat for US$200. Sengphet did not have any money, not even enough to buy clothes for his children. However, when Sengphet was first married, they lived with an Australian diplomat for one year. When the diplomat's second term ended in 1975, he asked if they would leave with him. Sengphet and his wife declined, but the diplomat told them that if they ever needed money, they were to go to a certain person who would send a telex message and he would send them money. Knowing he had to make a second escape attempt, Sengphet found this person who, unbeknownst to him, happened to be his old science professor. Sengphet said, "I want to go, I cannot stay … He gave me US$600. At that time, 1978, US$600 is a lot of money … I don't know if he telexed him [his diplomat friend in Australia] … or it's his own money."

Sengphet paid US$200 for the boat and gave the old farmer an extra US$200 to bribe the soldier patrols along the Mekong River. Sengphet crossed the river one day in October 1978 at 9:00 a.m. with his wife and two small children, his uncle and aunt's family of five, and a friend of his wife. His brother-in-law drove the boat, so there were eleven people. "I looked to the side. I saw the patrol soldiers with the gun. I thought, 'Oh no, they're going to shoot us.' But they don't shoot; they just let us go."

Sengphet and his family arrived in Si Chiang Mai District, Thailand, on the west shore of the Mekong at 11:45 a.m. Sengphet sold the boat for 500 baht (US$25), and the purchaser drove them to the police station in Si Chiang Mai, where they stayed for two to three nights in a house full of people. A Thai man told them that since they had young children, they would not want to go to jail as it was dirty and the children might get sick. So they paid the man to drive them from the police station to Nong Khai refugee camp.

Nong Khai refugee camp was "overcrowded. About 40,000 people lived in that refugee camp. Yeah. We had to buy a small hut … It's very, very, not, not standard. Very poor building. We bought that for 1,900 baht [US$93]." To survive in the refugee camp, his brother-in-law sold water, and Sengphet and his wife, who was a nurse, set up a pharmacy to treat people. They obtained permission to go to the town of Nong Khai to buy medicines and resell them in the refugee camp. Sengphet set up a school for other refugees and helped them fill out applications for resettlement in third countries. "So, I teach French and English to the refugees, and I earned some money from that. And when I made an application for them, they also paid me a certain amount of money. We had to survive. We had to do everything we can." Sengphet and his family stayed in the refugee camp for almost a year, from October 1978 to July 1979.

His first interview was with Australian immigration. Australia only accepted him, his wife, and their children. His nineteen-year-old brother-in-law, interviewed as a single adult, was not accepted. His wife would not leave her younger brother at the refugee camp, so they waited for an interview with Canadian immigration. After the interview he checked the camp's information board daily. One day, he saw all five of their names. On 8 or 9 July 1979, the family left the refugee camp on a bus with other refugees to go to the Bangkok transit centre where many people were staying in the same room.

Sengphet arrived in Canada at age thirty-one as a government-assisted refugee. He and his family landed in Toronto on 13 July 1979, and from there went to Ottawa where a Manpower official picked them up and took them to the Beacon Arms Hotel. The family stayed there for one month until the government found them an apartment. It was summer, and the weather was nice and warm, but later their first experience of winter was very tough. People who were responsible for assisting refugees helped them get warm clothes, coats, and boots.

Sengphet was an educated man in Laos, a principal, and a language teacher, who already spoke French and English when he arrived in Canada. His wife also spoke some English and was able to attend ESL classes at a government centre for six months, along with her brother. His first job was at a factory. While he was grateful for it, he soon wanted something more stimulating and in line with his love of education. He applied for and was accepted to a three-year nursing program in French at Algonquin College. However, after his first day of orientation, Catholic Immigration Services offered him a job as a translator and ethnic counsellor to help new arrivals. This was a difficult decision for the family, as his wife was working a minimum-wage job and they could not afford to have him go to school. He decided to go to work for Catholic Immigration Services for three years. He helped people look for jobs and housing as well as arrange visits with doctors, lawyers, and government agencies. His clients were Laotians, Thais, and Cambodians who spoke Lao. After six months, his wife began to work as a cook in a restaurant. "She's a nurse, but we cannot get the certificate." His brother-in-law went to high school for two years and then to the University of Ottawa to become an engineer. "He's the first person who graduates as an engineer for the Laotians. Yeah, for the Lao community. Yeah, he graduated in 1984, I think, a mechanical engineer."

While working at Catholic Immigration Services, Sengphet was contacted by the Mennonite Central Committee Canada to translate for a Laotian family it had sponsored. After that, he had the opportunity to ask a Mennonite church to sponsor the rest of his family, living in an unsafe and dangerous situation in Laos. In 1988, the church sponsored his mother, two nieces, one nephew, and his brother's family of five. The church took care of them for one year, rented a house for them, sent them to ESL classes, and found jobs for them. After that, the church sponsored Sengphet's two sisters and their families, for a total of nineteen people. The latter came to Canada in 1991. This was a miraculous event for Sengphet, who feared that his sisters would be repatriated back to Laos from Thailand. He had personally called UNHCR Bangkok and asked them to allow his sisters' families to remain in Thailand as they had sponsors in Canada willing to resettle them.

Sengphet was involved in many volunteer jobs. When working with Catholic Immigration Services, he applied for a grant to set up a heritage language school to teach Lao language and culture to Laotian students. The parents of these Laotian students often worked minimum-wage jobs and were not able to drive their children, so Sengphet would pick these students up and take them to Laotian school. He operated the school for six to seven years and always struggled to compensate the teachers adequately with only a small student population. He states, "If you're a principal, they pay well, almost thirty bucks an hour. But a normal teacher, like they pay $14–15 an hour. It's too bad that we don't have students. That's why I had to give [it] up." He also volunteered at the Laotian community organization as a consultant. As part of his work with them, he obtained a government grant to operate a camp for students.

Sengphet's final jobs were good ones. He became a quality auditor with JDS Uniphase. He started as an assembler and moved up to inspector, final inspector, quality control, and then quality auditor, inspecting fibre optic cables before shipment to customers. His wife stayed with the same job in Canada. Sengphet feels that the lifestyles in Canada and Laos were very different. In Laos, women focused on homemaking while men focused on paid employment. In Canada, there is more equality between the sexes. He describes how "we have to help each other. My wife cooking, I do the dishes. Still doing [this] now."

Two of Sengphet's children were born in Laos and another daughter was born in Canada in 1986. The elder daughter works as a computer engineer for the Canada Revenue Agency, the son works as an electrical and high-tech engineer, and the younger daughter has a master's degree in social sciences and works as the secretary of the Canadian High

Commissioner. Sengphet encouraged his children to study: "'Don't work like me, like your mother. You're going to have to study. This country has a lot of opportunities for young children.' That's why I have three successful kids. All of them have good jobs. I'm so proud of them too."

Politically, Sengphet does not like the communist system:

> I don't like it at all … They're like a supreme power. They do whatever they want. They don't listen to people. People talk about them behind [their back]. They come to catch you if they know, if someone reports to them. Like, they create hate … hate in the same family. Like your brother/sister become enemies, like they don't trust each other. Make your family don't trust each other. It's terrible. I don't see any future for the children. That's why I decide, you know, decide to take them out very young and have a better system here in Canada.

Sengphet has no desire to visit Laos and feels it is still dangerous.

Sengphet states that "everybody knows that this country [Canada] has the best opportunities for building families, for the children … Yeah, to have good future for the children. Freedom … You can do whatever you want. Nobody's going to keep an eye on you. Free … free[dom] of speech and so on. This system is the best in the world. I like it. Yeah, that's why I decided to come to Canada."

Kingkeo Savejvong

The quotes in this story are translated from an interview conducted in French (Interview HOF060 2019).

Kingkeo Savejvong was born in Vientiane. In 1966, when she was six years old, her family moved to France; they returned to Laos in 1973. She was the oldest of six children. Her father was a civil servant for the Royal Lao Government, and her mother was a midwife and radiology technician at the hospital.

Kingkeo's father was taken to semina when the new regime came into power. He was one of two hundred civil servants from his district sent to rehabilitation camps, leaving his wife to care for six children. Kingkeo's family lived six years in communist Laos. During that time, she felt oppressed and forced to follow the government's rules – dressing and thinking the way the regime required. She states, "People, especially students, if you were creative or if you had imagination, you died a little bit because you no longer had your own personality at all. So, at this moment I was fifteen years old in 1975 when there was the abolition of the monarchy, it was like your adolescence was gone overnight." Furthermore, "I found myself as an adult so I could be the right hand for my mother. My father was taken to the camps. So we had no childhood my sisters and I, because we became adults not out of spite but out of necessity." According to Lao culture, the oldest is often expected to take on the "second mother" role to help with the younger siblings. After two years, her father was released from semina and was able to rejoin the family.

She describes how she was able to attend only one week of her first year in the Faculty of Medicine. Then the government changed the system, and she was only allowed to study for three days a week and then required to work in the rice fields for the other four days. "The priority was to rebuild the country." However, no money was being circulated and people could not purchase what they needed to survive. Her mother worked in the hospital as a nurse and "she got rice rations of ten kilograms of rice per month, two kilograms of sugar, and three dozen eggs or boxes of sardines, and that was it." Kingkeo states, "Our mother was like our hero because she went out of her way for her daughters. She took rolls … from the hospital to make us [sanitary] pads because there was none. We were only girls, so for us that was heroic, because if she got caught, she would be locked up for ten years because for them it was stealing; but for us and our mother, we did not see it as stealing." Kingkeo's family had to sell their clothes through the black market to Cubans and Russians who had arrived in Laos. Even with any extra money they had, it was difficult to purchase anything due to limited supplies in stores, so they would give money to their Russian language professors, who bought things for them from the stores for foreigners. "So that's it, we were very crushed. We had no freedom of thought, no freedom at all, we were dying. I thought of this as a silent, silent death."

Kingkeo recalls the traumatic disappearance of her sister:

> I had a sister who was younger than me – she was fifteen – and one day she never returned home, but her friends returned with her bicycle. We said, "Is she dead, was there an accident?" But they said that your daughter left with two hundred other students to Vietnam. Yes, so I went to the minister of education and said my sister never returned home and she isn't the only one – there's two hundred, look, there is a list posted somewhere. When I found the list, there was only first names and numbers, no last names. It was like the children didn't belong to their parents, they belonged to the state. It's like they brainwashed them, so two hundred students were okay with leaving to study in Vietnam to learn more about the socialist system. It was a shock for my parents ... That triggered it [the departure].

The family could not share their thoughts or plans for departure with anyone because "there was a lot of people around who were always listening. Everyone was monitoring." Fearful of losing other children, her parents told Kingkeo, "'Listen, we are going to leave because we have no choice.' We had no future."

Kingkeo's parents planned for eight months to escape from Laos without telling the younger children. During that time, the children went to school, their mother went to work at the hospital, and their father, who needed time to recover after his time in semina, worked in the garden. On the day that they were leaving, they needed to get to their father's hometown near the Mekong River without arousing suspicion. If they all went together, soldiers were more likely to intercept and incarcerate them. So, her two sisters rode their bikes, and Kingkeo followed three hours later. During the night, the three younger children and parents went in a car. Her great-aunt risked her life by hiding them until the smugglers arrived at two or three in the morning to help them cross the river. The boat was very small for the family of eight and an uncle, so they were not allowed to take even their small clothing packages. As they were crossing the river, Kingkeo recalls vividly how "the coast guards fired at us because that was their job. It was their way – they knew people crossed, so they fired to make us scared and to make us return." After thirty minutes they made it to Thailand.

Kingkeo describes spending the first night in Thailand hiding in a tobacco plantation before walking to a village to seek asylum. They had no papers, and were cold, stressed, and anxious. The chief of police was compassionate; he allowed them to take showers and gave them food. He then offered to bring them beds to stay in the office rather than in the jail cells with gangsters and sex workers. Her father said, "No, we do not want exemption from your rules – take us where the others are supposed to go." The women were sent to the women's cell and the men to the men's cell for the night. Fortunately, Red Cross personnel came the next morning to help them begin their life as refugees. Kingkeo's first stop was a detention centre housing five thousand refugees, where they were not allowed to leave. They were shocked to witness the lawlessness. "There was no rules, so people were swiping things right and left. Everyone was together, and we were scared." After ten days, Kingkeo and her family were taken to Nong Khai refugee camp, where they were able to register. They found friends who had been there for three to five years and feared that they might have to stay six or seven years in the camp. Kingkeo describes living in huts and having to line up for water. She describes how in "the first ten days, me and my sisters barely ate anything because we were too scared to use the washroom when we saw the state of it. So we didn't eat."

Kingkeo taught French in the camp to earn some money while her mother assisted in the hospitals. The family participated in the life of the camp, but never went out at night as it was unsafe and lawless. A month later, in 1979, the camp administration needed female interpreters. Because Kingkeo spoke French, she was assigned to assist immigration officials coming to the camp to interview refugees. During that time, she also worked for the UN. They lived at the camp for ten months before going to the transit camp in Bangkok. Her family was required to wait in the transit centre in Bangkok as the Thai officer said her younger sister had tuberculosis. The family understood that this was a tactic to obtain money from them. As they did not have any money, they had to remain for her sister to do a second X-ray that was sent to Singapore. After two months, the test finally came back negative. Corruption was often a problem, especially in the transit camps. In recalling her sister's medical examination, Kingkeo says, "We lost two months. And it seemed like in big families, they tried to do this" – delay processing until a bribe was offered. "This was a shock." She also recalls that when "the Red Cross brought clothing, they [the camp workers] chose the nicest pieces and left the rest for the refugees." Stories like this are common among vulnerable refugees who are powerless to prevent being taken advantage of.

She worked for the UN and Quebec Immigration, interpreting for families being interviewed for resettlement. After a few months, a Quebec official suggested she and her family apply to go to Quebec as they spoke French. He said, "Your whole family is French. There's no problem at all. Quebec can be your home." However, her mother refused as she wanted to return to the sunshine in Marseille, France. She said, "What will we do in Quebec?" But Kingkeo defied both her mother and the cultural expectation to defer to one's parents. She said, "If you want to wait for France, I can understand that, but for me I won't. We lost seven years to the communists. We were patient enough; we won't lose all of our youth here. No, we are going." In the end, her parents accepted the challenge and agreed to apply to Quebec for the future of their children. They applied in August 1979, and in October they went to the transit camp in Bangkok to prepare for their departure to Quebec. They were certain that they would go to Montreal.

Kingkeo was nineteen years old when her family arrived in Canada, sponsored by a private group. They arrived in Montreal and were taken to Longue-Pointe military base on 12 December 1979. The family remembered it was snowing and raining, and it felt deserted. Her mother was distraught and said, "You see, this is Canada!" There were five hundred people on the plane, and the old people and children were crying. At the military base, they completed more paperwork and were given social insurance numbers, medical insurance, and blood tests to see if the family was in good health. After two days, they were told, "Listen, you are ten people. There are no apartments in Montreal who can take you, and we can't let you be on your own … This group of sponsors will come get you and bring you to Louiseville." In their minds, they were supposed to go to Montreal, and they cried when this was not possible. Kingkeo shares, "It was the unknown because we clung to Montreal. It was like a goal, Montreal the big city. We come from a small country, but we still came from the capital." They were sponsored by Saint-Antoine-de-

Padoue parish of Louiseville, consisting of a priest, doctors, and lawyers. This group of sponsors had experience with Southeast Asian refugees as they had already sponsored two other Laotian families.

On arrival, they were taken to the basement of the church to pick out winter clothes. Her mother feared that the clothes were from people who had died, and she did not want them. Kingkeo and the rest of the family assured her that the clothes were from those who had moved away. The sponsors were great in helping her parents with groceries, rent, and integration into Quebec society, and the younger children were placed in schools. They rented a house for the family, but there was no work.

The sponsors were shocked that Kingkeo and her family spoke French, as the other two Laotian families did not. Kingkeo was surprised that the sponsors did not realize that Laos had been part of the French protectorate in Southeast Asia and that they did not ask about their experiences. She felt, "They saw us as impostors and my nineteen-year-old-self thought that they looked at us and thought we weren't real refugees." Kingkeo acknowledged that the program's objective was to bring the refugees quickly but wished that more information had been conveyed to the sponsors. Nevertheless, Kingkeo's family was grateful to their sponsors for their help.

Kingkeo was eager to work when her family arrived in Louiseville but was initially unable to find employment. She recalls, "I'm still thankful for this luck … The Laotian community called my parents to tell them that they needed women interpreters to help receive other refugees, because a lot of them were women who had gynecological problems and they did not want to speak to men." So Kingkeo went to work at the Longue-Pointe military base and was housed and fed there for five to six months while she helped the boat people from Vietnam. Much of her time was spent trying to give the refugees information on how things worked, how to do certain things, and where to get supplies. Kingkeo could not always reassure them that things would be okay as she was also new to Canada. People arrived in Montreal and were then "redirected to Alberta, to New Brunswick, all over Canada, so Montreal was just a drop-off point."

After her time at the military base, she enrolled in courses required by the Massage Therapy Federation to become a massage therapist. For the past thirty-one years she has found her calling as a massage therapist who incorporates Lao massage techniques. As she said, "All mothers know how to massage, the grandmothers know how to massage pretty well … Lao/Thai massage is practised in public – in the temples, in the communal rooms, and the person stays clothed!" She was careful to stress that she was not involved in the negative aspects of massage therapy sometimes portrayed in the media.

Kingkeo describes her family's connection to the Lao community and recalls how her father and his friends would organize gatherings for religious purposes to help the elders come together to meditate. She explains, "As Buddhists, there needed to be a temple to gather everyone, especially in difficult times." Lao Buddhist temples (Lao wat) were established in Laval, Sainte Julienne, and Lanaudière. Many events, including youth activities, take place at the temples. Her mother and other women established l'Association des Femmes Laotiennes du Quebec (Lao Women's Association of Quebec) and served on the council. Kingkeo is now the vice-president and incorporates aspects of Canadian society into the association.

Forty years ago, Lao refugees lived in Montreal's Côte-des-Neiges neighbourhood where the rent was cheap and where there was already a small population of Lao students that had been living near l'Université de Montréal. The neighbourhood did not have a good reputation as there were many sex workers and drug users, and the Lao people wanted to move to a different area. When the city of Montreal, with provincial and federal support, began a housing cooperative, her father and his friends decided to collect fifty names and visit sites for potential housing. The Mercier neighbourhood was a commercial, industrial area with fields, trains, junkyards, and syringes. They took up the challenge and "decontaminated the site, and they constructed thirty-six apartments." The six-building cooperative was named Santisouk (happiness). As it was only a small street in an industrial area, they asked City Hall and Mayor Jean Doré to name the street Rue du Laos (Street of Laos). Today, Rue du Laos is part of Le Plateau-Mont-Royal in the Mile End neighbourhood and is popular with artists. This project was the pride of her father and his friends and a contribution to Canadian society. Many activities take place there, including Montreal's 375th anniversary with a parade through the neighbourhood. Neighbourhood residents dressed in traditional Lao clothes in the parade. People learned "the story behind the name [of the street]. They welcomed us with open arms and said, 'Welcome home.'"

Her two sisters became nurses after finishing their studies in 1981, and her other two siblings also work in the public sector. Her father is now retired, in his eighties, and lives with one of her sisters. The three sisters bought houses beside one another so their father could live in the middle house. Her mother passed away three years ago from liver cancer. Kingkeo says, "It was earth shattering for us because our mother was the glue, the link holding us. Our parents were strong, solid together. It was very difficult, but it was serene. We were gathered all together, six kids with our dad. We accompanied him from the beginning to the end, in serenity, with the grandchildren, the great-grandchildren. That's why we continue, and we tell the story of our family."

Kingkeo's family experienced a wonderful miracle. As previously described, her sister was taken to Vietnam, along with two hundred children, for re-education. After four years, her sister found her way back to Laos in 1981. Kingkeo states, "Imagine two hundred families who lost their children like that overnight, and we didn't know she was in Vietnam." Even with the rest of the family now in Canada, they were able to connect with the lost sister. The family completed paperwork, and three years later, in 1984, her sister was able to come to Canada.

With the arrival of their sister, the entire family made Canada their home. Kingkeo states, "So, of course after forty years, we are definitely at home, and we share all of this with our Quebecois friends. It's extraordinary ... We were told we had nothing, we were stateless, so we had to set roots and enrich ourselves before we could share. It's a nice experience. We feel good. We're involved in everything. It's our contribution – it's giving back to the people who welcomed us." Kingkeo says, "I think Quebec is extraordinary, Canada is extraordinary. They've given us the opportunity to a second chance in life, to live again."

Thomas Vang

The quotes in this story are from an interview (Interview HOF090 2019).

Thomas Vang is Hmong, an ethnic minority group in Laos. Historically, the Lao people were divided into three groups according to dwelling elevation: the Lao Loum, or Lowland Lao; the Lao Theung, or Midland Lao; and the Lao Soung, or Highland Lao, including the Hmong (Evans 1999). Thomas was born in Oudomxay, in the northwest of Laos, but grew up in Sayaboury (Sainyabuli), approximately 150 kilometres south of Oudomxay. Both his parents were farmers, planting corn and rice and raising animals. Thomas was the fifth of seven children. He was a student at a private college in Sayaboury until 1975. Due to the war, he did not complete his studies.

Thomas's life as a Hmong teenager was scary under the new government. He states, "Even before the Pathet Lao took over Laos, they already publicly announced that the Hmong, who affiliate with the CIA, are going to be singled out to prosecute and persecute." Thomas did have several uncles and cousins who were soldiers under the Hmong general Vang Pao, who was trained by and worked for the CIA. Concerns about these threats led the whole family, along with their cousins, to hastily leave Laos on 30 May 1975, shortly after the Pathet Lao came to power.

For the most part, the Mekong River is the border that divides Laos from Thailand. However, in one area the river runs to the east of the border, and there is a land crossing. Sayaboury is located west of the Mekong River close to the northern Thai border. Thomas's family walked from their home through the remote, thick jungle toward the Thai border. Thomas describes leaving everything behind and only packing some food, mostly vegetables, for their journey that lasted many days.

When Thomas's group arrived in Thailand, the "Thai army and police officials tried to stop us [from entering] the city or the urban area, and they tried to push us back to the border, into the bush or the forest to stay there, until the authorities made a decision." The family was stuck on the Thai side of the border for almost one month. Even though there were over three thousand people at the border, there was no refugee camp, and people just stayed wherever they could. The refugees tried to relocate to another town, but the authorities pushed them back into the bush, so they had to build their own camp there. Because of increasing numbers at that border crossing, an official camp called Soptuang was set up in late 1976.

Thomas met his wife at the refugee camp and they were married by Thai officials. Their first child was born in the refugee camp. Thomas's family remained in the camp for four years, until 1979. He explains why they remained so long in the camp: "The reason is that I study. The Red Cross, International Red Cross, and UNHCR officials, they had a program to recruit young people to be trained as paramedics to help back at the camp. So, I was trying to help ... to be a paramedic to help foreign medical doctors there. And they asked me to stay longer there to help them. That's why we stayed there long." He became a paramedic, trained by one Australian and two English medical doctors. Thomas recalls the remoteness of the refugee camp and how the "Thai authorities and the local Thai population, they didn't like refugees, so they did so many awful things to refugees."

Thomas's family was taken to a transit camp in Bangkok in December 1979. They remained there until 3 February 1980 as there had been a mix-up with their initial sponsors, and immigration officials needed to find other sponsors for them. Thomas felt that they were supervised and treated well at the transit camp.

Thomas was twenty years old when his family came to Canada. On 3 February 1980, they landed in Montreal. They spent a week in a temporary shelter to process documents and complete physical exams. Upon completing the exams, they flew to their final destination, Burlington, Ontario, where they were greeted at the airport by their sponsors. Their large family was divided into three families; two of the families had the same sponsor and the other family had a different sponsor in the same city. The sponsors provided housing and the basics for the family. Thomas did not speak much English or French on arrival. After thirty days in Burlington, Thomas found work as a janitor at the Holiday Inn, and shortly thereafter, "I paid myself all my rent, my food, and the sponsor still looking after me to make sure I'm fine. And after twelve months in their supervision, then I just moved to Kitchener and then living here until now."

In Kitchener, Thomas first worked as a janitor at a McDonald's restaurant and went to night classes. He says, "I tried to take credits to qualify to go to high school. I study at nighttime in English, science, and mathematics for a couple years, I think from 1983 until 1985. Then, I qualified to go to study full time at the high school." He spent two years completing his high school diploma and went on to study history at the University of Waterloo before completing a business administration diploma program at Wilfrid Laurier University. His wife did not have the opportunity to study as she was caring for their children.

Later, Thomas was "invited to organize the association, the mutual association to help our people resettle into this area." At the time there was no Hmong church or any other association to assist refugees. There were about seven Hmong families living in the Kitchener-Waterloo area, but the majority of Hmong were scattered across Canada. So he developed a Hmong Christian church for refugees and the Hmong Association to help refugees find jobs and housing, and to help translate for immigration officials and at doctor's appointments. The Hmong Association worked with Peter Vang, who was hired by the Mennonite Central Committee Canada to find work for refugees, and Thomas helped with translating.

Thomas has spent most of his Canadian life working for and organizing the Hmong Association, which was extremely busy in the first five years assisting with settling refugees. Now the association focuses on keeping the Hmong culture alive. As Thomas states, "The people have been here longer; long enough they know the language. And the kids have been growing up and learning the language too. So they can help themselves, so we don't have many things to help the people." Now the Hmong Association runs Angel festivals, New Year's festivals, summer picnics, and other community events. They are also involved in helping families resolve disputes before using the legal system and running various workshops on topics such as health awareness. The association started to run Hmong language programs in 1983, but this ended in 2018 due to the lack of students. Thomas laments, "I think the language or the program is not going to last long, and the children are not going to speak the language for long. Few people can speak … By the third generation only very few can speak the language." Thomas has written a book, *A*

History of the Hmong: From Ancient Times to the Modern Diaspora (2008), which is an important contribution to the Hmong community and its place in the world. It describes the history of the Hmong in Laos, their life as refugees, and their new life in Western countries.

Thomas's first child was born in a Thai refugee camp, his second child was born in Burlington, and the remaining four were born in Kitchener. He has talked to his children about why they left Laos and their refugee camp experience. He says, "It's part of the motivation and encouragement for them to study hard here … I've been telling them that life is hard unless they put their time and focus on education first, before moving to something else." His second child attended Carleton University to study industrial design. He laughs at how he and his children were in school at the same time when he completed high school and went to university. Four of his children went to university and two attended college. All the children have their own families and jobs. He states, "That's like any other Canadians."

In describing opportunities in Canada, Thomas says,

> A refugee person, they have nothing except themselves. And I'd just like them to know, to understand the life of a refugee, and how they struggle to survive a new country, in a new country like Canada. They have to start to learn a language, to start to learn a culture, try to adapt to a society, and learn to work from the beginning. And it's quite hard. And if they have someone or some people to help them, it will make their life easier. Especially for the Hmong community, we didn't have any people or community existing here in this country to help us. Compared to the Vietnamese and the Laotians and the Chinese, we had more difficulty to adjust and resettle here.

Conclusion to Part Five

The stories of Sengphet, Kingkeo, and Thomas show the courage, strength, and resilience in surviving the war, enduring the refugee camps, and resettling in a new country. Their lived experiences demonstrate the importance of education and hard work, family support, and assisting those in need. Their work with Catholic Immigration Services, heritage language schools, Lao Buddhist temples, housing cooperatives, Hmong Church, and the Hmong Association were instrumental in helping to settle refugees in Canada. These programs and services continue to help integrate newcomers and build Canada's multicultural communities.

Conclusions and Reflections

Like a beautiful spider web, the narratives outlined in this book contain many strands. The 145 individual life stories of refugees from three distinct countries in Southeast Asia over four decades are described against a backdrop of vicious wars, harsh oppression, and rapid political and social changes. From the interwoven individual threads of dangerous escapes, life in refugee camps, and choosing to rebuild their lives in Canada, the authors have pulled together a pattern of the key factors that shape the collective experiences into an important chapter in Canadian history. The most significant outcomes are a sponsorship program that made it possible for individual Canadians to actively participate in fulfilling Canada's humanitarian commitments, and the substantial contributions that these refugees have made in reshaping the social and economic fabric of Canadian society for generations to come. Participant after participant gave of their valuable time to sit down with us and share their most heartfelt memories, and this would not have been possible without the oral interviews. We appreciate the emotions that were exposed. We recognize the weight of their words. And we undertake the task of capturing and preserving their knowledge through oral history.

Oral History

> Oral History is a history built around people. It thrusts life into history itself and widens its scope. It allows heroes not just from the leaders, but also from the unknown majority of the people … It brings history into, and out of, the community. It helps the less

> privileged … towards dignity and self-confidence. It makes for contact – and hence understanding – between social classes, and between generations … In short it makes for fuller human beings.
>
> Oral history is a method of historical and social scientific inquiry and analysis that includes life histories, storytelling, narratives, and qualitative research. (Thompson 2002, 35–42)

British oral historian Paul Thompson's above definition of oral history describes the Hearts of Freedom (HOF) experience in gathering oral histories from Vietnamese, Cambodian, and Laotian refugees who survived war, genocide, oppression, and potentially fatal escapes to rebuild their lives, raise their families, and create a respected place for themselves in the Canadian mosaic.

The "heroes" of the HOF project and this volume are ordinary people who found themselves in the direst of circumstances and risked all to find a better future. The telling of their stories, often for the first time, is an exercise in courage and self-confidence. Their accounts "thrust life" into the history of the terrible Vietnamese, Cambodian, and Laotian wars and their catastrophic aftermaths. The project has brought history "into and out of" Canada's Southeast Asian communities. In a very deliberate sense, the HOF project is a conduit through which the memories of the refugee generation are passed to their contemporaries, their children and children's children, and Canadian society as a whole.

Victimhood versus Agency

Refugees are often portrayed, especially in the literature about sponsorship, as helpless victims rescued by kind Canadians. In the face of vindictive, even murderous regimes, perilous escape circumstances, and hostile neighbouring countries, their ability to act was often severely, and sometime mortally, constrained. In the HOF oral histories, a recurring theme is that people came to the conclusion that if they remained in their country of birth, death was certain. On the other hand, they believed that while they might die in trying to escape – and of course thousands did – there was at least a chance they would succeed and live.

The accounts of the survivors who made it to Canada demonstrate that being victims was a passing phase quickly left behind. The impression that emerges is of people who were fiercely determined to take control of their own lives and futures and willing to work very hard and take bold decisions to do so. While those lucky enough to be matched with sponsors express appreciation for efforts made on their behalf and frequently report friendships that endured for decades, the goal they articulate in their interviews was always to become independent and self-sufficient as quickly as possible.

We often find people like Tran Chi Hieu independently finding their own accommodations and employment within months of arrival, leaving their sponsors, and never looking back. For those who ended up in small towns, like Michael Do Duy Tien (Kapuskasing, Ontario), Zung Trinh (Summerland, British Columbia), and Minh Karlsson (Kamloops, British Columbia), often the most critical first decision was to move to a large city for employment or educational opportunities and to have access to a larger Southeast Asian community and, very importantly, familiar food.

In the case of Nguyen Thi Kim Loan, the decision to move across Canada to Edmonton was motivated by the availability of better services for an autistic child. While most people headed for the big cities, the family of Huynh Vinh moved to the small town of Rossburn, Manitoba, where they purchased and operated a restaurant that provided them the income to put the children though university.

Professionals had to overcome their own challenges. Some managed to requalify; others had to find alternative occupations. Neither veterinarian Huynh Hien Thanh nor his physician wife was able to qualify in their professions, but after years of effort he became the supervisor of a medical laboratory and she a nurse.

Dentist Hoang Dinh Tri survived several years in a re-education camp and an escape by boat, but he had to acknowledge in writing that his qualifications would not be recognized in Canada before getting his visa. Following a stint as a dishwasher and several years working in a dental lab, he saved enough to take a two-year upgrading course in Montreal, after which he passed the Quebec and national dental exams and returned to Edmonton to establish a successful dentistry practice.

On arrival in Quebec, Nguyen Trung Thu was offered a well-paying job as a technician, but as an engineer with considerable experience, he was wary of getting stuck at the technician level. Instead, he obtained a master's degree in engineering with help from the federal Department of Manpower and Immigration, which led to a successful engineering career in Canada and abroad.

These are not the attributes of helpless victims, but rather of people determined to make the best of the opportunities their new country affords them and their children.

Escape

In the oral history interviews, the refugees describe the disruption of their lives by the communist victories, the experience of the re-education camps and new economic zones, and the particular horrors of life under the Khmer Rouge in Cambodia. They recall deep personal suffering in their homelands and extremely dangerous escape journeys. Many of them witnessed deaths, and many had near-death experiences. They lost family members; some were killed by the new governments, some perished trying to escape, and others were left behind. Like all refugees, they fled because they could no longer endure or survive life in their homelands.

After days or weeks on the high seas crammed into overcrowded, unseaworthy boats at the mercy of pirates and weather, or struggling through thick jungles, or crossing the perilous Mekong River sometimes under gunfire, they arrived at what they thought were safe havens. But for some, this was not the end of their suffering, as they could be pushed out to sea or back across the Thai-Cambodian border through minefields. Once they made it to refugee camps, they faced uncertainty about the future.

The primary consideration for most refugees was escaping. They were not thinking of life beyond the refugee camps, but most hoped to go to the United States while others had ties to France. They knew little or nothing of Canada but went because Canada was willing to accept them and to resettle them, often quickly.

As they arrived in Canada, they had to create new lives while they were still suffering from the fears and traumas of their past. On arrival, many found it difficult to believe that in a cold, seemingly inhospitable country, strangers offered them help for no apparent reason; their previous life experiences did not prepare them for this.

The interviews tell of severe initial settlement difficulties, culture shock, deep loneliness, and anxiety regarding relatives left behind. They had problems with language, the shocking cold, unfamiliar food, strange cultural practices, and fitting into Canada's work life. In general, the first jobs they found were far below their competence. But they also recall the welcome and initial assistance they received from Canadian authorities, private sponsors, and other helpful Canadians.

The HOF Interviews

These are not formal histories. They are individual memories inscribed in the consciousness of human beings who survived the experiences they recount. While there are common threads from interview to interview, each story is different. For the reader, individual stories present the broad spectrum of the refugee experience, including deep suffering, but also much joy and many successes. As such, they have great immediacy.

The storytellers are Vietnamese, Cambodians, and Laotians. Some are Buddhists; others are Catholics, or Animists. National identities do not always define ethnicities. Some belong to the Chinese minorities in Vietnam, Laos, or Cambodia, or the highland Hmong from Laos, or the Khmer minority in Vietnam.

The stories are told by both men and women. Some fled and arrived in family groups; others were single, while still others were children. Some were military officers and others common soldiers. Some were government functionaries; others were highly trained, often multilingual professionals or businesspeople; others were working people or farmers.

Most of the interviewees are passionate anticommunists whose views are rooted in their experiences under communist rule. In his exhaustive history *Vietnam: An Epic Tragedy, 1945–1975*, Max Hastings states:

> By the end of 1975, many people in the South were struggling for subsistence, and severe hunger struck a few months later … The suffering of the South Vietnamese in the years thereafter, with the failure of Hanoi's economic policies and the pillaging of the vanquished to serve the victors, were cruel indeed. Communists of all ranks wandered into homes, removing anything that took their fancy. (Hastings 2019, 632)

Conditions in communist Laos, a North Vietnamese puppet state, were like those in South Vietnam, but in Pol Pot's Cambodia people had to fear not only hunger, looting, and corruption, but mass murder.

Settlement Experiences: Employment

Examples of initial settlement challenges in finding appropriate employment are described in most interviews. In Montreal, two medical doctors, Dr Le Van Chau and Dr Tran Van Dung, started their lives in Canada as orderlies and, according to Le, "earning minimum wage on the graveyard shift at the St Jean de Dieu hospital for the mentally ill in the far east end of Montreal." The nurses' union blocked their attempt to obtain higher wages. In Toronto, the father of Dr Le Thuan Kien, who had been a high-ranking naval officer in Vietnam, became a stationary engineer maintaining furnaces in a hospital, while his mother, who had been a teacher in Vietnam, became a hairdresser. The examples can be multiplied across the stories of the interviewees. Most started their working lives as manual labourers, and many remained in positions below their qualifications for the duration of their working lives.

On the other hand, a number of the interviewees managed to reach senior professional and business positions in Canada very rapidly. Within three years of arriving with a newborn baby, Nguyen Bui Thi Mui qualified as a pharmacist and had her own pharmacy. Almost immediately after arrival, merchant marine captain Ha Phu Cuong found a job as a ship's captain. He captained ships mostly on the Great Lakes, but also in international shipping, until the end of his working life.

Settlement Experiences: Relations with Sponsors

Most private refugee sponsorships worked well. Canadians organized over 7,000 private sponsorships that accounted for over 34,000 arrivals in 1979 and 1980 alone. Having Canadians personally welcome the refugees to Canada and provide essential needs, including accommodation, orientation, and financial assistance, for the first year usually alleviated initial settlement challenges. And many sponsors assisted the refugees beyond the mandated first year and remained friends long after. The example of Dang Van Nghiem (Interview HOF084 2019) and his family, sponsored by a Mennonite church in Hamilton, shows how far some sponsors were willing to go. "Unlike other Vietnamese families, who are sponsored maybe three, six months after they got a job and have to go to work, my family, fortunately, we were sponsored maybe nine years, [including] rental and also food." This meant that the earnings of Dang and his wife could be sent to poverty-stricken relatives in Vietnam, and Dang could finish his education at Queen's University.

On the other hand, there were some serious private refugee sponsorship failures. Author Stephanie Phetsamay Stobbe (Interview HOF113 2019) provides an example in her account of how her family was placed in a "two-room house with no running water … no heat except for a wood-burning stove, no washroom. There was an outhouse nearby, located in a church graveyard … Coming from a Buddhist culture that feared ghosts, that was an extreme shock for our family." This type of negative experience with private sponsorships was relatively rare, but several other interviewees suffered similar experiences.

Some government-assisted refugee interviewees had problems with government bureaucracy. Bokhara Bun, who arrived in Windsor in April 1984, was provided one bedroom at the Holiday Inn for about two months and registered in ESL classes, but otherwise left on his own. A Canadian priest he had met in Cambodia moved him to Winnipeg, where he was accommodated at the Archbishop of St Boniface and enrolled in a French school. Bun's story demonstrates that for some government-assisted refugees, private Canadians sometimes stepped in when officialdom failed.

Racism

Many interviewees describe a lack of cultural sensitivity on the part of Canadians, whether private sponsors, government officials, employers, or ordinary Canadians. For example, Kingkeo Savejvong's sponsors were unaware that many Laotians spoke French; "they saw us as impostors, and my nineteen-year-old-self thought that they looked at us and thought we weren't real refugees."

The medical staff at the rural hospital considered the yellow appearance of Do Thi Kim Luong's newborn baby to be normal, since the baby was of Southeast Asian ethnicity. Fortunately, a visiting Halifax doctor diagnosed jaundice and rushed mother and child to a Halifax hospital, thereby saving the baby's life.

Loneliness, bullying, and workplace exploitation were faced by many refugees during their early years in Canada. For many interviewees, there may be a reluctance to refer to incidents of Canadian racism since they may not wish to appear too critical of Canada or be seen as complaining. They overcame horrific situations upon their escapes from Southeast Asia that make these issues less relevant to them. Most interviewees who drew attention to racist experiences in Canada arrived as children or teenagers. They speak English with a Canadian accent, and to the superficial observer only their facial features differentiate them from Canada's European majority. Thus, Nguyen Duong states that as a child in school in Ottawa he was sometimes told that he is not "a real Canadian. I find it very hurtful when they say, 'You Chink, go home.'" Nguyen Quyen, the vice-president of a major Edmonton corporation, states that he experienced some racism in the workplace, and he had to work twice as hard as his Canadian-born colleagues to reach his position, while Du Chang (Interview HOF140 2020), a successful lawyer, recalls that as a child she experienced some incidents of racism.

Nevertheless, overt observations about experiencing racism in Canada are relatively rare in the interviews. This does not mean that some refugees did not experience racism. However, in comparing the generally positive way Canadians have treated them and the opportunities they had for a better life in Canada after the terrible experiences in their homelands, the refugees emphasize, in interview after interview, that Canadians may look different from them, but treat them kindly, unlike their former compatriots. This attitude is especially pronounced in the stories of Cambodian refugees who had experienced the genocide of Pol Pot's regime. For example, Paulie Phoeuk (Interview HOF038 2019) comments that during the Pol Pot regime, the Khmer Rouge looked like him but treated him very badly – "I almost died by them."

Rural versus Urban Destinations

Before the start of the Southeast Asian refugee movement there were very few Vietnamese, Cambodian, or Laotian nationals anywhere in Canada. With the beginning of the movement in 1975, both the federal and Quebec immigration departments made efforts to resettle many refugees outside major urban centres, considering that this may make their adaptation more rapid. Once the private refugee sponsorship program was implemented in 1979, many sponsors, especially religious congregations, were from small towns, and the refugees were destined to go to those locales.

However, most refugees felt lost in small towns. For example, on arrival in Canada, the government-assisted refugee Minh Karlsson (Interview HOF171 2020) was sent to Kamloops, British Columbia, where she felt lonely and depressed. "I cried every day. I lost a lot of weight. It was very stressful." But her English teacher and new Canadian friends facilitated her move to Vancouver, where her life immediately became better. Nguyen Van Thoi (Interview HOF155 2020) was commissioned by the federal Department of Manpower and Immigration to visit rural communities in Alberta and found his newly arrived compatriots "isolated in small settlements, not knowing the language or the culture ... lost far from their homeland."

The refugees' stories show that within two to three years of arrival, many of them moved to large urban centres, and this movement continued over the following decades. In the cities they found better jobs, more educational, professional, and business opportunities, and familiar food. And very importantly, they found companionship in the growing populations of their compatriots and could join ethnic associations. A touching description of this is found in the interview of Nguyen Ba Trieu, which describes how, in the late 1970s, newly arrived Vietnamese refugees gathered in his modest apartment to eat the first bowls of pho (Vietnamese soup) cooked in Ottawa. Eventually, Nguyen became the first president of the Ottawa Vietnamese Association. Thomas Vang founded a Hmong Association in Kitchener-Waterloo to help refugees find jobs and housing and to help translate for immigration officials and at doctor's appointments. Now the Hmong Association runs Angel festivals, New Year's festivals, summer picnics, and other community events.

Starting in the late 1970s, the growth of Southeast Asian ethnic communities in major urban centres across Canada overlapped with the gradual acceptance of multiculturalism by Canadian society and contributed to the process of the refugees "becoming Canadian." Hard work, family, community, and education are very important for the Vietnamese, the Cambodians, and the Laotians. Most of the newly arrived refugees eventually discovered that they could find satisfactory jobs, care for their families in Canada, sponsor family members left behind in Southeast Asia, and support their children in getting a good education from within their communities in Canada's major cities.

Statistical Analysis: Vietnamese Refugee Community Experience

The Resettlement of Vietnamese Refugees across Canada over Three Decades by Feng Hou of Statistics Canada contains a comprehensive statistical analysis of the adaptation to Canada of Vietnamese refugees who arrived in Canada in 1979–80 at the height of the boat people crisis over the next three decades (Hou 2017).

Using census data and Statistics Canada surveys, Hou's analysis demonstrates that adult Vietnamese refugees upgraded their language knowledge and education rapidly. As well, "adult Vietnamese refugees were successful enough in finding jobs that, within a year or two after arrival, they were more likely than other immigrants to be gainfully employed" (Hou 2017). They experienced faster earnings growth; after twenty years in Canada their average earnings were almost up to the Canadian average.

> In spite of the hardships of the refugee experience and limited family resources, childhood Vietnamese refugees who went on to postsecondary education were much more likely to complete a university degree than other childhood immigrants or their Canadian-born counterparts … Probably because of their high educational attainment, childhood Vietnamese refugees had much higher annual earnings than other childhood immigrants and the similar-aged Canadian-born population in the early stage of their working careers (ages 20–37). (Hou 2017, 15)

Although Hou's study covers a relatively limited cohort of refugees (1979–80) in comparison with the total Southeast Asian refugee movement between 1975 and 1997, its conclusions largely coincide with what was observed through the HOF project's comprehensive research on Vietnamese, Cambodian, and Laotian refugees in Canada that included 145 interviews from these communities.

The Meaning of Freedom for the Refugees

The name Hearts of Freedom, the title of this book and of the project upon which this book is based, comes from the refugees themselves. The word "freedom" has a strong connotation for the refugees. It means living in peace free from government harassment and intimidation and from the fear of being reported to the authorities. It means living in a country where you can get an education and, if you work hard, you can succeed. For Samath Yi, it means being able to buy a house and provide for your family. It means having a small business. It means a country that accommodates people like himself with disabilities. For him, Canada is the best country in the world. For Minar Chhor (Interview HOF077 2019), Canada is a country where he has never felt like an outsider. Here, "Our children have also contributed a lot. They are proud Canadians, and I am proud of them too."

Many Southeast Asian refugees have been able to enjoy the freedom that Canada offers through their children. Manisorn Vong (Interview HOF116 2019) shared, "I want to let them know that they should be proud to be here in Canada … [to] learn from us and from them to be good, study, have a good job … I want them to know that I am proud to be Lao Canadian." In interview after interview, we learned that the children of Southeast Asian refugees have acquired a good education, and many of them are contributing to Canada through business, the professions, education, and the arts.

The freedom to make of your life what you yourself want, based on your own talents and hard work, is a quality of Canadian life most appreciated by the refugees. Having endured, survived, and escaped terrible oppression in Southeast Asia, they really understand the concept of personal freedom.

Multiculturalism

Minar Chhor (Interview HOF077 2019) says, "There is the Canadian charter which respects a lot of beliefs on multiculturalism … We have been welcomed and we have been able to integrate well … We have contributed to the richness of art and to the economy of the host country."

As they began to create institutions across the country, the emerging leadership of the three communities learned that the government of their new country not only supported the creation of ethnic community organizations but was willing to make funding available. Canada's official policy of multiculturalism was new and untested, having been announced on 8 October 1971, just four years before the fall of Saigon. The Canadian government's financial support and encouragement of ethnic community association formation were strong factors in helping the refugees build meaningful lives and feel at home in Canada. For the former Southeast Asian refugees, maintaining their cultures came to be seen as an essential element of their Canadian identities.

Sense of Belonging; Becoming Canadian

The interviews provide a cross-section of the views of former refugees about the development of their lives over several decades in Canada. They have thought deeply about this subject. Their opinions vary a great deal but reflect several distinct trends.

Many interviewees express deep gratitude to Canada and Canadians. Many refugees describe Canada as a land of kind people that gave them a new start in life. To a certain extent this is surprising, since, as the foregoing attempts show, the interviews contain stories of numerous difficulties, including problematic interactions with Canadians. But we must recall where the refugees came from and their previous experiences. Despite problems on arrival, Canada provided them with a haven from intense violence and oppression in their homelands.

This is perhaps most clearly expressed by Ho Cong Thanh (Interview HOF133 2020), who considers that Vietnam abandoned him and made him stateless. According to Ho, the minute he received his Canadian immigration visa in a refugee camp, he became Canadian. "For us refugees, we don't have a state, we don't have a nationality. Canada is a home country that took me, took my family. This is home to me."

Several interviewees, who say they feel fully Canadian and for whom Canada is their only home, were children when they arrived in Canada. Vu Thanh Uyen Tanya (Interview HOF143 2020), a member of an extended Vietnamese family in Edmonton, recalls that she visited Vietnam as an adult: "Back in Vietnam I found it very strange. I did not feel that Vietnam was my country. I felt like a tourist."

For most interviewees, feeling at home in Canada is part of a process. They report that once they had jobs, satisfactory living conditions, a grasp of an official Canadian language, and a knowledge of how to get around in their new communities, it was sufficient for the demands of daily life and they felt at home. The fact that Canada's family reunification provisions made it possible to reunite with family members that had been left behind added to their positive feelings for their new home. (By 1997 over sixty thousand relatives had been brought to Canada under the Orderly Departure Program; see appendix 1.) It is impossible to determine an exact amount of time required for people to feel Canadian; it varies from interviewee to interviewee, but generally it appears to be between seven and ten years.

Identity Issues/Dual Identity

It should be noted that for many interviewees, feeling at home in Canada and feeling fully Canadian are different concepts. The primary allegiance of some refugees is still to their idealized, noncommunist homelands. An example of someone with this mindset is Nguyen Ngoc Duy (Interview HOF072 2019). He calls Canada his "second country," not his home. After thirty-nine years in Canada, he still hopes that someday, once the communists are not in power, he will be able to return to Vietnam.

Some of the interviewees, especially well-educated professionals, consider their identities, usually after internal struggles, as fully Canadian, but also fully Vietnamese, Cambodian, or Laotian and, in some cases, Chinese. Thus, Du Chang (HOF140 2020) felt for a long time that she had "cultural schizophrenia" (her words). She was a Western woman whose only fluent language was English, and yet some of her most profound cultural patterns were those she learned from her Vietnamese and Chinese parents. She has accepted her inherited Asian cultural identity but considers herself fully Canadian now that she has Canadian children with no Asian identity. Tran Duc Chi, a gifted mathematician who feared that by feeling fully Canadian he was betraying Vietnam, used mathematical reasoning – infinity divided by two is still infinity – to prove that it was possible to have dual loyalties and a dual identity.

Overall, many of the refugees, unless they had arrived in Canada as children, continue to consider their Southeast Asian ethnicity their primary identity, with Canada being the country that saved their lives and provided them with the possibility to flourish in a free and peaceful environment with their families.

Southeast Asian Contribution to Canadian Multiculturalism

Fifty years later, in contemporary Canada, former Southeast Asian refugees are part of Canada's cultural mosaic; some of them are in leading positions in business, the arts, and the professions. Most of them describe good lives and report that their children are, on the whole, doing well. In cities, and even in smaller towns, where fifty years ago Southeast Asian foods were unavailable, there are now many stores and restaurants that feature products that are routinely consumed by Canadians. It is a rare Canadian city that does not have Vietnamese, Cambodian, or Laotian restaurants. Major cultural events like Tet New Year festivals, the Cambodian Sangkran festival, or the Lao That Luang festival take place in Canadian cities from coast to coast. Former refugees are part of a multicultural Canada which they have helped to transform over the decades.

Southeast Asian communities have become active parts of the societies of Canada's different regions. For example, Kingkeo Savejvong describes how Montreal's Laotian community created a Lao housing cooperative at the edge of the city's trendy Plateau-Mont-Royal neighbourhood with the help and cooperation of federal, provincial, and municipal authorities. With the blessing of the Montreal mayor, the street on which the cooperative was built was named Rue du Laos, and the Laotian community has become a valuable and vibrant participant in many of the city's cultural events.

Contribution of Southeast Asians to Communities and to Canada

At the same time as they are grateful for what Canada has given them, the HOF interviewees are also aware of what they have contributed to Canada and are very proud of their contributions. Former refugees are part of a diverse multicultural Canada which has been transformed over the past half-century. Southeast Asian refugees have played an important and active role in the country's transformation.

Several interviewees are actively giving back to Canada through a range of benevolent volunteer activities. These include helping newcomers – both refugees and other immigrants – with their settlement by providing mentoring, mental health, and counselling services, and being private sponsors to new refugees. The interviewees and their children are professional businesspeople, accountants, medical doctors, dentists, engineers, professors, teachers, nurses, and so forth, providing services to Southeast Asians and the larger Canadian community. Some have also established medical, educational, and legal aid services and programs for poor people in Vietnam, Cambodia, and Laos and have led medical or developmental missions to those countries.

Former refugees and their children have become involved in a range of artistic and cultural activities in Canada, and some have become widely known, prize-winning Canadian authors in both English and French. Cultural functions presented by Southeast Asian ethnic organizations have enriched Canadian culture.

Impact of the HOF Project

As an important deliverable of Hearts of Freedom, the Canadian Southeast Asian Refugee Historical Research Project at Carleton University, this book is the cultural vehicle through which Southeast Asian refugees, both as individuals and as communities, contribute to the record of this important chapter in Canadian history in a highly visible manner. The HOF website, which provides public access to 163 of the 173 oral interviews that were conducted, has become an important source of information for Southeast Asian communities, academic researchers, and larger Canadian society.

Principal Lessons of the HOF Project

Canada's private sponsorship program, introduced just in time in 1978, initially proved its worth as a settlement strategy during the boat people emergency of 1979–80 and has continued to increase Canada's capacity to absorb large numbers of refugees and provide them with a personal welcome for five decades. In 2016, the UN General Assembly recognized the Canadian private refugee sponsorship system and recommended that other countries consider creating similar programs. Through the Global Refugee Sponsorship Initiative, Canada's Private Sponsorship of Refugees Program is a model for similar programs in Argentina, Ireland, New Zealand, the United Kingdom, Spain, Germany, and the United States.

The oral histories reveal that while material support for government-assisted refugees delivered through Canadian Manpower centres in English-speaking Canada was adequate for survival, it was the many instances of kindness and assistance on the part of officials that they most appreciated. At the same time, there were cases of government-assisted refugees, like Cambodians Chamroeun Lay, Kong Bun, and Channa Kong, where new arrivals were registered in a hotel and essentially left to fend for themselves.

These shortcomings did not go unnoticed by the Canadian government, and the Department of Immigration in particular. The impressive network of robust, community-based settlement agencies that have welcomed subsequent waves of government-assisted refugees grew out of the lessons learned. In Quebec, the Centre d'orientation et de formation des immigrants (COFI) system, which provided both intensive language and orientation for government-assisted Quebec-bound refugees, worked very well, though it initially struggled to accommodate the large number of arrivals.

It is difficult to express in words the magnitude of the impact that these refugees made in reshaping the social and economic fabric of Canadian society. They arrived at a time when multiculturalism was new and the general Canadian public knew very little about Southeast Asia. Their arrival not only served to unite individual Canadians behind a humanitarian cause; it also spurred faith and community organizations to apply their resources to assist the refugees. For most Canadians at the time, multiculturalism was something that politicians talked about on Canada Day. When over 7,000 sponsoring groups welcomed 32,000 refugees into their communities, their places of worship, and their homes in 1979–80, multiculturalism became a lived experience.

The arrival of the refugees in such large numbers galvanized federal, provincial, and municipal governments to cut through the red tape to create needed legislation, institutions, programs, and processes in record time. And at a fundamental level, the media brought the very real horror of war and its refugee aftermath to a new generation of Canadians for the first time since World War II. Their influence is immeasurable.

The HOF project underscores through these very personal accounts the risks and losses that the refugees incurred in escaping their home countries and their determination to start a new life in their new country.

The HOF project team wishes to express its gratitude for the courage and generosity of those who relived and recorded their experiences for this research project, making it possible to save and preserve stories, memories, and experiences that would otherwise have been lost, and that constitute such an important chapter in our shared history.

The single overwhelming lesson imparted through the Southeast Asian refugee experience is that when Canada and Canadians welcome refugees with compassion, respect, and dignity, and facilitate their road to becoming Canadian, the refugees will repay Canada by becoming valuable participants in the Canadian cultural mosaic.

APPENDIX 1

Statistical Analysis of the Refugee Movement from Vietnam, Cambodia, and Laos to Canada, 1975–97

The stories told by the Hearts of Freedom (HOF) interviewees are distillations of individual and family experiences over a long time. They are narrative samples of a large refugee movement sourced from three countries of origin, whose initial destinations were in eight main countries of first asylum in Southeast Asia, followed by third-country resettlement in a range of countries, including Canada. The statistical sources of such a multifaceted movement have gaps and are occasionally inconsistent with each other.

This appendix presents the statistical picture of the resettlement of Vietnamese, Cambodian, and Laotian refugees in Canada starting in 1975. It provides an analytical background to the HOF refugee interviews. Its methodological approach consists of a numerical analysis and comparison of all available statistical sources, taking special care to find the best possible estimates when the sources contain gaps or inconsistencies.

A full statistical analysis of the refugee movement to Canada had not been undertaken prior to this project. The movement was too diverse and multifaceted, including many geographic locations and several ethnic groups across Southeast Asia over a period of twenty-three years. There were many national and international institutions involved, and the reporting about the refugees in various locations was not always entirely dependable. The most obvious example of uncertain statistics mirroring terrible events is the number of refugees who perished at sea. Different commentators provide widely differing numbers. The average number from a range of sources is 300,000; it is at best an educated guess.

However, based on information garnered from the interviews, we consider that the figure of 300,000 contained in the most detailed published statistical analysis (Rummel 1997) may be slightly too low.

A careful analysis can provide relatively few exact figures about this refugee movement. However, estimates based on available numerical statistics can be provided.

The resettlement of Southeast Asian refugees in Canada consisted of the following components (Molloy et al. 2017):

1975–78: Over 8,000 refugees from Vietnam, Cambodia, or Laos, most of whom escaped in the immediate aftermath of the war, were selected in accordance with Canadian Cabinet decisions.

1979–97: Following a UNHCR consultation in December 1978 and a UN conference in July 1979, Canada made a two-year commitment to resettle 50,000 Vietnamese, Cambodian, or Laotian refugees. This figure was later increased to 60,000. Between 1979 and 1997, these refugees were selected under the 1976 Immigration Act as government-assisted and privately sponsored members of the Indochinese Designated Class, plus a small number who were sponsored by family in Canada. The vast majority were in camps in Southeast Asia for extended periods. Some were in private accommodations, and a few were in countries outside the region.

1979–94: Family members residing in Vietnam sponsored by refugees already resettled in Canada were allowed to leave Vietnam directly for Canada under the provisions of the Orderly Departure Program (ODP). This program was based on an agreement concluded between the UNHCR and the Vietnamese government in 1979 and supervised by the UNHCR. Canada accepted these refugees using family reunion regulations.

Sources

To get a reasonable numerical estimate of the overall numbers of Southeast Asian refugees resettled in Canada the following sources were used (listed here by the range of years covered by each source):

1975–96: *Immigration Statistics = Immigration, statistiques* (Citizenship and Immigration Canada, annual reports published between 1966 and 1999). Recorded the country of birth of immigrants, including refugees, landed in Canada each year, but did not separately record refugee landings.
1979 AND 1980: *Indochinese Refugees: The Canadian Response, 1979 and 1980* (Employment and Immigration Canada 1982). Recorded all Indochinese refugee landings in Canada for these two years.
1975–97: *Terms of Refuge: The Indochinese Exodus and the International Response* by W. Courtland Robinson (1998). Orderly Departure Program (ODP) statistics in appendix 2 of *Terms of Refuge* cite the UNHCR's records of Vietnamese and Cambodian nationals resettled in Canada under the family reunion element of the ODP between 1975 and 1997 (295).

The above sources were cross-checked with UNHCR statistics drawn from the UNHCR publication *The State of the World's Refugees 2000: Fifty Years of Humanitarian Action* (UNHCR 2000).

The numerical analysis of Indochinese refugee resettlement in Canada is an approximation. We do have exact numbers, by country of birth (COB), for Indochinese refugees resettled in Canada in 1979 and 1980 (see table A1.2). The Government of Canada was committed to resettling 60,000 refugees during this two-year period; COB statistics were carefully maintained and reported in *Indochinese Refugees* (Employment and Immigration Canada 1982). It is important to note that in addition to reporting a combined 57,210 refugee arrivals from Cambodia, Laos, and Vietnam, *Indochinese Refugees* also lists 2,839 Indochinese refugee arrivals with a COB of "Other." Therefore, of the 60,049 Indochinese refugees that landed in Canada in 1979 and 1980, 57,210 (95.3%) were born in Vietnam, Cambodia, or Laos, while 2,839 (4.7%) were born outside of the three major refugee source countries (Employment and Immigration Canada 1982, 20; and see table A1.2).

In 1979–80, a substantial percentage of the Vietnamese refugees were Chinese minority (Hoa) people. Of the 60,049 Indochinese refugees resettled in Canada during these two years, 18,021 (30%) identified Chinese as their mother language. While most of the Hoa refugees were born in

Vietnam, a minority were not. These are among the Indochinese refugees with a COB of "Other" shown in table A1.2.

Another category where exact numbers are available is the number of Cambodian and Vietnamese immigrants resettled in Canada through the family reunion provision of the Orderly Departure Program (ODP) (see table A1.5). According to the terms of this program, established through an agreement between the UNHCR and the Government of Vietnam in 1979, the UNHCR was responsible for monitoring its progress. Because its modus operandi was direct transportation from Vietnam to Canada of family members sponsored by refugees who were already resettled in Canada, the UNHCR kept exact numerical statistics containing an accurate count of direct departures to Canada.

Two elements of the ODP should be highlighted. First, in facilitating the legal departure from Vietnam of members of refugee families left behind, it reduced the high risks associated with escapes by sea. Through the intermediary of the UNHCR, the United States pushed Vietnam to accept the program and Vietnam, wishing to reduce irregular refugee departures by sea following the expulsion of Chinese from South Vietnam, accepted the ODP. Second, an additional reason for Vietnam's acceptance of the ODP was its wish to use the program to remove from Vietnam some of the 170,000 Cambodian refugees who had escaped (or were expelled) to Vietnam from the Khmer Rouge regime. Under the ODP, Canada resettled 60,285 Vietnamese and 4,670 Cambodians for a total of 64,955 (Robinson 1998, 295).

Annual immigrant landings by immigrant class were only reported in *Immigration Statistics* between 1983 and 1996 (Citizenship and Immigration Canada 1975–99), including both Family Class and Assisted Relative landings, classes used by Immigration Canada for family reunion. Thus, we have Canadian family reunion numbers for fourteen of the nineteen years during which the ODP functioned. As well, for three of the five missing years (1979, 1980, and 1997), the ODP and family reunion from Vietnam were functioning in a very limited manner, with low numbers. In 1979–80, at the beginning of the program, the ODP was running into serious implementation problems because of Vietnamese government obstruction. By 1997, the program was essentially over.

Therefore, by comparing the available Canadian family reunion numbers from *Immigration Statistics* with UNHCR's ODP numbers (Robinson 1998, 295), we do have a rudimentary control mechanism for ODP statistics. Between 1983 and 1996, *Immigration Statistics* reported 58,570 Vietnamese and 1,700 Cambodians resettled in Canada through family reunion. The Vietnamese number is very reasonable when compared to the UNHCR's Vietnamese ODP total of 60,285. The discrepancy in the Cambodian number when compared to UNHCR's Cambodian ODP total of 4,670 is relatively easy to explain. Many (probably most) Cambodian refugees expelled from Cambodia to Vietnam were members of the Vietnamese minority in Cambodia. While UNHCR statistics counted them as Cambodian nationals, Canadian landing statistics probably counted them as Vietnamese residents. Therefore, UNHCR's Canadian ODP statistics appear, after applying all available controls, to be reliable.

Overall, in combining COB landing numbers from archived *Immigration Statistics* (Citizenship and Immigration Canada 1966–99) with the exact statistics available through *Indochinese Refugees* (Employment and Immigration Canada 1982) and *Terms of Refuge* (Robinson 1998, 295), we arrive at numbers of Vietnamese, Cambodian, and Laotian nationals resettled in Canada between 1975 and 1997 (see table A1.6). It should be noted, however, that while both *Indochinese Refugees* data (table A1.2) and our estimated total number of Indochinese immigrants (table A1.6) include Indochinese refugees whose COBs were outside Vietnam, Cambodia, and Laos, *Immigration Statistics* (tables A1.1, A1.3, and A1.4) and UNHCR data reported in *Terms of Refuge* (table A1.5) do not.

Conclusions

Several observations need to be made about the above statistical tables.

1 The *Immigration Statistics* reports from 1975 to 1997 were checked against UNHCR's statistics from appendix 2 of Robinson's *Terms of Refuge* (1998, 295). According to the UNHCR, the total number of Indochinese refugees resettled in Canada between 1975 and 1997,

TABLE A1.1

1975–78: Cambodian, Laotian, and Vietnamese immigrants (primarily refugees) resettled in Canada.

Country of birth	Immigrants resettled
Cambodia	671
Laos	244
Vietnam	7,767
Total (Cambodia, Laos, and Vietnam)	8,682

Sources: Citizenship and Immigration Canada, 1966–99, *Immigration Statistics = Immigration, statistiques* [annual reports 1975 (20), 1976 (20), 1977 (20), 1978 (20)], catalogue no. MP22-1-PDF (Ottawa: Manpower and Immigration = Main-d'œuvre et immigration), publications.gc.ca/pub?id=9.500621&sl=0.

TABLE A1.2

1979–80: Indochinese refugees resettled in Canada, by country of birth.

Country of birth	Refugees resettled
Cambodia	4,697
Laos	9,849
Vietnam	42,664
Combined total, Cambodia, Laos, and Vietnam	*57,210*
Other	2,839
Total (Indochina)	60,049

Source: Employment and Immigration Canada, 1982, *Indochinese Refugees: The Canadian Response, 1979 and 1980*, 20, catalogue no. MP23-60/1982E-PDF (Ottawa: Employment and Immigration Canada), publications.gc.ca/pub?id=9.804208&sl=0.

TABLE A1.3
1979–80: Cambodian, Laotian, and Vietnamese immigrants (primarily refugees) resettled in Canada.

Country of birth	Immigrants resettled
Cambodia	4,785
Laos	9,881
Vietnam	43,707
Total (Cambodia, Laos, and Vietnam)	58,373

Sources: Citizenship and Immigration Canada, 1966–99, *Immigration Statistics = Immigration, statistiques* [annual reports 1979 (20), 1980 (26)], catalogue no. MP22-1-PDF (Ottawa: Manpower and Immigration = Main-d'œuvre et immigration), publications.gc.ca/pub?id=9.500621&sl=0.

TABLE A1.4
1981–96: Cambodian, Laotian, and Vietnamese immigrants (primarily refugees) resettled in Canada, including all classes of immigrants.

Country of birth	Immigrants resettled
Cambodia	16,829
Laos	7,272
Vietnam	117,248
Total (Cambodia, Laos, and Vietnam)	141,349

Sources: Citizenship and Immigration Canada, 1966–99, *Immigration Statistics = Immigration, statistiques* [annual reports 1981 (26), 1982 (14), 1983 (14), 1984 (18), 1985 (18), 1986 (18), 1987 (20), 1988 (20), 1989 (20), 1990 (20), 1991 (20), 1992 (24), 1993 (24), 1994 (24), 1995 (24), 1996 (24)], catalogue no. MP22-1-PDF (Ottawa: Manpower and Immigration = Main-d'œuvre et immigration), publications.gc.ca/pub?id=9.500621&sl=0.

TABLE A1.5

1979–97: Cambodian and Vietnamese immigrants resettled in Canada through the family reunion provision of the Orderly Departure Program (ODP), by country of birth, as reported by UNHCR.

Country of birth	Immigrants resettled through family reunion
Cambodia	4,670
Vietnam	60,285
Total (Cambodia and Vietnam)	64,955

Sources: W. Courtland Robinson (1998), "Cumulative Indo-Chinese Resettlement Statistics, 1975–97," appendix 2 of *Terms of Refuge: The Indochinese Exodus and the International Response* (New York: Zed Books), 295.

TABLE A1.6

1975–97: Total estimated number of Indochinese immigrants resettled in Canada (the overwhelming majority refugees or family members of refugees).

Country of birth	Immigrants (primarily refugees) resettled
Cambodia	22,197
Laos	17,365
Vietnam	167,679
Other	2,839
Total (Indochina)	210,080

Sources: Citizenship and Immigration Canada (1966–99), *Immigration Statistics = Immigration, statistiques*, annual reports [1975 (20), 1976 (20), 1977 (20), 1978 (20), 1979 (20), 1980 (20), 1981 (26), 1982 (14), 1983 (14), 1984 (18), 1985 (18), 1986 (18), 1987 (20), 1988 (20), 1989 (20), 1990 (20), 1991 (20), 1992 (24), 1993 (24), 1994 (24), 1995 (24), 1996 (24)], catalogue no. MP22-1-PDF (Ottawa: Manpower and Immigration = Main-d'œuvre et immigration), publications.gc.ca/pub?id=9.500621&sl=0; Employment and Immigration Canada (1982), *Indochinese Refugees: The Canadian Response 1979 and 1980*, 20, Catalogue no. MP23-60/1982E-PDF (Ottawa: Employment and Immigration Canada), publications.gc.ca/pub?id=9.804208&sl=0; W. Courtland Robinson (1998), *Terms of Refuge: The Indochinese Exodus and the International Response* (New York: Zed Books), 295; UNHCR [UN High Commissioner for Refugees] (2000), "Chapter 4: Flight from Indochina," in *The State of the World's Refugees 2000: Fifty Years of Humanitarian Action*, 79–104 (Oxford: Oxford University Press), https://www.unhcr.org/publications/state-worlds-refugees-2000-fifty-years-humanitarian-action.

including (i) refugees resettled from countries of first asylum and (ii) family reunion immigrants resettled directly from Vietnam through the ODP, was 202,178 (Robinson 1998, 295). This is 3.8% less than the grand total estimate of 210,080 obtained from *Immigration Statistics*. However, the UNHCR statistics only contain refugees who were resettled in Canada from first countries of asylum. They do not include thousands of refugees who were first transferred to the US in 1975, resettled in Canada from US military facilities, and appear in Canada's immigrant landing statistics for 1975 and 1976. Other refugees who ended up in European countries and again qualified for resettlement in Canada without reference to the UNHCR. Therefore, UNHCR's Canadian refugee resettlement numbers are lower by a few thousand than the actual immigrant COB resettlement numbers recorded in the *Immigration Statistics* reports.

2 The most reliable Canadian immigration statistics we possess are immigrant country of birth (COB) statistics. In 1979–80, the only two years with accurate refugee (rather than immigrant) landing statistics, 2,839 refugees resettled in Canada were not born in one of the three refugee source countries. For the remaining twenty-one years of the movement, we have no way to capture those refugees resettled in Canada who were not born in the three source countries. Admittedly, the "Other" category in table A1.2 is higher than for other years, since 1979–80 were the highest years of Chinese minority refugee resettlement, which gradually petered out after 1981. Most "Other" COB refugees in table A1.2 were probably born in China. Nevertheless, it is also probable that, during the twenty-one years when we have no access to the "Other" figure, some of the refugees resettled in Canada were not born in the three source countries of Indochina and cannot be accessed from the *Immigration Statistics* reports.

3 There is a small number of Vietnamese, Cambodian, and Laotian immigrants to Canada during the twenty-three years of the Indochinese refugee movement who were not refugees or ODP family reunion dependents of resettled refugees. This can be demonstrated by comparing the 58,373 Cambodian, Laotian, and Vietnamese im-

> migrants resettled in Canada in 1979–80 (table A1.3) with the 57,210 Cambodian, Laotian, and Vietnamese refugees resettled in Canada in 1979–80 (table A1.2). The variance is 1,163, meaning that during these two years Canada accepted 1,163 immigrants from the three source countries who were not classified as refugees.

In considering the above three observations, while we do not have an exact number for Vietnamese, Cambodian, and Laotian refugees resettled in Canada between 1975 and 1997, observations 1 and 2 tend to increase their annual numbers beyond the total number of Indochinese immigrants resettled by Canada between 1975 and 1997, while observation 3 tends to decrease their annual numbers. We emphasize that the maximum variance in either direction is less than 4% from the grand total of 210,080 from *Immigration Statistics*.

Therefore, using available numerical statistics, we estimate that the total number of Vietnamese, Cambodian, and Laotian refugees and family-sponsored dependents of refugees resettled in Canada between 1975 and 1997 was 210,000 plus or minus 3.8%, meaning a mean figure of 210,000 with a possible maximum of 218,000 and a possible minimum of 202,000. Of these, 167,600 plus or minus 3.8% were Vietnamese, 22,200 plus or minus 3.8% were Cambodians, 17,400 plus or minus 3.8% were Laotians, and 2,800 plus or minus 3.8% were "Other." Note that all estimates have been slightly adjusted up or down to provide round numbers.

Using the UNHCR's ODP numbers, the above total may be divided into:

Refugees selected through a Government of Canada refugee program: 145,000
Family reunion with refugee sponsors in Canada through the ODP: 65,000

We do not have a statistical breakdown for privately sponsored and government-assisted refugees between 1981 and 1997. (Note: neither the ODP nor the private refugee sponsorship program existed before 1979.) On this aspect of the Indochinese refugee movement, we can only make a rough guess. Since between 1975 and 1978 there was not yet a private sponsorship program, for these four years, 8,692 Indochinese refugees were government assisted (Citizenship and Immigration Canada 1966–99 [1975–78]). For 1979–80, the breakdown as reported in *Indochinese Refugees* (Employment and Immigration Canada 1982) was:

> Privately sponsored refugees resettled in Canada in 1979–80: 39,904
> Government-assisted refugees resettled in Canada in 1979–80: 20,145

For the remaining years of the Indochinese refugee resettlement program, based on the breakdown in the above figures, and knowing that there was a special push in 1979–80 to accommodate private sponsorships, we guess (and we emphasize that this is a guess) that the rest of the program was 45% government assisted and 55% privately sponsored.

In conclusion, based on the above analysis, we estimate that a total of 210,000 Vietnamese, Cambodian, and Laotian refugees and family-sponsored dependents of refugees resettled in Canada between the falls of Saigon, Phnom Penh, and Vientiane in early 1975 and the end of Canada's Indochinese Designated Class in 1997. Of these, 167,600 were Vietnamese (including Chinese minority), 22,200 were Cambodians, 17,400 were Laotians, and 2,800 were residents of the three refugee source countries, but not born there (designated as "Other"). Of the total, 65,000 were selected through the UNHCR's Orderly Departure Program, and 145,000 were selected through a government of Canada refugee program; of the latter, roughly 80,000 were privately sponsored and 65,000 were government assisted. (All final numbers are rounded up or down.)

APPENDIX 2

Statistical Analysis of the Hearts of Freedom Project Interviews

Most refugee interviewees were selected through contacts with, and recommendations from, the Vietnamese, Cambodian, and Laotian ethnic communities in Canada. There were interviews with refugees and with Canadian officials, facilitators, private sponsors, and ex-politicians; interviews took place in ten Canadian cities/regions from coast to coast, including Halifax, Montreal, Hamilton, Kitchener/Waterloo, Ottawa/Gatineau, Toronto/Southwest Ontario, Winnipeg, Edmonton, Calgary, and Vancouver. Thus, the Hearts of Freedom project provided a broad representation of the Southeast Asian refugee resettlement experience across Canada.

The project was based in Ottawa. Because of financial and time limitations, the three central Canada cities – Montreal, Toronto, and Ottawa/Gatineau – were slightly overrepresented as interview locations, while Vancouver was underrepresented. Nevertheless, as shown in Table A2.1, we succeeded in having a representative sample across Canada of interviewees from each refugee group and a limited number of interviews with Canadian officials, nongovernmental organization facilitators and private sponsors, as well as interviews with two senior Canadian ex-politicians who were closely involved in Canada's Southeast Asian refugee program.

Table A2.2 contains the interview breakdown by refugee nationality plus Canadian facilitators and sponsors as well as two senior Canadian ex-politicians (Joe Clark and Lloyd Axworthy). It should be noted that although the Chinese minority (Hoa) population in Vietnam formed an important part of the refugee movement to Canada, we could not reliably

TABLE A2.1
Number of interviews by location.

Location	Number of interviews
Halifax	3
Montreal	32
Ottawa/Gatineau	41
Toronto/Southwest Ontario	40
Winnipeg	15
Edmonton	15
Calgary	13
Vancouver	14
Total	173

TABLE A2.2
Number of interviews by interviewee group.

Interviewee group	Number of interviews
Vietnamese	73
Hoa (Chinese minority in Vietnam)	14
Cambodians	30
Laotians	28
Canadian officials, NGO facilitators, and private sponsors	26
Senior Canadian ex-politicians (Joe Clark and Lloyd Axworthy)	2
Total	173

form a statistical estimate of its share of the overall movement in appendix 1. We do, however, have an estimate of the number of Hoa people interviewed, which is included in Table A2.2. This remains an estimate, because some of the interviewees identify as members of both Vietnamese and Hoa ethnic groups, and some are in mixed marriages, with one marriage partner being Vietnamese and the other Hoa.

TABLE A2.3
Number of interviews by language.

Language of interview	Number of interviews
English	122
French	32
Vietnamese	11
Khmer (Cambodian)	7
Lao	1
Total	173

The number of English- and French-language interviews in table A2.3 mirrors the settlement patterns and official language acquisition in Canada of the three refugee source communities. According to the 2016 Canadian census, 21% of Vietnamese, Khmer, and Lao mother language Canadian residents reside in Quebec and 79% in the rest of Canada. Of the official language interviews, 20% were in French and 80% in English, closely corresponding to the census linguistic division of Vietnamese–, Khmer–, and Lao–mother language residents between Quebec and the rest of Canada. In addition, there were eighteen interviews conducted in the interviewees' Southeast Asian mother languages. The latter were translated into an official language through the cooperation of the three ethnic communities.

APPENDIX 3

Canadian Government and Civil Society Interviews

While the Hearts of Freedom (HOF) oral history project focused mainly on the Vietnamese, Cambodians, and Laotians who came to Canada as refugees between 1975 and 1997, the Research Committee was keenly aware that more than four decades later, many of the Canadians involved in the resettlement effort are no longer with us. It was decided, therefore, to capture the memories of people from government and civil society while it was still possible. This decision led to twenty-eight interviews covering a broad spectrum from prime minister to frontline settlement workers and sponsors.

Political Leaders

At the political level, we were fortunate to record interviews with former Conservative prime minister Joe Clark (Interview HOF173 2021), whose government authorized the admission of 50,000 Southeast Asian refugees in July 1979, and with former Liberal minister of employment and immigration Lloyd Axworthy (Interview HOF110 2019), who added another 10,000 refugees to the total in the spring of 1980.

Public Servants

The public servants who were interviewed included coauthor Michael Molloy (Interview HOF026 2019), who helped design the resettlement system including the private refugee sponsorship program that came into effect in 1978, and who was senior coordinator of the Indochinese Refugee Task Force at Employment and Immigration Canada that oversaw the admission of 60,000 refugees in 1979 and 1980. Also interviewed were visa officers Margaret Tebbutt (Interview HOF168 2020) and Scott Mullin (Interview HOF095 2019), along with Quebec immigration agents Lucile Horner (Interview HOF063 2019) and Florent Fortin (Interview HOF062 2019), who interviewed, screened, and documented Vietnamese, Laotian, and Cambodian refugees in nine Asian countries and territories and over seventy refugee camps. Naomi Alboim (Interview HOF093 2019) and Jim Pasman (Interview HOF0163 2020) coordinated federal sponsorship and settlement services in Ontario and British Columbia respectively. Hulene Montgomery (Interview HOF088 2019) was a refugee liaison officer with Canada Employment and Immigration in Kitchener-Waterloo who worked jointly with a coalition of churches, communities, and government partners to support incoming refugees. In addition to their video-recorded HOF interviews, each of the former officials in this section told their stories in *Running on Empty: Canada and the Indochinese Refugees 1975–1980* (Molloy et al. 2017).

Civil Society

Having ordinary Canadians step forward to assist waves of refugees was not new in Canada's history, but it was the magnitude of the public response to the boat people and the refugees from Vietnam, Laos, and Cambodia that was unprecedented. Micheline Levesque (Interview HOF122 2019) ran a unique school in Phanat Nikhom refugee camp in Thailand to prepare refugees for life in Quebec. Former Air Canada flight attendants Joyce Ernyes (Interview HOF096 2019) and Patricia Talbot-Begin (Interview HOF158 2020) served on refugee flights during the 1979–80 operation.

Leadership from Faith-Based Communities

John Wieler, the Mennonite Central Committee Canada's director of overseas services, appointed William Janzen (Interview HOF049 2019) as director of MCC Ottawa to negotiate the first refugee sponsorship master agreement in 1979. Art DeFehr (Interview HOF106 2019), a member of the Mennonite community, worked with World Relief and CARE in Southeast Asia. Rev. Arie Van Eek (Interview HOF097 2019), a minister with the Dutch Christian Reformed Church of Canada in southern Ontario, negotiated a sponsorship master agreement on behalf of his church with the federal government and coordinated its sponsorship efforts.

Community Coordination

Appalled by the suffering of the refugees in Southeast Asia, York University professor Howard Adelman (Interview HOF094 2019) organized a neighbourhood meeting to do something about the refugees and, almost by accident, ended up founding Operation Lifeline, which expanded to over one hundred chapters across Canada dedicated to coordinating and promoting refugee sponsorship. Simultaneously in Ottawa, Mayor Marion Dewar decided that her city could resettled 4,000 refugees. Barb Gamble and Eleanor Ryan (Interview HOF039 2019) and Sue Pike (Interview HOF040 2019) became actively involved and helped to organize the 12 July 1979 Project 4000 rally that drew close to 3,000 people to Lansdowne Park.

The Front Line: Settlement Workers

Patricia Marshall (Interview HOF017 2019), a settlement worker for the Ottawa Carleton Immigrant Services Organization, organized volunteers under the Canadian Friendship Program that provided support and friendship to government-assisted refugees. Anna Hemmendinger (Interview HOF088 2019) of Kitchener-Waterloo saw a gap in English-language training and developed the English in a Workplace Setting program. Brice Balmer and Lao Vang (Interview HOF087 2019) recognized many of the challenges facing Hmong refugees due to their lack of experience in cities and assisted in the creation of a Hmong Association in Kitchener.

Sponsors

Finally, the HOF oral history website, heartsoffreedom.org, contains accounts from four refugee sponsors. John and Helen Cornies (Interview HOF091 2019), members of the Hamilton Mennonite Church, emphasize that it is the sponsor's responsibility to learn about the culture of the refugees they sponsor. They also reflect on what remarkable citizens the Vietnamese have become. In 1978, with $150,000 from various Catholic religious communities, Monsignor Pierre Blanchard (Interview HOF 065 2019) and a colleague started doing sponsorships with the school in Montreal where he was working. Between 1981 and 1991 they sponsored almost 2,000 people, most of whom quickly found jobs and became independent. In 1979, Bob and Carol Liddle (Interview HOF150 2020), a professional engineer and a teacher with four children, reported that St David's United Church in Calgary had sponsored eight refugee families and that the key to success is to be prepared to raise the money and to have a significant number of people willing to do the hands-on work. Finally, Vicki Baril (Interview HOF138 2020), along with her husband and four other couples in Edmonton, responded to their priest's suggestion that they sponsor a widow with six children. The youngest daughter of their sponsored family, Nhung Tran-Davies (Interview HOF141 2020), eventually became a physician and gained national attention by sponsoring a Syrian single mother with several children.

It is people like John and Helen Cornies, Msg. Pierre Blanchard, Vicki Baril and her husband, and Bob and Carol Liddle that pioneered the private sponsorship system that subsequently resettled hundreds of thousands of refugees.

Canadians' response to assisting Southeast Asian refugees is wonderfully summarized by former immigration minister Lloyd Axworthy in the report *Indochinese Refugees: The Canadian Response, 1979 and 1980*:

Never before had Canada been involved in a refugee movement which arose so dramatically or persisted in such large numbers for so long. Never had the distances been so vast, the cultural differences so pronounced. Never had a group of Canadians motivated by conscience and a determination to relieve suffering, become so personally involved; and, never before had they joined with their federal and provincial governments in a formal partnership to provide a new homeland for refugees. (Employment and Immigration Canada 1982)

APPENDIX 4

Hearts of Freedom Project Management and Teams

It is the dedication and support of the following individuals and organizations that has made the Hearts of Freedom (HOF) project possible.

HOF Project Funders
Canadian Heritage, Canada History Fund; the DeFehr Foundation; Immigration, Refugees, and Citizenship Canada; Canadian Immigration Historical Society; Canadian Mennonite University; Carleton University – Future Funder Program

HOF Project Partners
Vietnamese Canadian Federation; Cambodian Association of the Ottawa Valley; Lao Association of Ottawa Valley; Canadian Museum of History; Canadian Museum of Immigration at Pier 21; Menno Simons College, Canadian Mennonite University

Hearts of Freedom Management Committee
Co-chairs
Allan Moscovitch, principal investigator, Carleton University; Colleen Lundy, principal investigator, Carleton University

Members
Anne Arnott, Canadian Immigration Historical Society; Xay Bounnapha, Lao Association of Ottawa Valley; Emily Burton, Canadian Immigration Museum at Pier 21; Richard Dang, Rich Cinematics;

Peter Duschinsky, Canadian Immigration Historical Society; Charlene Elgee, Canadian Immigration Historical Society; Tri Hoang, Vietnamese Canadian Federation; Dau-Thi Huynh, Vietnamese Canadian Federation; Tuyet Lam, Vietnamese Canadian Federation; Vuthy Lay, Cambodian Association Ottawa Valley; Kien Le, Vietnamese Canadian Federation; Luong Le Phan, Vietnamese Canadian Community of Ottawa; Charlie Lim, Cambodian Association Ottawa Valley; Mike Molloy, Canadian Immigration Historical Society; Mai Nguyen, Vietnamese Canadian Community of Ottawa; Sheila Petzold, documentary filmmaker; Som Phouangpraseuth, Lao Association of Ottawa Valley; Laura Sanchini, Canadian Museum of History; Stephanie Phetsamay Stobbe, Menno Simons College, Canadian Mennonite University; Chris Trainor, Carleton University, Archives and Collections; Van Nha Tran, Association des Vietnamiens de Sherbrooke; Minh Nguyen, independent curator (until February 2019)

HOF Research Committee

Co-chairs

Allan Moscovitch, principal investigator, Carleton University; Colleen Lundy, principal investigator, Carleton University

Members

Peter Duschinsky, Canadian Immigration Historical Society; Mike Molloy, Canadian Immigration Historical Society; Stephanie Phetsamay Stobbe, Menno Simons College, Canadian Mennonite University

Project Management Team

Ginette Thomas, project coordinator; Mondy Lim, media coordinator/web designer; Zoey Feder, accounts (until January 2021); Amy Ma, graduate social work student practicum (winter term 2021)

Cambodian Interview Team

Rivaux Lay, coordinator; Ran Dawn Long, interviewer; Richard Dang, camera operator

Laotian Interview Team
Som Phouangpraseuth, coordinator; Jean Legault, interviewer; Meaghan Brackenbury, camera operator

Vietnamese Interview Team
Mai Nguyen, coordinator; Uyen Vu, interviewer; Hanh Hua, camera operator

Government and Sponsor Interview Team
Jean Legault, coordinator and interviewer

City Coordinators
Mai Nguyen, Calgary; Jean Ngan Tran, Edmonton; Phuong Nguyen, Halifax; Stella (Nhung) Davis, Vancouver; Pam Sharp, Vancouver; Ari Phanlouvong, Winnipeg; Stephanie Phetsamay Stobbe, Winnipeg

Students
Aliyah Campbell, Megan Evans, Meaghan Fallak, Simran Joura, Alexandra Koslock, Amy Ma, Uyiosa Osunde, Ari Phanlouvong, Malinda Pich, Korri Schneider

Translation
Sylvie Doucet, Jean Legault, Mondy Lim, Phi-Vân Nguyen, Sinclair Robinson, Stephanie Phetsamay Stobbe, Ginette Thomas

Research Papers/Literature Reviews
Filipe Duarte, Clare Glassco, Jamie Lenet, Lisa McLean, Stephanie Phetsamay Stobbe, Ginette Thomas

Book Committee
Coordinator
Mike Molloy

Members
Peter Duschinsky, Mondy Lim, Colleen Lundy, Allan Moscovitch, Stephanie Phetsamay Stobbe, Ginette Thomas

Documentary Film Committee

Chair

Sheila Petzold

Members

Richard Dang, Mondy Lim, Stephanie Phetsamay Stobbe, Uyen Vu

Documentary Film Team

Sheila Petzold, producer, director, writer; Norm Sawchyn, editor; Kathie Mckenna, archive producer; Judy Trinh and Uyen Vu, narrators; Edmund Eagan and Norm Sawchyn, sound design; Edmund Eagan, original music and mix; Pham Duc Thanh, traditional music; Jamie Muntean, map animations; Allan Moscovitch, executive producer

Special Thanks

Affinity Productions, Amy Ma, Zoey Feder, Thi Bach Mai Nguyen, Barbara Gamble, Karl Roeder, Som Phouangpraseuth, Rivaux Lay, Malcolm Hamilton, Tuyet Lam, Donald Cameron, Major (Ret.), Jacques Coiteux, Joyce Ernyes, Hoang Dinh Tri, Huan Huu Nguyen, Lucile Horner, Murray Mosher, Nguyen Mai Chi, (Pham) Buchan Trong Tho, Eleanor Ryan, Robert J. Shalka, Stephanie Phetsamay Stobbe, Ly Mao, John McEachern, Michael Molloy, Mean Bonn Taing, Tran-Le Hong Phuc, Le Tuyet

Travelling Museum Exhibition Committee

Chair

Stephanie Phetsamay Stobbe

Members

Emily Burton, Laura Sanchini (replaced by Saeedeh Niktab Etaati August 2022), Tri Hoang, Som Phouangpraseuth, Rivaux Lay; initial consultations included Mondy Lim, Richard Dang

Exhibition Creation Team

Stephanie Phetsamay Stobbe, creator/curator; Emily Burton, Dan Conlin, and Catherine O'Sullivan, consultants/advisors; Stephanie

Phetsamay Stobbe, text (travelling exhibition); Peter Duschinsky and Mike Molloy, text (digital exhibition); Stephanie Phetsamay Stobbe and Emily Burton, English editors; Paula Sousa, French editor/translator; Grant Murray, overall travelling exhibition designer; Mondy Lim, digital exhibition designer; Stephanie Phetsamay Stobbe, exhibition tour coordinator; CMU and Shayne Wong, exhibition shipping coordinator; SSHRC and private donors at CMU (see https://heartsoffreedom.org/sponsors-and-donors-for-museum-exhibition/), exhibition tour funders

Special Thanks

Catherine O'Sullivan and the team at Canadian Museum of History; Emily Burton, Dan Conlin, and the team at Canadian Museum of Immigration at Pier 21; Winnie Cheung, Wendy Yip, Pat Parungao, and the team at Pacific Canada Heritage Centre – Museum of Migration; Dorota Blumczynska, Roland Sawatzky, Seema Hollenberg, Zoe McQuinn, Anya Moodie-Foster, and the team at Manitoba Museum; research assistants and volunteers: Ari Phanlouvong, Korri Schneider, Uyiosa Chukwuka, Alexandra Koslock, Meaghan Fallak, Megan Evans; Phi Van Nguyen; research assistants for the Canada tour: Shayne Wong, Cassie Dong, Mahbub Zaman, and Taewook Bae; and our partners and volunteers in all the tour cities

References

Primary Sources

Oral history video interviews of Southeast Asian refugees that resettled in Canada are the primary sources of this book. Conducted for Hearts of Freedom (HOF), the Canadian Southeast Asian Refugee Historical Research Project at Carleton University, they are cited as references by interview number throughout the book's text. The video interviews are available on the Hearts of Freedom project website, except in cases where an interviewee declined to have their interview published. To access the video interviews, go to heartsoffreedom.org and click on "Interviews." The interviews are listed in numerical order, using their HOF numbers, under the headings "Vietnamese Interviews," "Cambodian Interviews," and "Laotian Interviews," as well as interviews with government officials and sponsors, and can be searched by name or interview number.

Secondary Sources

Adelman, Howard. 1980. *The Indochinese Refugee Movement: The Canadian Experience*. Proceedings of a conference in Toronto, 19–21 October 1979. Toronto: Operation Lifeline.

– 1982. *Canada and the Indochinese Refugees*. Regina: Weigl Educational Publishers Limited.

Amer, Ramses. 1996. "Vietnam's Policies and the Ethnic Chinese since 1975." *Sojourn: Journal of Social Issues in Southeast Asia* 11 (1): 76–104.

Appy, Christian G. 2003. *Patriots: The Vietnam War Remembered from All Sides.* New York: Penguin.

Batarseh, Robert C. 2016. "Inside/Outside the Circle: From the Indochinese Designated Class to Contemporary Group Processing." *Refuge* 32 (2): 54–66.

Beiser, Morton. 1999. *Strangers at the Gate: The Boat People's First Ten Years in Canada.* Toronto: University of Toronto Press.

Bersma, René. 2024. *Don't Take the Boats.* Unpublished manuscript. Ottawa: The Canadian Immigration Historical Society.

Borch, Fred L. 2018. "A Look at the My Lai Incident Fifty Years Later: What Really Happened on 16 March 1968? What Lessons Have Been Learned?" *On Point* 23 (4): 36–44.

Bording, Tove. 2014. *Description of Events at Immigration HQ*. Ottawa: Canadian Immigration Historical Society (CIHS) Collection.

Bredo, William. 1970. "Agrarian Reform in Vietnam: Vietcong and Government of Vietnam Strategies in Conflict." *Asian Survey* 10 (8): 738–50.

Brune, Lester H. Dean Burns. 1992. *America and the Indochina Wars, 1945–1990: A Bibliographic Guide.* Claremont: Regina Books.

Buchignani, Norman. 1988. "Towards a Sociology of Indochinese Canadian Social Organization: A Preliminary Statement." In *Ten Years Later: Indochinese Communities in Canada,* edited by Louis-Jacques Dorais and Kwok B. Chan, 13–36. Montreal: Canadian Asian Studies Association.

Buckley, Brian. 2008. *Gift of Freedom: How Ottawa Welcomed the Vietnamese, Cambodian, and Laotian Refugees*. Renfrew: General Store Publishing House.

Bun, Chan Kwok, and Louis-Jacques Dorais. 1998. "Family, Identity, and the Vietnamese Diaspora: The Quebec Experience." *Sojourn: Journal of Social Issues in Southeast Asia* 13 (2): 285–308.

Chan, Kwok B. 1988. "The Chinese from Indochina in Montreal: A Study in Ethnic Voluntary Associations, Community Organization and Ethnic Boundaries." In *Ten Years Later: Indochinese Communities in Canada,* edited by Louis-Jacques Dorais and Kwok B. Chan, 141–64. Montreal: Canadian Asian Studies Association.

Chan, Kwok B., and Lawrence Lam. 1987. "Psychological Problems of Chinese Vietnamese Refugees Resettling in Quebec." In *Uprooting, Loss, and Adaptation: The Resettlement of Indochinese Refugees in Canada,* edited by Kwok Chan and Doreen Indra, 27–41. Ottawa: Canadian Public Health Association.

Chernoff, David. 1986. *The Vietnamese Gulag*. New York: Simon and Schuster.

Citizenship and Immigration Canada. 1966–99. *Immigration Statistics = Immigration, statistiques* [annual reports 1975–96]. Catalogue no. MP22-1-PDF. Ottawa: Manpower and Immigration = Main-d'œuvre et immigration. publications.gc.ca/pub?id=9.500621&sl=0.

C-Span Q&A. 2020. "James Taing." 01:00:27. 6 October. Accessed 29 July 2024. https://www.c-span.org/video/?476652–1/qa-james-taing.

Cutts, Mark. 2000. *The State of the World's Refugees, 2000: Fifty Years of Humanitarian Action*. Geneva: UNHCR, Oxford University Press.

Davidson, Phillip B. 1991. *Vietnam at War: The History, 1946–1975*. New York: Oxford University Press.

Denov, Myriam, Pok Panhavichetr, Sopheap Suong, and Meaghan Shevell. 2022. "'We Vowed by Force, Not by Our Heart': Men's and Women's Perspectives on Forced Marriage during the Cambodian Genocide." *International Journal of Human Rights* 26 (9): 1547–70.

Deschamps, Gilles. 1987. "Economic Adaptation of Indochinese Refugees in Quebec." In *Uprooting, Loss, and Adaptation: The Resettlement of Indochinese Refugees in Canada,* edited by Kwok Chan and Doreen Indra, 97–115. Ottawa: Canadian Public Health Association.

Dommen. Arthur J. 1972. "Laos: The Year of the Ho Chi Minh Trail." *Asian Survey* 12 (2): 138–47.

Dorais, Louis-Jacques. 1991. "Refugee Adaptation and Community Structure: The Indochinese in Quebec City, Canada." *International Migration Review* 25 (3): 551–73.

– 2000. *The Cambodians, Laotians and Vietnamese in Canada* 28. Ottawa: Canadian Historical Association.

– 2010. "Politics, Kinship, and Ancestors: Some Diasporic Dimensions of the Vietnamese Experience in North America." *Journal of Vietnamese Studies* 5 (2): 91–132.

Dorais, Louis-Jacques, Kwok B. Chan, and Doreen Marie Indra. 1988. *Ten Years Later: Indochinese Communities in Canada.* Montreal: Canadian Asian Studies Association.

Duiker, William J. 1985. *Vietnam since the Fall of Saigon*. Athens: Ohio University Center for International Studies.

Elliott, David. 2003. *The Vietnamese War: Revolution and Social Change in the Mekong Delta 1930–1975*. New York: Routledge.

Elliott, Mai. 2010. *Rand in Southeast Asia: A History of the Vietnam War Era.* Santa Monica: RAND Corporation. https://www.rand.org/content/dam/rand/pubs/corporate_pubs/2010/RAND_CP564.pdf.

Employment and Immigration Canada. 1982. *Indochinese Refugees: The Canadian Response, 1979 and 1980.* Catalogue no. MP23-60/1982E-PDF. Ottawa: Employment and Immigration Canada. Ottawa. publications.gc.ca/pub?id=9.804208&sl=0.

End Slavery Now. 2024. "Legal Support for Children and Women." https://www.endslaverynow.org/legal-support-for-children-and-women-lscw. Accessed 29 July 2024.

Evans, Grant. 1999. *Laos: Culture and Society.* Chiangmai: Silkworm Books.

Fifield, Russell H. 1997. "The Thirty Years War in Indochina: A Conceptual Framework." *Asian Survey* 17 (9): 857–79.

Frankum, Ronald. 2007. *Operation Passage to Freedom: The United States Navy in Vietnam, 1954–1955*. Lubbock: Texas Tech University Press.

Goscha, Christopher. 2010. "Hell in a Very Small Place: Cold War and Decolonisation in the Assault on the Vietnamese Body at Dien Bien Phu." *European Journal of East Asian Studies* 9 (2): 201–23.

– 2016. *Vietnam: A New History*. New York: Basic Books.

– 2022. *The Road to Dien Bien Phu: A History of the First War for Vietnam*. Princeton: Princeton University Press.

Hammond, William M. 2009. "The Tet Offensive and the News Media: Some Thoughts on the Effects of News Reporting." *Army History* 70 (Winter): 6–16.

Hastings, Max. 2019. *Vietnam: An Epic Tragedy, 1945–1975*. London: Williams Collins.

Hathaway, James C. 1993. "Labelling the 'Boat People': The Failure of the Human Rights Mandate of the Comprehensive Plan of Action for Indochinese Refugees." *Human Rights Quarterly* 15: 686.

High, Steven. 2008. *The Montreal Life Stories Project.* Concordia University's Centre for Oral History and Digital Storytelling. https://thenhier.ca/en/content/oral-history-concordia-university-steven-high.html.

Hinton, Alexander Laban. 2005. *Why Did They Kill? Cambodia in the Shadow of Genocide.* Berkeley: University of California Press.

Hirschman, Charles, Samuel Preston, and Vu Manh Loi. 1995. "Vietnamese Casualties During the American War: A New Estimate." *Population and Development Review* 21 (4): 783–812.

Holcombe, Alec. 2020. *Mass Mobilization in the Democratic Republic of Vietnam, 1945–1960.* Honolulu: University of Hawai'i Press. https://library.oapen.org/handle/20.500.12657/37328.

Hou, Feng. 2017. *The Resettlement of Vietnamese Refugees across Canada over Three Decades.* UN-WIDER Working Paper 2017/188. Accessed 29 July 2024. https://www.wider.unu.edu/sites/default/files/Publications/Working-paper/PDF/wp2017-188.pdf.

– 2021. "The Resettlement of Vietnamese Refugees across Canada over Three Decades." *Journal of Ethnic and Migration Studies* 47 (21): 4817–34. https://www.tandfonline.com/doi/full/10.1080/1369183X.2020.1724412.

Indra, Doreen M. 1987. "Bureaucratic Constraints, Middlemen and Community Organization: Aspects of the Political Incorporation of Southeast Asians in Canada." In *Uprooting, Loss, and Adaptation: The Resettlement of Indochinese Refugees in Canada*, edited by Kwok Chan and Doreen Indra, 147–70. Ottawa: Canadian Public Health Association.

Institut National de l'Audiovisuel. 2010. "Ile de lumière: navire hôpital." DailyMotion. Uploaded by @ina. 00:03:24. Accessed 21 August 2024. https://dai.ly/xfd63h.

Jackson, Tony. 1987. *Just Waiting To Die? Cambodian Refugees in Thailand.* Oxford: Oxfam GB. https://policy-practice.oxfam.org/resources/just-waiting-to-die-cambodian-refugees-in-thailand–134989/.

Kamm, Henry. 1979. "Cambodia Says Thai Troops Killed 300 Refugees Forced over the Border." *New York Times*. 23 June 1979. https://www.nytimes.com/1979/06/23/archives/cambodia-says-thai-troops-killed-300-refugees-forced-over-border.html.

Kiernan, Ben. 1989. "The American Bombardment of Kampuchea, 1969–1973." *Vietnam Generation* 1 (1): 3. https://digitalcommons.lasalle.edu/vietnamgeneration/vol1/iss1/3/.

– 1990. "Roots of Genocide: New Evidence on the US Bombardment of Cambodia." *Cultural Survival Quarterly* 14 (3): 20–2.

– 2002. *The Pol Pot Regime: Race, Power, and Genocide in Cambodia under the Khmer Rouge, 1975–1979*. New Haven: Yale University Press.

Kumin, Judith. 2008. "Orderly Departure from Vietnam: Cold War Anomaly or Humanitarian Innovation?" *Refugee Survey Quarterly* 27 (1): 104–17.

Labman, Shauna. 2016. "Private Sponsorship: Complementary or Conflicting Interests?" *Refuge* 32 (2): 67.

Lipman, Jana K. 2020. *In Camps: Vietnamese Refugees, Asylum Seekers, and Repatriates*. Oakland: University of California Press.

Mam, Kaylanee. 2006. "The Endurance of the Cambodian Family Under the Khmer Rouge Regime: An Oral History." In *Genocide in Cambodia and Rwanda: New Perspectives*, edited by Susan E. Cook, 119–62. New Brunswick: Transaction Publishers.

McLean, Lisa, and Stephanie P. Stobbe. 2019. *Laotian Resettlement and Integration in Canada: A Literature Review*. Ottawa: Canadian Southeast Asian Refugee Historical Research Project: Hearts of Freedom.

– 2020. "The Evolution of Canadian Settlement Programming from the Mass Resettlement of Indochinese (Southeast Asian) Refugees to the Present." *Peace Research* 52 (1–2): 81–112. https://www.peaceresearch.ca/pdf/52/PRJ-52–1-2-2020-McLean-Stobbe.pdf.

Merziger, Patrick. 2016. "The 'Radical Humanism' of 'Cap Anamur'/ 'German Emergency Doctors' in the 1980s: A Turning Point for the Idea, Practice and Policy of Humanitarian Aid." *European Review of History: Revue européenne d'histoire* 23 (1–2): 171–92. https://www.tandfonline.com/doi/full/10.1080/13507486.2015.1117423#d1e114.

Mishra, Patit Paban. 2001. "Laos in The Vietnam War: The Politics of Escalation 1962–1973." *Proceedings of the Indian History Congress* 62: 873–85. Indian History Congress.

Molloy, Michael J. 2014. "In Memoriam – Tove Bording." *CIHS [Canadian Immigration Historical Society] Bulletin* 71 (October): 11. https://cihs-shic.ca/wp-content/uploads/2014/10/Bulletin-71-Final.pdf#page11.

– 2020. "How Canada Defined Indochinese Refugees: Principle and Pragmatism." In *Beyond 2020: Renewing Canada's Commitment to Immigration, Metropolis Canada eBook* 2, edited by Jack Jedwab and Miriam Taylor, 61–81. Montreal: Association for Canadian Studies. https://acsmetropolisca-wpuploads.s3.ca-central–1.amazonaws.com/wp-content/uploads/2022/04/08230559/609_Metropolis_eBook_Vol2_2020_V9_LR.pdf.

Molloy, Michael J., Peter Duschinsky, Kurt Jensen, and Robert Shalka. 2017. *Running on Empty: Canada and the Indochinese Refugees 1975–1980.* Montreal: McGill-Queen's University Press.

Molloy, Michael J., and James C. Simeon. 2016. "The Indochinese Refugee Movement and the Launch of Canada's Private Sponsorship Program." *Refuge: Canada's Journal on Refugees* 32 (2): 3–8.

Nguyen, Andrew. 2023. *The Skyluck Journals.* On CBC First Person. 28 April 2023. https://www.cbc.ca/radiointeractives/docproject/the-skyluck-journals.

Nguyen, Van Canh, and Earle Cooper. 1983. *Vietnam Under Communism, 1975–1982.* Stanford: Hoover Institution Press.

Operation Frequent Wind: The Helicopter Airlift from the US Embassy. First Days Story Project: Voices of the Vietnamese Refugee Experience. Accessed 29 July 2024. https://www.pbs.org/wgbh/americanexperience/lastdays/firstdaysstoryproject/slideshow/operation-frequent-wind/.

Opper, Marc. 2020. *People's Wars in China, Malaya, and Vietnam.* Ann Arbor: University of Michigan Press.

Oral History Centre. Copyright 2004–2024. Winnipeg: University of Winnipeg. https://oralhistorycentre.ca/.

Owen, Norman G. 2005. *The Emergence of Modern Southeast Asia: A New History – Vietnam 1700–1885.* Honolulu: University of Hawaii Press.

Pappone, Rene. 1982. *The Hai Hong: Profit, Tears and Joy.* Ottawa: Employment and Immigration Canada.

Path, Kosal. 2012. "China's Economic Sanctions against Vietnam 1975–1978." *China Quarterly* 212 (December): 1040–58. https://repec.vietstudies.com/kinhte/ChinaSanctions_ChinaQuart2012.pdf.

Paul, Christopher, Colin P. Clarke, Beth Grill, and Molly Dunigan. 2013. "Laos, 1959–1975: Case Outcome: COIN Loss." In *Paths to Victory: Detailed Insurgency Case Studies*, 147–56. Santa Monica: RAND Corporation. https://www.rand.org/pubs/research_reports/RR291z2.html.

– 2013. "South Vietnam, 1960–1075: Case Outcome: COIN Loss." In *Paths to Victory: Detailed Insurgency Case Studies*, 177–97. Santa Monica: RAND Corporation. https://www.rand.org/pubs/research_reports/RR291z2.html.

Refugee Camps.info. 2018. "Remembering the Vietnamese Exodus." Accessed 28 November 2024. https://refugeecamps.net/index.html.

Robinson, W. Courtland. 1998. "Cumulative Indo-Chinese Resettlement Statistics, 1975–97." Appendix 2 of *Terms of Refuge: The Indochinese Exodus and the International Response*, 295. New York: Zed Books.

– 2000. "Refugee Warriors at the Thai-Cambodian Border." *Refugee Survey Quarterly* 19 (1): 23–37. https://www.jstor.org/stable/45053197.

Rosenau, William. 2001. *Special Operations Forces and Elusive Enemy Ground Targets: Lessons from Vietnam and the Persian Gulf War*. Santa Monica: RAND Corporation.

Rummel, R.J. 1997. "The Vietnamese War State." Alternate title: "Statistics of Vietnamese Democide, Estimates, Calculations, and Sources." Chapter 6 of *Statistics of Democide*. Honolulu: University of Hawaii. https://www.hawaii.edu/powerkills/NOTE5.HTM.

Schoepfel, Ann-Sophie. 2019. "Boat People Rescue Operation and Memory. Interview with Anh Tuan Dinh-Xuan, a Franco-Vietnamese Medical Doctor at Parisian Cochin Hospital." In *Reconstructing Memory in European Cities*, posted on 21/11/2019. https://memcit.hypotheses.org/915.

Singh, Sudhir Kumar. 2015. "Colonialisms, Nationalism and Vietnam's Struggle for Freedom." *Proceedings of the Indian History Congress* 76: 620–30. https://www.jstor.org/stable/44156629.

Snepp, Frank. 1997. *Decent Interval: An Insider's Account of Saigon's Indecent End.* New York: Random House.

Southgate, Laura. 2019. "The Third Indochina War." In *ASEAN Resistance to Sovereignty Violation: Interests, Balancing and the Role of the Vanguard State*, 71–116. Bristol: Bristol University Press. https://doi.org/10.51952/9781529202212.ch003.

Statistics Canada. 2017. *Canada [Country] and Canada [Country]* (table). *Census Profile.* 2016 Census. Statistics Canada Catalogue no. 98-316-X2016001. Ottawa. 29 November. Accessed 4 December 2024. https://www12.statcan.gc.ca/census-recensement/2016/dp-pd/prof/index.cfm?Lang=E.

Statistics Canada. 2023. *Census Profile* [table]. 2021 Census of Population. Statistics Canada Catalogue no. 98-316-X2021001. Ottawa. 15 November. Accessed 4 December 2024. https://www12.statcan.gc.ca/census-recensement/2021/dp-pd/prof/index.cfm?Lang=E.

Stobbe, Stephanie Phetsamay. 2006. "Cross-Cultural Experiences of Laotian Refugees and Mennonite Sponsors in British Columbia and Manitoba." *Journal of Mennonite Studies* 24: 111–28.

– 2016. *Conflict Resolution and Peacebuilding in Laos: Perspective for Today's World.* London: Routledge: 120. https://www.taylorfrancis.com/books/mono/10.4324/9781315774312/conflict-resolution-peacebuilding-laos-stephanie-phetsamay-stobbe.

Stuart-Fox, Martin. 1997. *A History of Laos.* Cambridge: Cambridge University Press.

– 2008. *Historical Dictionary of Laos.* 3rd edition. Historical Dictionaries of Asia, Oceania, and the Middle East. Lanham: Scarecrow Press.

– 2010. *The A to Z of Laos.* 3rd edition. Lanham: Scarecrow Press.

Stursberg, Peter. 2006. "Oral History." *Canadian Encyclopedia.* Historica Canada. Last edited by Michelle Filice, 30 October 2020. *Canadian Encyclopedia.* https://www.thecanadianencyclopedia.ca/en/article/oral-history.

Tarling, Nicholas, ed. 1993. *The Nineteenth and Twentieth Centuries.* Volume 2 of *The Cambridge History of Southeast Asia.* Cambridge: Cambridge University Press. https://doi.org/10.1017/CHOL9780521355063.

Thompson, Paul. 2002. *The Voice of the Past: Oral History*. 3rd edition. Oxford: Oxford University Press.

Thomson, S. 1980. "Refugees in Thailand: Relief, Development and Integration." In *Southeast Asian Exodus: From Tradition to Resettlement*, edited by Elliot L. Tepper, 125–31. Ottawa: Canadian Southeast Asian Studies Association.

Toronto Star. 1979. "Viets Storm Hong Kong." 30 June. 1–2.

Treviranus, Barbara, and Michael Casasola. 2003. "Canada's Private Sponsorship of Refugees Program: A Practitioners Perspective of Its Past and Future." *Journal of International Migration and Integration/ Revue de l'integration et de la migration internationale* 4: 177–202.

UNHCR [UN High Commissioner for Refugees]. 2000. "Chapter 4: Flight from Indochina." In *The State of the World's Refugees 2000: Fifty Years of Humanitarian Action*, 79–104. Oxford: Oxford University Press. https://www.unhcr.org/publications/state-worlds-refugees-2000-fifty-years-humanitarian-action.

Van Esterik, Penny. 2003. *Taking Refuge: Lao Buddhist in North America*. 3rd edition. Tempe: Arizona State University Center for Asian Research.

Van Nguyen, Duong. 2008. *The Tragedy of the Vietnam War: A South Vietnamese Officer's Analysis*. Jefferson, NC: McFarland.

Vickery, Michael. 1990. "Refugee Politics: The Khmer Camp System in Thailand." In *Revival: The Cambodian Agony*. 2nd edition, edited by Davis A. Ablin and Marlowe Hood, 293–331. New York: M.E. Sharpe.

Vietnamese Heritage Museum. 2024. "Koh Kra – Hell on Earth." Accessed 29 July 2024. https://vietnamesemuseum.org/our-roots/refugee-camps/thailand/koh-kra/.

Willbanks, James H. 2008. *The Tet Offensive: A Concise History*. New York: Columbia University Press.

Winland, Daphne. 1992. "The Role of Religious Affiliation in Refugee Resettlement: The Case of the Hmong." *Canadian Ethics Studies* 24 (1): 96–120.

– 1994. "Christianity and Community: Conversion and Adaptation among Hmong Refugee Women." *Canadian Journal of Sociology/ Cahiers canadiens de sociologie* 19 (1): 21–45.

– 2006. "Revisiting a Case Study of Hmong Refugees and Ontario Mennonites." *Journal of Mennonite Studies* 24: 169–76.

Yuen, Mary. 1990. "Vietnamese Refugees and Singapore's Policy." *Southeast Asian Journal of Social Science* 18 (1): 81–93.

Contributors

Authors

PETER DUSCHINSKY is a retired Canadian foreign service officer. Born in Budapest, Hungary, he came to Canada in 1957 as a Hungarian refugee. As a graduate student of history at the University of British Columbia, he was, along with his wife Christiana Epp Duschinsky, principal researcher of John Norris's *Strangers Entertained: A History of the Ethnic Groups of British Columbia* (Vancouver: Evergreen Press, 1971). Along with Michael J. Molloy, Kurt Jensen, and Robert J. Shalka, he is a coauthor of *Running on Empty: Canada and the Indochinese Refugees, 1975–1980* (Montreal: McGill-Queen's University Press, 2017). He is the author of several articles on subjects related to refugees and immigration. Between 2011 and 2021 he was on the board of the Canadian Immigration Historical Society. He had foreign postings in Paris, Chicago, Cairo, and Budapest. During his Cairo posting he established and oversaw the movement of Ethiopian refugees from camps in Sudan to Canada. Between 1998 and 2001 he served as director, international liaison, responsible for the international multilateral relations of the Department of Citizenship and Immigration.

COLLEEN LUNDY, MSW, PhD, is a social work professor emeritus at Carleton University, a former director of the School of Social Work, and the previous academic director of the Centre for International Migration and Settlement Studies, a former Carleton University research centre.

She has been involved in several international research initiatives including on violence against women in Sweden and Canada and the impact of economic transformation on women in Cuba and Russia and was a component leader on a five-year funded partnership between Carleton University and the University of Havana. A second edition of her authored book, *Social Work, Human Rights and Social Justice: A Structural Approach to Practice* (Toronto: University of Toronto Press, 2011), makes an important contribution to the understanding of structural social work and a social justice/human rights perspective. She is a coauthor (with Therese Jennissen) of *One Hundred Years of Social Work: A History of the Profession in English Canada 1900–2000* (Waterloo: Wilfrid Laurier University Press, 2011), the first complete history of social work in Canada.

MICHAEL MOLLOY is a retired Foreign Service officer who served in Japan, Lebanon, Uganda, Minneapolis, Geneva, Jordan, Syria, and Kenya. He was involved in a series of refugee resettlement operations (Czechoslovakia 1969, Uganda 1972, and Southeast Asia 1979–80) and led the design of the refugee provisions of the 1976 Immigration Act, including the private refugee sponsorship program, the Convention refugee class (for refugees as defined under the 1951 UN Refugee Convention), and designated classes (additional humanitarian classes for displaced and persecuted people in need of resettlement). Later in his career he was Canada's ambassador to Jordan and special coordinator for the Middle East Peace Process at the Department of Foreign Affairs. In retirement he is an adjunct research professor at Carleton University and the coauthor of *Running on Empty: Canada and the Indochinese Refugees 1975–1980*.

ALLAN MOSCOVITCH is professor emeritus at Carleton University, where he was a member of faculty for more than forty years and a previous director of the School of Social Work. His most recent publication is an introduction to the new edition of *Report on Social Security for Canada* by Leonard Marsh. During his career he was director of planning for the Social Services Department of the Regional Municipality of Ottawa Carleton, the chair of the (Ontario) Minister's Advisory Committee on Social Assistance Reform to the minister of community and social services, and (with Andrew Webster) the author of a monograph for the Royal Commission on Aboriginal Peoples. He was president of Jewish Family Services of Ottawa, chair of the Allocations Committee of the Jewish Federation of Ottawa, and chair of the Friends of the University of Hargeisa, School of Social Work.

STEPHANIE PHETSAMAY STOBBE, PhD, is a professor in conflict resolution studies and business at Canadian Mennonite University. She is a leading expert on Southeast Asian dispute resolution processes and has conducted conflict resolution and peacebuilding workshops around the world with political leaders, nongovernmental organizations, and civil societies. As an educator and Alternative Dispute Resolution (ADR) practitioner, she has worked and conducted research in Canada, United States, South America, Europe, India, and Asia. Stephanie has served on the ADR Institute of Manitoba and ADR Institute of Canada boards; on the American Bar Association team of experts advising the UN Development Programme; and as a visiting professor/researcher at Matsunaga Institute for Peace and Conflict Resolution at University of Hawaii. She was an Expert Advisory Board member for Asia Pacific Refugees Studies at Auckland University in New Zealand and is a fellow of McLaughlin College at York University and president of the Canadian Association for Refugees and Forced Migration Studies. Stephanie has authored several books and is the Lexington Book Series editor for *Conflict Resolution and Peacebuilding in Asia*. She is the curator of the museum exhibition *HOF – Stories of Southeast Asian Refugees*, which is travelling across Canada.

Research, Technical, and Editorial Contributors

MONDY LIM is a seasoned technology professional with over twenty-five years of experience in the high-tech industry. He is fascinated by the intersections and effects of art, design, and technology on society. He has a strong interest in the field of privacy, data collection, and visualization and the ways in which these areas can be utilized to gain valuable insights. He understands the importance of utilizing these insights to effect behavioural change and promote positive outcomes. He currently works as a consultant for the Government of Canada, assisting with its digital transformation.

GINETTE THOMAS, PhD, is a retired public servant with a career in the development of national Indigenous health policies. She participated in the launch of the then Institute for Aboriginal Health at the Canadian Institutes of Health Research in Ottawa, as well as the then National Collaborating Centre for Aboriginal Health at the University of Northern British Columbia in Prince George, BC. At Carleton University, she conducted research on the impact of Canadian public policy on the health of Indigenous Peoples and taught courses at the School of Social Work. She maintains a passion for social policy with a critique titled *The Conservative Government and the Re-emergence of Tuberculosis in First Nations and Inuit Communities* and a technical report coauthored with Allan Moscovitch proposing a new Social Care Act for Canada.

Index